1918 THE LAST ACT

derisively
derisively

salient

sacrosanct
implacable

cri de coeur
insoluble

1918
The Last Act

BY

BARRIE PITT

Pen & Sword
MILITARY

First published in 1962 by Cassel Co Limited

Published in 2003
and re-printed in this format in 2013 by

Pen & Sword Military
an imprint of
Pen & Sword Books Ltd
47 Church Street
Barnsley
South Yorkshire
S70 2AS

The right of Barrie Pitt to be identified as author of this work has
been asserted by him in accordance with the Copyright, Designs and
Patents Act 1988.

ISBN:- 978-1-78346-172-1

Printed and bound in the UK by CPI Group (UK) Ltd, Croydon, CRO 4YY

Pen & Sword Books Ltd incorporates the Imprints of Pen & Sword Aviation,
Pen & Sword Family History, Pen & Sword Maritime, Pen & Sword Military, Pen
& Sword Discovery, Wharncliffe Local History, Wharncliffe True Crime,
Wharncliffe Transport, Pen & Sword Select, Pen & Sword Military Classics, Leo
Cooper, The Praetorian Press, Remember When, Seaforth Publishing
and Frontline Publishing.

For a complete list of Pen & Sword titles please contact
PEN & SWORD BOOKS LIMITED
47 Church Street, Barnsley, South Yorkshire, S70 2AS, England
E-mail: enquiries@pen-and-sword.co.uk
Website: www.pen-and-sword.co.uk

TO

JOHN MICHAEL CHARLES

'JOHNNYMIKE'

THE LAST OF THE LINE

WITH LOVE

Author's Note

I WOULD like to record my gratitude to the many people who have helped me during the writing of this book. The officials of many Public Libraries – especially those of Reading and Basingstoke – have co-operated to a degree, as have the owners of several private collections of books and papers.

For his help in the time-consuming task of research through a wealth of material I am greatly indebted to Mr. V. A. Mosey; and to Wing Commander P. W. G. Burgess, O.B.E., Mr. F. Wallwork, Mr. F. P. Ridsdale, and especially Captain B. H. Liddell Hart, I owe thanks for reading my typescript and correcting my errors of syntax and fact. For the preparation of that typescript from my own virtually indecipherable notes, I must express my gratitude to Miss Shirley White.

And for her faith, hope and charity throughout that period of domestic chaos which seems inevitably to engulf us as soon as book-writing commences, I must once again thank S.D.P. Without her, the book could not have been written.

BARRIE PITT

Contents

Illustrations

*Unless otherwise indicated, all photographs are
the property of the Imperial War Museum.
R.T.H.P.L. - Radio Times Hulton Picture Library*

ILLUSTRATIONS

Mark V tanks of the 4th Battalion, Tank Corps, at Meaulte, August
  22nd, 1918
British armoured cars at Biefvillers, August 25th, 1918
Wire belts in the Siegfried Line, stormed by the Australians
German machine-gunners
British Mark IV Female tank attacked by flamethrowers
From the German angle
Near Dury, after the battle of the Drocourt-Quéant Switch,
  September 2nd, 1918
The cost of the assault
Scene on the battlefield
Canadians in the Wotan Line, September 2nd, 1918
German machine-gun post
Americans in the Argonne *(U.S. National Archives)*
German trench, summer 1918
Concrete defences in the Siegfied Line, under attack
British artillery crossing the Canal du Nord
Canadian patrol in Cambrai, October 9th, 1918
Prince Max of Baden *(R.T.H.P.L.)*
General von Seeckt (Tita Binz)
Grand Hotel Britannique, Spa
The Kaiser and his suite on Eysden railway station, November 10th, 1918
(R.T.H.P.L.)
The King and his generals

Maps

*   *   *

GERMAN SPRING OFFENSIVE
WESTERN FRONT 1918

Front Line 20 March ━━━━━

MILES 0   20   40   60   80 MILES

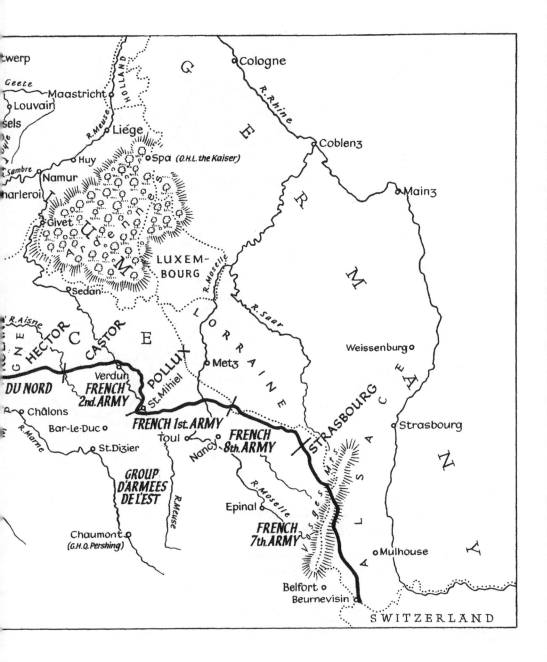

North Sea

ENGLAND

Zeebrugge
Ostend
Nieuport
BELGIAN ARMY
Bruges
Ghent
Antw
R. Schelde
R. G

Dover
Dunkirk
Calais
Straits of Dover

28 SEPT
Ypres
Passchendaele
BRITISH SECOND ARMY
Hazebrouck
Armentières
F L A N D E R S
B
E
L
G
R. Lys
R. Zenne
R. Dyle
Bruss

Boulogne

Lille
Mons
Valenciennes
Maubeuge
Che

BRITISH FIFTH ARMY
2 OCT
Béthune
Lens
Douai
26 AUG
BRITISH FIRST ARMY
21 AUG
BRITISH THIRD ARMY
Flesquières
Cambrai
R. Selle
Le Câteau
R. Oise
Montreuil

E n g l i s h
C h a n n e l
Abbeville
Albert
Péronne
St. Quentin
Mézi
R

BRITISH FOURTH ARMY
Amiens 8 AUG
Moreuil
R. Somme

Dieppe
FRENCH FIRST ARMY
F
R
A
N
la Fère
Laon
Re
R. Aisne

FRENCH THIRD ARMY
Compiègne
17 AUG
Soissons
Rheims

Rouen
R. Seine
R. Oise
FRENCH TENTH ARMY
17 AUG
R. Marne
20 JULY
Châlo
19 JULY

18 JULY
FRENCH SIXTH ARMY
19 JULY
Gd. Morin
19 JULY
FRENCH NINTH ARMY
FRENCH FIFTH ARMY
C
H
A
M

Paris

R. Seine

THE ALLIED OFFENSIVE
AUTUMN, 1918

Front line, 18 July, 1918 ▬▬▬▬
Armistice line, 11 Nov. 1918 ▬ ▬ ▬ ▬

MILES 0   20   40   60   80 MILES

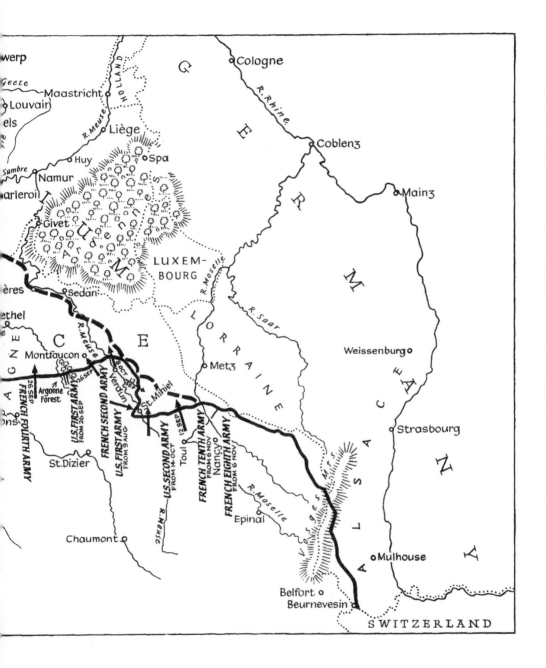

Prologue

WHEN Europe went to war in 1914, it did so in a mood of joyous certainty. Both sides were confident that their causes were just, that their armies were invincible, and that their consequent victories would be glorious, overwhelming and practically immediate. So inexhaustible are the springs of human optimism that it was some time before the nations as a whole realized that the war was not progressing in accordance with their first ingenuous suppositions, and that they would be called upon to pay for their days of splendid ardour throughout years of pain and anguish. National reserves of fortitude and endurance were to be drawn upon to the full, and Germany's dominance among the Central Powers increased as time passed.

Among the Allies, however, the relative seniorities of the partners subtly altered. Russia and France had possessed the enormous forces which first flung themselves upon the enemy in August 1914, when Britain's contribution was her Navy (in Continental eyes of no account) and an original expeditionary force so small as to enable her own propagandists to coin the historic appellation 'contemptible little army', and then to attribute its origin to her foes. Time was to alter this, and by 1916 Britain had an army in the field which Germany recognized as the major block to Kaiserlich ambitions. Britain had thus replaced France as the senior partner on the Western Front; but although the power had changed hands, the philosophy remained the same.

For years before the war, the official policy of the French Army had been based upon the 'Spirit of the Offensive' with which their soldiers had been thoroughly imbued – and time and occasion combined to infect their British ally with the same principles. When, eventually, the French were to pause and reflect upon the wisdom of their creed, their erstwhile junior partners regarded them with a disdain not unmixed with malice, and assumed the tradition of the offensive themselves. Victory, however, still eluded them, but in a moment of doubtful inspiration was produced the 'Doctrine of

Attrition' which, if lacking in imagination, possessed the supreme appeal of simplicity. All it required for its operation and success was an unlimited supply of men for the trenches – and Britain's Empire was vast.

But by the end of 1917, it was becoming evident that even Britain could not afford such wild extravagance as that in which her army commanders had been indulging. True, the enemy had suffered considerably as a result of the vast conflicts which had been forced upon her, but despite these losses there was as yet little sign of disintegration among the Central Powers. Russia's losses had been even greater than Germany's, France's losses had come near to crippling her. Europe was thus on the verge of bankruptcy – and a bankruptcy far more vitiating than one to be declared in some centre of commercial law, for it was of blood and spirit, of manhood and human hopes. Grim despondency was the mood which now dominated the peoples of the warring nations – not yet plunged into defeatism, but unable to perceive the means of victory.

Yet two events had occurred in 1917 which would offer the golden prize, first to the Central Powers, then to the Allies.

In March had begun the Russian Revolution. It did not immediately release German and Austrian divisions from the Eastern Front – indeed the Russian General Brusilov was to launch yet another offensive against them – but it was obvious to the German rulers that by early 1918 they should be able to concentrate their strength in the West. In order to expedite the Russian collapse, the German Government even allowed the passage of Lenin across the country ('in a sealed carriage, like some dangerous bacillus'), for they knew that if they were to grasp their chance of victory, they must do it quickly. Germany's chance was *now*, for in April had occurred the second event which might well serve to snatch victory from her: America had entered the war, and her vast potential of men and materials would undoubtedly tip the scales against the Central Powers if given the time to do so. So it became a race, *against* time for Germany, *for* time for Britain and France.

As 1918 dawned, half in fear and half in hope, Europe looked towards America. She alone seemed to possess the key to the situation. Whether she would arrive in time to turn it was another matter.

*　　*　　*

1. The Deadlock

It was bitterly cold in the trenches during the last fortnight of the year 1917 and there were many successive days of frost. Snow mantled the ground, softening the edges of the trenches, the gun-pits and the shell-craters, covering for a while the ugly detritus of bitter fighting. For most of the men in the line it was to be remembered as a good time, for they had learned by now the best ways of keeping warm, and hard ice was infinitely preferable to the treacherous, stinking and engulfing mud in which they had fought and bled during the last interminable months. It was quiet, too, the armies on both sides more concerned with their own comfort than with enemy disturbance.

The soldiers had lived in trenches for a long time. To many indeed, it seemed that their whole adult lives had been spent thus, mole-like below the surface of the earth, in circumstances of varying danger but invariable discomfort. There were few among them now to recall the early days of the war, the counter-marches, the cavalry screens, the street-fighting; and those who did were listened to – when they were listened to at all – with scepticism and open disbelief; for they seemed to speak of another war, another life. In any case, it was all past history, dead and gone.

But it was the essential preface to present adversity.

*　　*　　*

At the war's outbreak, the Schlieffen Plan had flung the German armies across Belgium and the north-eastern provinces of France in a gigantic wheel which pivoted on the Vosges Mountains and was intended to sweep westwards of Paris, then eastwards to entrap the French armies and crush them against their own fortifications and the Swiss border. The plan had failed because of the impossibility of feeding, supplying and reinforcing the armies on the outer edge of the wheel across the enormous expanse of the battleground they had covered, combined with weaknesses of mind and nerve in the German High Command. As a result, the radius of the wheel was

3

shortened, the outer armies swung in east of Paris and exposed themselves to flank attack from the French garrison in the capital, while the remainder of the French armies, instead of being trapped, had been merely pressed back along their own lines of communication.

Thus when the exhausted German troops reached the Marne, sweltering in the August heat, they were held as though in the bottom of a sack by the re-formed and recuperating Allied line. Every attempt they made to thrust across the top of the sack and renew their sweep westwards was countered by extensions of the Allied line to the north until it stretched up through Amiens, across the Belgian frontier and the Flanders plain, and ended on the sea between Nieuport and Ostend. In the meantime, pressure on the bottom of the sack had forced the central German armies to recoil along their own tracks – and now the situation developed as before, but in reverse: as the German lines of communication shortened, the French were stretched. Eventually, positions of balance were reached where the forces facing each other could not move forward without additional strength – and feverishly, each unit dug defensive positions to hold until reinforcements should come up in sufficient numbers to enable them to break through the enemy line opposite.

But they never arrived.

No matter how strong the force assembled, how heavy or numerous their artillery, how devoted and valiant their soldiers – always the defence was too strong. Power in defence proved easier and quicker to build than power in offence to assemble. Time after time this was proved – in the Ypres Salient and at Loos in 1915, at Verdun and on the Somme in 1916, and in April 1917 the Nivelle offensive drove the point home so hard to the French poilus in the line that they mutinied and refused to have anything more to do with the offensive. 'We will hold the line,' they said, '... but we will not attack.'

And *faute de mieux*, while the French weakened what little strength remained to them by internal dissension and strife, the British infantry were sacrificed in hundreds of thousands to hold the attention of the German High Command away from the dangerous sectors of the line. The British did not swarm over the Passchendaele Ridge or burst out of the Ypres Salient – the weather and power of defence saw to that – but for month after squalid month the slaughter went on while for every man that fell to enemy fire, one was drowned in mud. Eventually weather and utter exhaustion closed down the fighting, leaving, as usual, more difficult tactical problems for the attackers to solve than those with which they had originally been faced.

Late in November 1917 there was a sudden and brilliant burst of hope for the Allies. Despite an engrained belief among the Staffs that horses provided the only permissible means of transport for troops in action, sanction had been obtained for an attempt by massed British tanks to penetrate the enemy line opposite Cambrai.

It was brilliantly successful – too successful in fact – for the tanks and their supporting infantry penetrated four miles during the first few hours. This was so extraordinary a feat for those days that the Staff, being unused to feeding such a rapid advance and in any case short of men as a result of their recent extravagance, were unable to reinforce the thrust with sufficient reserves to maintain momentum, and there existed for several hours a two-mile wide gap in the German defences through which the two cavalry divisions in reserve should have poured. But nobody gave them orders to do so and they remained where they were until it was too late; meanwhile the tank crews were exhausted and their comparatively primitive engines were in dire need of attention or replacement.

The positions were held – and improved – by supporting infantry for nine days, at the end of which the Germans launched a counter-attack against the haunches of the two flanks of the advance. They did not win back all their lost ground, but they did cause a considerable withdrawal – to the line of what was to become known as the Flesquières Salient – and the hopes which had rocketed both in England and in the Allied trenches, fell accordingly. However, not everyone's morale suffered, and members of the Cavalry Club were able to congratulate themselves upon the attitude of sceptical disgust with which they had always regarded the new-fangled petrol engine.

And in order to deflect opprobrium which might fall upon his own head, the Army Commander in whose area the attack had been carried out (and who on November 25th could confidently have expected honours and the Nation's gratitude), in early December wrote unfairly and uncharacteristically: 'I attribute the reason for the local success on the part of enemy to one cause and one alone, namely – lack of training on the part of junior officers and NCOs and men.' Sir Douglas Haig, however, the Commander-in-Chief, would not support this attitude, sacked several of his subordinate commanders and assumed full responsibility for the set-back himself.

The episode was thus concluded, cavalrymen believing that their traditional position on the pinnacle of the military hierarchy was unchallenged, the tank men angry but obstinately certain of the ultimate justification of their ideas. The infantrymen consoled their dashed hopes of an end to their appalling tribulations with their customary mordant cynicism, and life in the line continued as before.

It was not a pleasant life for either side, for it was characterized by mud, the stench of decomposition, and feelings of almost unbearable strain and futility – strain as a result of the conditions, futility as a result of the utter lack of success which had attended all efforts on both sides to break the appalling deadlock on the front. It had existed now for three whole years, blocking the progress of nations, robbing their populations of happiness, and ending so many lives in futile and inconsequential agony – for delusive hope had tantalized ten million men with dreams of breaking it, and in so doing had led them forward to a million deaths.

From the Belgian coast near Nieuport, the trench lines and the strips of ground between and behind them which war had wasted, lay smeared across the land like the trail of a gigantic snail. It left the sand-dunes of the coast in a fifteen-mile southerly curve, then bulged out eastwards and back again like the outline of a chancre around the murdered landscape of the Ypres Salient. Then from Messines to just east of Rheims it wobbled in an uncertain curve of small salients and re-entrants, making an overall bulge to the south-westward, after which it ran due east for nearly sixty miles to the Verdun fortress complex which anchored it firmly.

Then came the St. Mihiel salient – two thirty-mile long sides of an equilateral triangle which jutted into France – after which the line curved gently and comparatively evenly south-eastwards, until it rounded the northern end of the Vosges to run south along their eastern flank. Opposite Mulhouse it commenced its final stretch – southwards across the Belfort gap, to end just in front of the little village of Beurnevesin on the Swiss frontier.

The strip was sealed at its northern end by the sea – augmented

6

by a murderous tangle of underwater wire, booby traps and contact mines sown by both sides – and at its southern end by the Swiss frontier, jealously guarded by troops of that naturally apprehensive neutral. Between these points the web of trenches ran in a swathe of danger and discomfort – across rivers which flooded them for months on end, across main pavé roads whose surfaces had long been blown to granite chips or ground to powder, across minor roads which had been completely obliterated. Villages had stood on the line when it had first been formed – they had sometimes been the anchorage points upon which company or battalion flanks had rested: now their remains were perhaps a collection of shattered, roofless buildings, deserted by their owners, inhabited only by transient poilus 'resting' in a quiet part of the line, while in sectors held by the British the villages had gone completely, only a crude placard reading 'Site of Pozières', 'Site of St. Julien', 'Site of La Boiselle', reminding passers-by of their erstwhile existence. From the air, pilots or balloonists would sometimes observe a pinker tinge in the ground where brick rubble had filled the craters and stained the mud.

The French right wing – along the flank of the Vosges – was a discontinuous line of forts and outposts, but along the rest of the line it was, in theory, possible to walk below ground from Nieuport to Verdun. (It would have taken at least two months, and enormous determination.) In practice such a journey could never have been made through the Allied trenches and is of doubtful possibility through those of the Central Powers. So far as the British were concerned, although parts of the line had been very strongly fortified with deep trenches and cavernous dug-outs, such practice was in general discouraged by the Staff, who recognized the difficulties of waging offensive warfare once the men who had to carry it out had been allowed to provide themselves with any degree of comfort or protection. This, of course, did not prevent them on their infrequent visits to the line from complaining angrily about the untidy and generally inadequate state of the trenches, the men's uniforms, and the general attitude of thinly-veiled contempt with which they felt themselves, correctly, to be regarded.

The French attitude to fortification was similar, coloured by the fact that the trenches were in their own soil and a considerable area of their country was occupied by the hated Boche: the sooner the foe was evicted the better – and by 1918, the great majority of the vaunted French Army were unconcerned as to whether this desired end was obtained by a treaty of victory or one of defeat. They had realized that even victory can be bought at too high a price and were beginning to suspect that they had already paid it – so it was illogical to waste time and effort forming anything but the flimsiest and most temporary defences. It was also hard work, and would raise suspicions in the Boche mind that offensive activity was contemplated. This would bring retaliation and more French blood would be spilt. No – let the trenches be deep enough for the men to shelter in them as necessary, and if the Americans when they took them over wanted something better, then they could dig them themselves.

So if the British trenches were in places shallow and unsafe, the French trenches were in places virtually non-existent.

But the most serious obstructions to an undercover pilgrimage from the sea to Switzerland would be provided by nature. There were long periods when large portions of the line were flooded, and indeed the majority of the British line had been dug in country where it was estimated that the water-table was only a matter of two or three feet below the surface. Nevertheless, Field Regulations and Staff Orders demanded trenches seven feet deep, and by such devices as high sandbag parapets and quite extensive projects of civil engineering coupled with continual pumping operations, there were even times when the trenches were habitable.

But when bombardment destroyed the intricate drainage system, or heavy rainfall overburdened it, the trenches flooded and mud lay across the battlefront like a gigantic squid awaiting its prey. During 1916 a piece of German propaganda called *The Archives of Reason* was circulated in the Americas offering advice to those who wished their countries to join the Allies. 'Dig a trench shoulder high in your garden,' it suggested, 'fill it half full of water and get into it. Remain there for two or three days on an empty stomach. Furthermore, hire a lunatic to shoot at you with revolvers and machine-guns at close range. This arrangement is quite equal to a war and will cost your country very much less.'

Few pieces of propaganda have contained so high a proportion of the truth – not that this prevented the combatant Governments from condemning ever-increasing numbers of their countrymen to exactly such an existence. Neither were those countrymen allowed in training so graphic and accurate a description of their future abode and activity. They were, instead, shown diagrams of impressive symmetry and then later sent to such dry and well-drained areas as Salisbury Plain in England, where they duly translated the diagrams into physical facts.

Here, the trenches traversed back and forth in beautifully accurate lengths, the chalk of the Plain lending itself to the clean lines of exact right-angles. Firesteps were level and wide enough for the heavy boots of the men who stood upon them, sandbags were clean and properly stacked, grenade and ammunition shelves convenient but deep enough for safety. There was ample material for full revetting, and the duckboards fitted snugly over the sump channels; the latrines brought smiles of delight to the most pernickety inspecting general.

In these ideal trench systems, saps zig-zagged forward to neatly dug listening posts or perhaps to well-sited and sandbagged machine-gun nests, and with no hostile interference to impede the work, the barbed wire was neatly and tightly strung between its pickets – at night too, to give reality to the exercise (the pickets having been accurately sited and driven during the afternoon period of instruction) unless, of course, it had been raining too hard for the instructors. Communication trenches snaked superbly back to the support lines, shallowing as they went at the fixed and statutory rate, and when they eventually shallowed up to ground level, it was usually alongside a deep pit with concrete base and semi-circular bastion in which stood a beautifully painted sign reading 'Gun Pit'. To see the real thing one had to journey to Happy Valley, Larkhill.

Such was the ideal, and elderly generals brought back from retirement saw to it, with the aid of long-service NCOs, that the rag, tag and bobtail of the New Armies were smart and soldierly in appearance, and moreover knew how to retain that smartness when they went overseas. A few younger officers, recovering from wounds and awaiting their return to the front, did occasionally try to introduce some reality into the picture, but their efforts did not receive a great deal of support.

For the reality at the end of 1917 was something quite different.

An official report made at the time stated firmly that the British line was in no state whatsoever to withstand a determined attack. It was rarely sited to good advantage, having invariably been formed

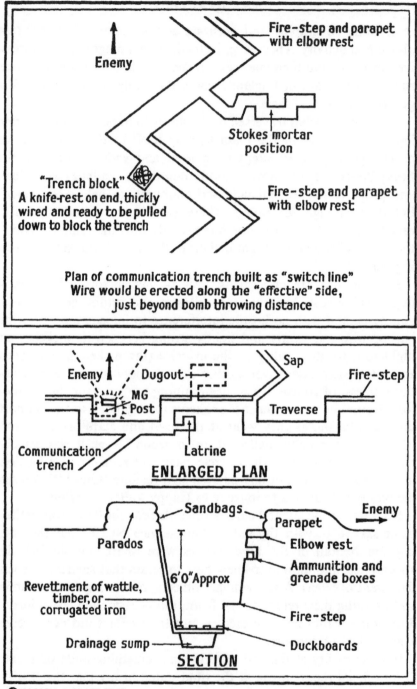

Plan of communication trench built as "switch line"
Wire would be erected along the "effective" side,
just beyond bomb throwing distance

ENLARGED PLAN

SECTION

In theory, trenches were to be constructed like this....

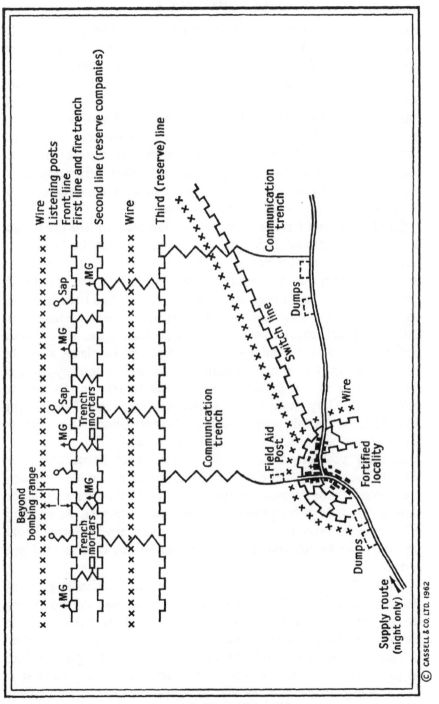

. . . and laid out like this

along the high-water mark of an attack. The protective wire belts were far too thin in number and flimsy in construction, machine-gun posts were inadequately sandbagged, traverses were sketchy, trenches insecurely revetted, while long stretches had little parados and no parapet: the sentries lay in grooves, or all too often behind barricades of piled bodies. There were few deep dug-outs, no deeply buried signal network, and the only concrete shelters were those captured from the Germans. (There is a decided note of pique in the report of one British Staff Officer, who indignantly complained that all the shelters which he inspected had been constructed with loopholes pointing in the wrong direction.)

Communication trenches were few in number and had often been allowed to fall into disrepair, switch-lines having been used as supply trenches: these in turn had been allowed to drop to the defensive level of the purpose they served. In the back areas, the old British lines from which the Somme and Ypres offensives had been launched should, in theory, have been available as lines of deep defence, but with the British effort concentrated for so long upon attack, there had been no labour available for their upkeep. In places also, the French civilians had actually begun to fill in and clear away some of the rear lines of the British area, in order to restore the land to cultivation. Oddly enough there seems little evidence of their being allowed to follow this practice behind their own lines – but perhaps they did not consider it worth while to do so.

Artillery positions were usually in somewhat better case than those of the infantry, but close up behind the front line gun-emplace-ments were shallow scoops in the ground and relied far more upon canvas camouflage for protection than upon concrete. After firing a few rounds, even in icy weather, the ground beneath often broke up under the recoil, and the guns had to be dug out, re-sited and re-laid.

A revealing comment on the life lived in the trenches is given by Robert Graves. 'The Western Front', he says, 'was known among its embittered inhabitants as The Sausage Machine, because it was fed with live men, churned out corpses, and remained firmly screwed in place.' It did so moreover in conditions of appalling discomfort. In past summers every bursting shell had spread dirt and dust in vast floating clouds, and the flies multiplied in the filth and spread sickness and intolerable irritation: in wet weather the chaos was coated with slime. The least unpleasant conditions a front-line soldier could expect were those now reigning – hard frost – when at least the trenches and dug-outs could be kept clean and dry, although it might take half an hour's energetic jumping up and down and arm-pounding to restore circulation after a spell on the firestep. But the climate in Flanders and Northern France had generally been too temperate to provide this relief. Humidity, not ice, had been the prevailing factor.

The stench, therefore, for most of the time was nauseating and inescapable. Stagnant mud, rotting half-buried bodies, stale human sweat and excrement, the pervading reek of chloride of lime, all these have haunted, for the remainder of their days, the memories of the men who occupied the trenches; and a malicious practice, common to both sides, was to lob occasional mortar bombs into enemy latrines with depressing effect. Often the lingering, sinister odour of phosgene or mustard gas condemned the soldiers to the sweating discomfort of rudimentary gas-masks for hours on end, while cordite and lyddite fumes were so much a part of the day-to-day existence as to be virtually unnoticeable; only the fragrance of burning wood, bubbling Maconachie stew (meat and veg) or frying bacon relieved occasionally the mephitic misery.

In the trenches, the British lived on bully-beef and stew, tasteless ration-biscuits which burnt well in time of fuel shortage, strong, dark brown tea made with condensed milk, and until the middle of 1917 there had been available for the front line troops an apparently inexhaustible supply of plum and apple jam; by 1918 some sectors were receiving jam of another flavour, but had been doing so for so long that they occasionally maundered nostalgically for the old days. A tot of rum for each man went into the tea at morning stand-to, but among the men there was little drunkenness in the line as, except for that ration, spirits were forbidden to them. Among the officers it was different, and gallons of whisky and cognac were consumed each night: but this may have been as palliative against the appalling strain and responsibility, and in any case there was little room in crowded dug-outs for furniture-smashing or riotous parties.

And all day and all night, along the entire length of the front and on both sides, were played the endless games of cards. The card-players were a race apart – uninterested in food except as essential fuel, uninterested in conversation other than call, curse or cackle of triumph, uninterested in the progress of the war or even the daily battle, except in so far as it took players from the table, or furnished new ones. These men may well have been the ones to find the most satisfactory cushion against the realities of life.

The realities of death were ever-present and inescapable, too; all but the most sensitive minds had grown callous in self-protection. Those too open and receptive drove their owners to madness, to suicide, or at best to bitter mockery, and the poets who retained their lives and sanities produced verse of searing power.

> To these I turn, in these I trust,
> Brother Lead and Sister Steel;
> To his blind power I make appeal,
> I guard her beauty clean from rust . . . .

wrote Siegfried Sassoon, and satirically offered it to a world which had become capable of believing that he meant it.

All day and every day, Death was present – and at night, the working parties and patrols went out to court it. From dusk until just before dawn they were out, hacking at the earth to carve connecting trenches between isolated posts or even between shell-holes which could be used by machine-gunners, driving iron screw-pickets or wooden stakes into the ground to support lines of hastily-draped barbed wire, lying close to enemy trenches all night in order to overhear their conversation; perhaps leaping into them, and after a few minutes' nightmarish activity with bomb and bayonet, dragging back to their own lines some whimpering, blood-smeared prisoner, for the sake of a few morsels of incoherent military intelligence.

Draped on the wire belts were the bodies of the men killed during these white, nerve-racked, back-breaking nights. Some were killed by rifle-bullets as they crawled over the ground carrying coils of wire, some caught by scything machine-gun fire as they stood to fix the wire, some bombed by prowling patrols as they worked, hearing above their own exertions only the last few footfalls of the oncoming enemy, or the soft thud of the grenade as it landed at their feet. The entire trench system from the Channel to the Swiss frontier was dug, fortified and held by pain and death.

At any hour of the day or night, death or mutilation came from the guns. On the ice-hard ground the shells would burst with devastating violence, slivers of steel sighing or screaming as they sped through the frost-laden air to clatter on the ground or to thud dully into animate or inanimate obstruction. Each type of gun had its own noise, each type of shell its own evil. German 77-millimetre field artillery spat 'whiz-bangs' which arrived with the noise of giant fire-crackers: 5·9s threw out their shells with a vicious bark, the shells whining and growling over the valleys and ridges before ending their lives with violent, ill-tempered crashes. Heavy guns pounded the back areas with shells that roared overhead like express trains and smashed to earth with tremendous and awful effect; and every now and then minenwerfers would cough their black burdens into the air to wobble uncertainly in a terrifying parabola, and burst with wide obliteration in the trenches.

The infantry hated the artillery. They hated its wantonness, its random, murderous power, above all their defencelessness against it. It was like a primitive god, uncertain, inconsistent and unjust.

Against enemy infantry, the soldiers had at least the defence of their own skill and their sentries' eyesight. During the day, these crouched for hours at their periscopes, constantly scanning the enemy positions and the ground between – and at night they lay out in forward posts, watching no-man's-land in the pale-green, spectral light of the flares, listening to the continuous muffled drum-beat of limbers and ammunition columns, of lorries, horses and the million men who shuffled interminably behind the battlefronts.

All men took this duty in turn, but in the times when they were not occupied on the firestep or about the trenches, there was talk of home, desultory reading – and sleep: by 1918 they had months of arrears to make up. Tarnished strains of music from mouth-organ or gramophone floated through the British trenches in quiet times, invariably playing the song-hits from the London shows: 'Keep the Home Fires Burning', 'If You Were the Only Girl in the World', 'Pack up Your Troubles in Your Old Kit Bag'. But the singers sang the trench ballads – obscene, ribald, some unbelievably bitter:

> The bells of hell go ting-aling-aling,
> For you but not for me,

15

The herald angels sing-aling-aling,
I'll be up there for tea.

or

If you want to find your sweetheart, I know where he is,
I know where he is, I know where he is.
If you want to find your sweetheart, I know where he is,
Hanging on the front line wire.

Rarely did the notes of classical music sound in the British lines
and a record of a sonata would remain unplayed or be quickly
broken unless jealously guarded by its owner, but oddly enough
strains of such music would be listened to in silence if they floated
across from the enemy lines. One infantryman tells of the existence
in 1916 of an old piano in the trenches opposite, upon which some
practised hand had played Schubertian melodies for hours on end.
When after a day of sporadic inter-trench raids the piano was silent,
there was no satisfaction expressed, and the following day the
infantryman heard a sentry softly whistling passages from the
second movement of the Unfinished Symphony.

Other sounds in the background of trench life were the scrape
and clatter of spades, the clank of dixies, the thud of earth-balled
boots on the duckboards in fine weather, the slop and squelch of
mud and the continual trickle of running water in wet: curses and
laughter, shouted orders and the high cry of 'Stretcher bearers!' –
these formed the tapestry of sound, rent by the crack of casual
bullet, burst open by the explosion of occasional rifle-grenade or
'minnie'.

The men themselves were not of the highest standards of either
physique or morale. It was impossible that they should be by 1918,
for the cream of the Empire's manhood had already been lost on the
Somme, and since. In the first day of that ill-conceived attack –
largely in the first hour – nearly 60,000 of the young, ardent enthusi-
asts who had rushed forward to join Kitchener's New Army had
fallen; and the slaughter of the following months plus Passchendaele
had taken most of the rest. Those who still lived and were fit enough
to serve in the trenches, did so with shattered nerves, and bodies
which cringed with expected agony at every rifle-crack and bomb-

16

burst. According to the casualty records, as many men had been wounded and returned to action as were serving in the front line – but some had been wounded several times, thus allowing a proportion of unscathed.

The old Regular Army – the Contemptibles – had gone; graves, hospitals and prison-camps held the majority, the residue served on the Staff.

There was still the continual influx of youngsters coming in as soon as they reached the minimum age – as their brothers had done in 1914 and 1915 – but now their ranks were mixed with conscripts and the ideals of service and sacrifice which had animated the original New Armies were corroded away. When everyone had been a volunteer, the sense of patriotic compact had engendered a fierce pride in being a front-line soldier. There had been a willingness to accept all hardship, all pain, and death: only the end of the war or a bullet could end a voluntarily entered contract. But now this atmosphere was gone, and the sly and the self-centred strove to set the pattern of behaviour. Often they were successful, and divisions with magnificent records gained at Delville Wood or Gallipoli were to prove of doubtful reliability during the closing weeks of the war.

Yet in many ways these men were more efficient soldiers. The cunning which they developed in avoiding the more obnoxious duties sometimes helped them to avoid the enemy bullets, and the almost dog-like devotion and reverence which the first volunteers had offered to their regular NCOs and officers, had been replaced by a deep and not ill-founded scepticism. 'Never obey orders – they're already cancelled', was a maxim which too often proved reliable, as young officers coming new into the line were quickly taught. Older officers were by now well aware of the fact that tomorrow a live soldier would be of more use than a hero uselessly killed today. Courage and fortitude were still available in abundance – but eager confidence was at a premium: the well of the soldiers' patriotism had been drawn upon too deeply, and too often had its waters been poured wastefully away. Now they wished to live, for they could not be certain that any cause but the enemy's would profit by their deaths.

For the enemy – the Jerries as they were called in envy of their coal-scuttle helmets – the Briton in the front line had considerable respect and a sympathy born of common experience. Among the

17

legends of enemy behaviour with which newcomers into the line were regaled were always a few to show Jerry in good light – the story of the 1914 Christmas fraternizations, the virtual cease-fire after Loos which had allowed the British to collect their wounded from no-man's-land, the unspoken agreements in some parts of the line at times, to fire high or to miss the unwary with the first shot. These stories leavened the main tale of hard, professional efficiency, and sweetened the bitterness caused by the web of booby traps left behind by the Germans when in 1917 they retreated behind the deep fortifications of the Hindenburg Line.

Even the hatred caused by these abominations had an admixture of reluctant, professional admiration. In all – as so often happens – the fighting soldier preferred his enemy to his ally, for the French were no more popular with the British than the British with them.

By this time, it was the Staff who were regarded by the British front-line soldier as his main enemy (a not uncommon development in any army) and for them he nursed a bitter hatred and an undying contempt. There were indeed, many occasions upon which members of the Staff acted with such unbelievable idiocy that no other effect upon the men who had to carry out their plans could have been expected. Upon one occasion a general ordered that gas should be released at all costs before an attack, despite the fact that the wind was blowing gently in his men's faces: on another, in order to 'raise the morale' of troops utterly exhausted by weeks of attack and counterattack, a daylight advance in November was ordered across ground clearly marked on the map as 'Marsh: sometimes dry in summer.'

Only one army commander seems to have made regular inspections of conditions at the front, and after 1914, no one in the higher ranks ever spent as long as one week living the life of the front-line infantry in the trenches. Thus, the crassest mistakes had been made due solely to ignorance of local conditions.

The fault lay basically in the peacetime structure of the Army, in which the officers were separated from the other ranks by an impassable social and mental barrier. Regular officers – especially in the favoured cavalry regiments which were to supply most of the top commanders – were scions of wealthy and aristocratic houses:

a very large proportion of the men, on the other hand, aptly deserved Wellington's description of his army at Waterloo – 'the scum of the earth, enlisted for drink.' There was thus no common ground between commissioned and non-commissioned ranks other than that forged by action – and action in 1914 had killed most of the regular officers and led to the rapid promotion of the rest.

The survivors were men used to expensive pleasures who had led lives of much physical but little mental exercise, and very few had any form of cultural interest which would serve to widen their intellectual field. They had been trained on the assumption that officers were gentlemen whose life was ordered by a set and clearly understood code, and that the men were shifty, idle, irresponsible and knavish – and although the vicissitudes of war compelled them now to accept as brother officers men with utterly different ideas, who obviously did not conform to the strict and peculiar tenets of their own code, they saw no reason to believe – few of them even suspected – that there could be any difference in the type of man who now served in the ranks.

In this they were enormously mistaken. Few events in Britain's history have been finer than the nation-wide flow of volunteers into the forces between the outbreak of war and the introduction of conscription at the beginning of 1916. From all walks of life they came, professional man and artisan, poet and plumber, coal-miner, craftsman and Cordon Bleu cook. The vast majority of them had proved themselves quite capable of supporting themselves (and often their families) in civilian life, and many were progressing satis-factorily up the ladders of their vocations when they had answered their country's call: they were cheerful, capable, industrious, eager to learn and aflame with enthusiasm. Altogether they represented the finest material ever offered to a military commander, and from them could have been moulded the greatest army the world had ever seen.

Yet what they accomplished was due far more to their own unquenchable spirit than to their professional mentors. These eager multitudes were the men with whom the regular officer on the Staff eschewed contact (the new, unacceptable officers could best act as channels of communication), and when circumstances rendered contact unavoidable, the majority of Staff officers approached the task with either feudal arrogance or unbearable patronage. At first this attitude was accepted by the men of the New Armies as just another inexplicable aspect in a new, rather incomprehensible life. But soon they responded with ribaldry, and when the iron of failure due to administrative inefficiency had entered their souls, with blistering contempt.

It was not an emotion which dimmed with the passage of time. After the war, A. G. MacDonnell was to pillory the Staff in several of his books, and C. E. Montague referred to the promotion of one officer from division to corps with relief, as it lessened the danger to the troops from that of a fatal accident to that merely of an obscure mortal disease. Another refers to members of the Staff striding about with hunched shoulders and riding-whips, endeavouring to give the impression that they had spent their entire lives in strained relations with a horse.

'Jerry's got a gun on our front,' one warrior is reported as telling another, '. . . with a fantastic range. Must be over forty miles.'

'That's nothing,' replied his companion. 'He's got one on our front that hit Corps Headquarters!'

This last comment was apt, and reveals a true but sombre state of affairs. One psychological hazard against which no commanding general of the Great War saw the necessity of protecting his Staff, was the fact that the longer a man remains out of danger, the less willing he becomes to face it. Officers who in 1914 would have thought nothing of walking unconcernedly along a bullet-swept ridge in order to hearten their men by showing an inspiring contempt for danger, by 1918 would not spend an hour within shelling range of the enemy if they could avoid it. Too often they were inept at concealing their emotions and extraordinarily tactless in their excuses for retreat.

'Must get back,' announced one of them loudly, as the evening 'hate' started in a particularly noisome sector of the line. 'Got veal for dinner, and if I don't get there in time the bloody servant won't have cooled the wine properly!'

Such men – GSOs in the lower echelons – and such incidents, raised the front-line infantry's fury to almost ungovernable heights, for they felt instinctively that these were the men who obscured the vision of the commanding generals, and who twisted or failed to pass on to them the representations of the fighting soldiers.

There was some truth in this, but there is more in the truism that generals get the staff they deserve. Men who were incapable of realizing the difference in the quality of those now under their command were not surprisingly also incapable of either adapting themselves to new conditions of warfare, or realizing that some of the ideas upon which they had been trained were basically incorrect. So far as the strategical and tactical problems which faced them were concerned, many of the Great War generals were, in one of the more brilliant analogies of modern literature, like savages trying to tear a screw from a baulk of timber: all they could think to do was to try to exert more and more direct pull on the head of the screw. The notion that it could be loosened by rotation would never have occurred to them, and would have been treated with the utmost contempt if made.

Most of them were also overwhelmed by the sheer magnitude of the forces under their command. Relatively unambitious men had suddenly found themselves commanding armies far larger than those of Wellington or Marlborough – whom they had been brought up to regard as the greatest military geniuses their country had produced. They endeavoured, honestly and sincerely, to grapple with the vast complexities which faced them, and they failed, most of them, because they were holding positions far above their professional ceiling.

This problem, in fact, vexed all armies, including the enemy's. Rudolf Binding, while serving on the Staff of one of the German armies, questioned whether there was a single general then alive who knew how to use armies numbered in millions:

One hears that there are people who can only count up to three. The Fueguian can count up to five, as many fingers as he has on his hand. Many company commanders can really only count up to one hundred, the sum of their cohort. I know myself men who could do anything with one regiment but nothing with two, and history teaches us that there have been men who could do this and that with one hundred thousand men, but could not move three hundred thousand.

Such then, were the intellectual limitations of many of the men who directed their countries' war efforts on the Western Front, and as invariably happens when men in command have great powers but neither the experience nor the mental ability to wield them, they all in their various capacities were soon surrounded by courts of flatterers and sycophants – indeed none but these could remain

21

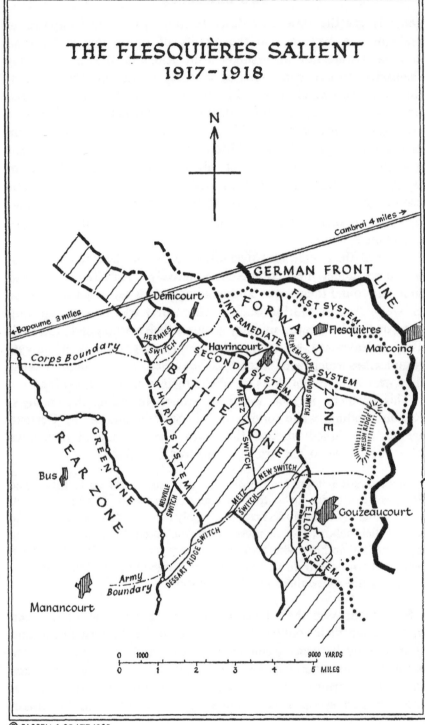

THE FLESQUIÈRES SALIENT
1917-1918

N

Cambrai 4 miles →

GERMAN FRONT LINE

Démicourt

← Bapaume 3 miles

FORWARD

FIRST SYSTEM

INTERMEDIATE

Flesquières

HERMIES SWITCH

Havrincourt

SECOND SYSTEM

BILHEN·CHAPEL·WOOD SWITCH

SYSTEM

Marcoing

Corps Boundary

BATTLE ZONE

THIRD SYSTEM

METZ SWITCH

ZONE

WELSH RIDGE

GREEN LINE

REAR ZONE

NEUVILLE SWITCH

NEW SWITCH

METZ SWITCH

DESSART RIDGE SWITCH

YELLOW SYSTEM

Gouzeaucourt

Bus

Army Boundary

Manancourt

0   1000   9000 YARDS

0   1   2   3   4   5 MILES

© CASSELL & CO. LTD. 1962

around the seats of power, for uncertainty of mind or purpose is exquisitely sensitive to contrary or critical opinion, and uses its power to suppress it.

There were thus many headquarter organizations of divisional, corps, or army status, composed essentially of one man endeavouring earnestly to carry out duties far beyond his capacities, surrounded by favourites whose main occupation was bolstering his confidence, eagerly endorsing his every opinion and often suppressing facts and figures which cast the unwelcome light of truth upon the effects of his decisions. It is no matter for wonder that the sight of red tabs on the uniform of a British officer provoked bitter anger in the men who paid with their lives for the egregious errors made by the men who wore them.

There were, of course, exceptions. Men would intrigue and bribe in order to be sent to the Second Army when Plumer commanded it and Harington was his Chief-of-Staff, and men in the Dominion divisions were not so bitter as those from England, once they had their own Dominion (and ex-front line) Staffs. Possibly because as Commander-in-Chief he was so utterly remote from them all, Sir Douglas Haig was not himself the object of great criticism from those in the front line: it was as though those between absorbed the anger and the scorn. Perhaps, too, faith in somebody, somewhere, was a psychological necessity for those in the trenches.

* * *

There had existed during the closing months of 1917, a place of weakness in the British line – and weakness inevitably invites attack. The position was that known as the Flesquières Salient, and it had been formed as a result of the tank breakthrough towards Cambrai in November, and the subsequent counterattack which had won back for the Germans most of the ground they had lost. The Flesquières Salient was, in fact, the truncated stub of the short-lived Cambrai Salient – and here, as the old year died, was fought a battle which typified the bitterness and the fury, the bravery and the squalor, the resolution and the waste of all the trench fighting which had taken place along the Western Front.

It was a microcosm of the war, and it happened in a locality which was to prove a most vital sector of the front in the months to come.

The front line – such as it was – was held by men of the British

63rd Division. For seven miles the salient bulged out towards the enemy from Demicourt in the north to Gouzeaucourt in the south, its apex lying just north of a derisory hillock called Welsh Ridge, and overlooking the German-held village of Marcoing. This was ground which a month before had been in the German rear – a stretch of the Hindenburg Line now served as first support trench behind the British front – with the result that when the men of the 63rd Division took it over, it was neither continuously trenched nor adequately protected by barbed wire belts. It was, in fact, a discontinuous line of outposts hurriedly improvised in the stress of battle.

It was as well that the nights were long, and the labours of the working-parties could thus be extended to the limit of their physical endurance. By Christmas Eve the trench system had been completed – or at least made continuous – running in three shallow, uneven lines which jutted back and forth like the edges of ill-used toothed wheels, for four miles in a curve around the apex of the salient. One line scarred the forward slope of the ridge, one line the crest, and the third lay at the foot of the steep reverse slope. At intervals, even shallower communication trenches zig-zagged back across the ridge to connect the three lines, while in the open areas more wire belts looped and sprawled, forming occasional dense thickets around the few sandbagged machine-gun posts. Ditches – they could not be called trenches – ran back from these posts to the trench lines behind them.

Just before dawn on December 30th, an intensive barrage was opened on the front line and advanced posts, and when the barrage abruptly shifted to the line on the crest of the ridge, white-garbed forms rose from the snow just beyond the outer wire belt, and stormed across it towards the trenches. The chaos and confusion of a trench battle descended on the forward positions with the immediacy and tragic inevitability of a nightmare.

Those British on the firesteps screamed warnings and opened fire, those in dug-outs rushed out thrusting their bayonets up towards the swathed and sheeted figures leaping down upon them, and knots of cursing, struggling men swayed back and forth, killing or maiming each other with club and bayonet, rifle-butt and boot, fighting too close and too quick to aim or fire. The first wave of attackers was beaten back or killed in the trenches, some of the second wave broke into the communication trenches and began bombing their way along them to the support trench, then the third attack wave came in and all the forward positions were submerged.

Troops in the support line counterattacked, at first along the communication trenches. These were always cut on the zig-zag, and to clear them of enemy occupants, it was necessary to lob bombs over the top from one arm into the next, using the resulting explosion as the signal for a charge around the corner – and twice enemy groups came at the British bombing parties from the further end of the arm to contest their way with pistol and bayonet. Eventually, the bombing parties were held up by yet another hazard – one of their own 'knife-rests', swathed in coils of barbed wire, had been toppled into the trench, and rifle fire from the far corner shot down two men trying to remove it. As the bombing party waited, baulked, whistles blew in the support trench behind them, and the rest of the support company clambered out into the open to charge between the shell-holes and the wire thickets towards the now ominously silent positions of the front line.

Immediately, the line pricked into life with German rifle and machine-gun fire, and as the charging men passed the position of the baulked bombing party they were enfiladed by the enemy in the front portion of the communication trench. Inevitably, their ranks thinned and the survivors went to ground, so the bombing party in their turn left cover, went overland to the next arm, cleared and dropped down into it, then resumed their systematic, bloody advance along the trench. As they reached the final arm leading to the front line, the survivors in the open arose and flung themselves across the last stretch of shell-pocked ground, over the parados and into the trench. The ensuing brawl was bitter, brutal, but brief.

By 8.25 a.m. the positions in the front line along one section had therefore been restored. True, the two companies holding them at dawn had been virtually annihilated – but so had the companies which had attacked them, so from the Staff point of view it remained merely to be seen who had the larger reserves. But in the meantime there was urgent business for the fighting men to attend to: bodies were flung out to build up the parapets, blown-in sections of the trench hastily re-built, dug-outs cautiously inspected for lurking foes, ammunition and bombs rushed up through the communication trenches.

But although this section of the front line had been retaken, the enemy still remained in a longer stretch to the left – and it soon became evident that no mere bombing party working along the trench line would shift them. So in the afternoon, a reserve battalion was brought up from the rear, put into the crest line and ordered to attack over the open ground. This battalion was the 1st Artists Rifles. At 2.15 p.m., without the benefit of support from either artillery or even trench mortars, the men of the battalion clawed their way out of the crest line, and against a background of snow-covered hill and grey sky, those who had not been immediately shot down, marched forward in obedience to their orders. Before they had covered twenty yards, the ground behind was blotched with khaki forms – some still, some writhing – and soon the wire thickets, the shell-holes and the inexorable pressure of mounting fear caused groups to form, as clusters of men automatically but unconsciously sought the chimerical protection of the herd. Officers shouted at them, waving them apart, beckoning them on – and the groups would split, inevitably leaving more of their number on the snow, to bunch again ten yards further on amid new wire belts, on the lips of more craters, still under the pitiless rain of fire and amid the crash and clatter of battle.

Halfway between the lines, the survivors went to ground in the exiguous cover of shell-holes and the slight – virtually imaginary – ridges in the snow. Officers scurried from group to group, encouraging the wounded, assessing the hopes for another advance. At last word was passed that no further movement would take place until dark, so with bayonet and entrenching tool they all began to dig themselves in; and if their efforts made little impact on the icy ground, the exercise at least kept their blood circulating. But it also made them thirsty and their water supply had been left far behind in the rush of the morning, while the noise of their activity revealed their positions to the observant German infantry. As dusk approached, rifle-grenades were arching slowly over the dividing ground, exploding viciously in the newly dug positions.

With dusk came a considerable increase in enemy rifle and machine-gun fire. More German troops crossed from their own lines and re-inforced those who had occupied the captured positions all day, bringing with them an apparently unlimited supply of flares, which climbed into the sky with slow and sometimes arresting beauty to

26

burst and flood the desolation with powdery light, giving it the stark, inhuman character of a charcoal sketch. With the help of this perilous illumination, men dragged or carried the wounded back to the doubtful protection of the support trench, a signals officer crept from trench to forward positions and from shell-holes to communication trench trailing out behind him an ever-lengthening skein of telephone wires (uselessly, for surface-laid communications are almost invariably the first casualties when action starts), and the Regimental Sergeant Major earned grudging tribute by organizing carrying parties with hot soup for the men in the shell-holes. The abandoned water was eventually brought up – no mean feat, for it lay at the bottom of a valley into which the enemy had been astutely pumping gas shells, which burst with loud pops of prudish affectation and left their lethal, creeping cargo insidiously to fill the trap.

By midnight, the Artists were ready to continue their advance. They lay on the edges of their shell-holes or within their own individually dug shallow ditches, gripping their rifles, counting the seconds, muttering their invocations, awaiting the signal. And just before it was due, shadowy forms arose from dead ground in front and advanced towards them behind a fulminating screen of stick-bombs. Some of the Artists rose and charged forward to escape the bursting bombs and meet their antagonists in the open, some stayed where they lay and if they survived the bombs coolly picked off their attackers: once again machine-guns chattered, and men of the support battalion poured in enfilading fire. The enemy went to ground, and those who could do so crawled back to their trenches.

Once more the wounded were collected, the signal lines re-laid, the survivors counted, the position re-assessed. It was not favourable, for casualties were mounting – but as suggestions for withdrawal would inevitably be countered with the irrefutable fact that the enemy had probably suffered the same proportion of losses, nobody made such a suggestion. At 2 a.m., another attempt was made by the Artists to advance, and a few more yards were gained before the survivors were once more driven to earth – to begin again the dreary, heartbreaking attempt to carve cover from the ice-hard ground. The wounded went back, the signals officer came out, a nineteen-year-old second lieutenant found that as the result of casualties he now commanded the company on the left flank, and because the intelligence officer found that the usual methods of

collecting information had become in the circumstances too uncertain and laborious, he rose to his feet and stalked rather officiously
about no-man's land discovering where the men were concentrated,
where the gaps lay, what obstructions would impede the next
advance. He then returned overland to the support trench and reported all this to his commanding officer.

At the same time as the Artists were ordered to re-take the lost
ground on the left, another reserve battalion of the 63rd Division
had been ordered to re-establish the position on the right. With,
however, a refreshing independence of mind, the battalion commander decided that in the existing situation his men's lives were of
more value than time, so he waited until dusk. Then, while there was
still just sufficient light for his men to see the ground immediately
in front but not sufficient for the enemy to see them, he sent out
probing patrols with orders to keep quiet, to keep low, and to lie
flat and still the moment they heard any sound indicative of hostile
presence. When their eventual positions were reported to him, he
slowly fed more men up towards them and in due course his attacking force were all lying close up under the shoulder of the ridge,
occupying the same sort of cavities as those in which the Artists had
passed their agonizing afternoon, but much nearer to the enemy
and in full strength.

Moreover it appears that the enemy were completely unaware of
their presence, for when at midnight the signal for the attack was
given, the men swarmed over the crest and into the trenches without
a shot being fired at them, and in the resulting mêlée with the astonished foe they re-took the line at a cost of only three casualties.

The position now was that the crest line was still held along its
entire length, and only one mile-long stretch of the forward positions
originally held by the division was still in enemy hands.

The rest of the night passed in ominous quiet.

Half an hour after dawn – following the customary prolonged
bombardment – the German infantry attacked again, in wave after
wave, with the heaviest concentration against what they had every
reason to believe was the soft spot in the line. Here lay the remnants
of the original attacking companies of the Artists, now reinforced
from the supporting companies whose men held the communication
trenches leading forward. The enemy, therefore, attacked into a

sack – after their own artillery had liberally plastered the area and while it was still shelling the crest.

There are in existence statistical tables which indicate that for every casualty caused by a rifle or machine-gun bullet, there were two caused by shell or shrapnel fire. The action fought on Welsh Ridge during the morning of December 31st, 1917, does not bear these figures out, for despite all the havoc intended by the German batteries, the British infantry were still in their trenches and mud-holes when the barrage lifted and they made extraordinarily good practice against the advancing hordes. The Germans had apparently learned nothing from the *coup de main* performed a few hours before by the British reserve battalion, and they used similar tactics to those which had decimated the Artists during the previous afternoon. They moved quicker – running, not walking – but they came upright across open ground in broad daylight, and what momentum they gained in the first rush from their own positions they lost when they reached the new shell-holes, blown a few minutes beforehand by their own guns.

Although some of the leading waves did reach the Artists' line, it was only a small proportion of those who had clambered out on to the churned and blood-bespattered snow, and as the German infantry advanced into the gap, they were subjected to a sustained and withering fire which melted them away. Some seemed to stumble and then quietly subside, some turned head over heels like shot hares, some were frozen in motion as though transfixed, then to fall in a paroxysm of threshing arms and legs; some continued their onward rush with blood spuming from them until nervous reflex ended and they crashed to the ground. Those few who reached the Artists' parapet were bayoneted or shot within seconds. Nowhere did they penetrate the crest line and as they had made no direct attacks on the flank position, the only results of the German attack were high losses for themselves, smaller losses for the British.

In the early afternoon attempts at attack and counterattack died away. Less than a mile of trenches had changed hands, and those who had been driven out now occupied the more favourable position. The Germans re-arranged the short lengths of line which they had occupied so as to face the other way; the men of the 63rd Division strengthened the junctions of their new positions, and flank companies drew back to the crest line, giving themselves better fields of fire and more protection; it was a pity that the position had not been utilized before.

The action at Welsh Ridge had lasted just over thirty hours. It had cost the 63rd Division 65 officers and 1,355 men in killed, wounded and missing. There is no reason to believe that the German losses were less. The unchanging pattern had been traced, at the unchanging cost in human life.

There was little other fighting along the Western Front that day – sporadic sniping, routine shelling, a few lengths of trench blown in by mortars: it is probable that the average daily 'wastage' of some two thousand men of all nationalities due to action or sickness caused by the conditions in which they lived, was maintained.

As light began to fail, the armies stood to. Flares and star-shells rose into the sky with the evanescence and sinister loveliness of tropical plants; the crater-studded, moon-like waste spasmodically vibrated to the percussion of desultory shellfire and explosion. More men were killed, more were wounded, more died. As midnight approached there were sounds of music and singing along the line of the German and Austrian trenches; there was a little mild celebration among the British but none, it seems, among the French.

Just south of the Ypres Salient a battalion of the Royal Sussex were in the line, and among their junior officers was the poet Edmund Blunden. Afterwards he wrote:

At the moment of midnight December 31, 1917, I stood with some acquaintances in a camp finely overlooking the whole Ypres battlefield. It was bitterly cold, and the deep snow all round lay frozen. We drank healths, and stared out across the snowy miles to the line of casual flares, still rising and floating and dropping. Their writing on the night was as the earliest scribbling of children, meaningless; they answered none of the questions with which a watcher's eyes were painfully wide. Midnight; successions of coloured lights from one point, of white ones from another, bullying salutes of guns in brief bombardment, crackling of machine-guns small on the tingling air; but the sole answer to unspoken but importunate questions was the line of lights in the same relation to Flanders as at midnight a year before. All agreed that 1917 had been a sad offender. All observed that 1918 did not look promising at its birth.

It was the fourth New Year's Eve of the war.

30

2. At Home

'A superficial review of the appearance of the vast battlefield as a whole [at the beginning of 1918] would lead to the conclusion that the Central Powers were winning the war,' wrote the Prime Minister of Great Britain in later years. If he felt this at the time, he was far too astute a politician to allow the slightest inkling of it to colour his public utterances.

Mr. Lloyd George had gained his pre-eminent position upon a declared policy of pursuing the war to a victorious conclusion, and despite the war-weariness with which he was surrounded, he knew the grim resolve beneath it. The slightest deviation upon his part from this aim, any suspicion that he might consider a negotiated peace, would result in the fall of his Government and his own dismissal from office – and he had laboured far too long and fought far too hard for the position to give it up lightly: not that Lloyd George was simply a narrowly and selfishly ambitious man, for no one can rise to high political rank – especially in time of crisis – unless he sincerely believes that his own policies, directed by himself, are the best for his country.

And it was Lloyd George's sincere conviction that the direction of Britain's war effort by her military leaders had already led her by successive bloodbaths to the brink of disaster, and that unless they were strongly curbed they would shortly plunge her in. The generals seemed to believe that they had a blank cheque upon the nation's manhood and that the reserve was inexhaustible.

During the past three years the British armies had managed to wrest from the enemy a wretchedly few square miles of worthless territory at an utterly prohibitive price, and it was poor consolation that the French losses had been as great. As for the contention that German losses had vastly exceeded those of the Allies, this remained to be proved, and was a point upon which Lloyd George was extremely sceptical. Verdun had cost the French 350,000 men, Allied losses on the Somme had been in all 600,000, and Passchendaele had cost the British alone some 300,000 men in killed, wounded and

31

missing. The last two years had cost Britain in numbers of young, fit men in the prime of life, something not far short of the entire population, men, women and children, of a very large city – and the High Command were decidedly nettled when more 'cities' were not immediately made available for their plunder.

By birth, race and temperament Lloyd George was naturally suspicious of any traditional and established form of authority (he had as a boy been in trouble for throwing stones at the local land-owner), and that of a military hierarchy headed in the field by a wealthy Scot of ancient lineage and close, plutocratic connections, aroused his strongest antipathy. To the battle against them, he brought immense talents, considerable resource and an almost demoniac energy.

He was possibly the most accomplished orator ever to occupy the highest office in British politics. Every tone from the raucous shout of violent abuse to the soft music of sweet reasonableness was his to command – and an agile brain and quick sensitivity laced his speeches with biting irony, broad humour or scintillating wit as occasion demanded. He was a compact man, with a striking head and gleaming eyes of intense vitality: few people were surprised that he had become Prime Minister once they met him, fewer people who came into continuous contact with him, trusted him, probably because they sensed that he was far quicker-witted than they were.

But the British public did because he had persuaded them that he was resolved upon total victory and nothing that he had done or said since assuming office gave them reason to believe that his resolve had weakened. His support outside Parliament was thus broad and firm; it was his position inside the House of Commons which necessitated the utmost care in manœuvre, and a combination of diplomacy and ruthlessness which must sometimes have taxed even his subtle brain to the limit.

For he was a Liberal Prime Minister ruling in Parliament only by the grace of the Conservatives, and the artifice and intrigue by which he had obtained his precarious position – according to current rumour – endeared him to nobody who heard of it.

At the outbreak of war, the position of Prime Minister had been held by Mr. Asquith, a man of wide culture and distinguished mind, leading a united country to war and supported by a House of Commons which recognized him as its greatest figure. Until the disasters of Neuve Chapelle and Loos in 1915, Mr. Asquith had not even deemed it necessary to form a coalition government, but even when the mismanagement of the Gallipoli campaign forced him to invite the Conservative Opposition to join the Cabinet (filling vacancies caused by the shelving of, among others, Mr. Winston Churchill), he still directed the business of the Government with a degree of inflexibility which was apparently inseparable from his temperament.

'His mind opened and shut smoothly and exactly, like the breech of a gun,' wrote one who knew him well – and herein lay both his strength and his weakness. His sure convictions gave him immense firmness and stature in the swirl and doubts of political life, but they made him extremely vulnerable when the truth of his convictions came into doubt. One of his convictions was that the business of politicians was to govern at home and that of generals and admirals to fight and win the war abroad – and if the generals had been able to show even moderate local successes at anything less than Pyrrhic cost, Mr. Asquith would have remained in office and his policy of non-intervention in military affairs would have been vindicated.

But the Battle of the Somme, despite its inconclusive results on the field, did produce two subsidiary effects at home which combined – with far-reaching consequences. It hardened into a firm conviction Lloyd George's belief that direction of the war must be taken from the generals, and it brought tragedy into Asquith's personal life by causing the death of his brilliant elder son, thus weakening him at a crucial moment. In December 1916 Asquith resigned, and the following day, with a few rather winsome gestures of protest, Lloyd George accepted the task of forming a Government – but as rumours of the intrigue and manœuvre by which he was credited with having attained his object filtered through the corridors of the House of Commons, the Liberal Party split. Some eighty members only supported Lloyd George; for the rest, he had to rely upon the support of the Conservatives, and to his inexpressible fury and frustration, four of the most influential only agreed to follow his leadership upon the condition that he retained his two *bêtes noires*, Generals Sir William Robertson and Sir Douglas Haig, in their offices as Chief of the Imperial General Staff and Commander-in-Chief of the British Armies in France respectively.

33

They also insisted that under no circumstances might he bring that astute politician Mr. Winston Churchill back into a position of power from which that young man might again try to launch one of his attractive-sounding but impractical schemes to out-manœuvre the enemy, instead of crushing him in head-on assault. Gallipoli had proved the fantasy of such schemes – as the generals pointed out to the statesmen upon every possible opportunity, until by 1917 constant repetition had caused all but the most independent-minded of them to accept the philosophy of the High Command.

And this was to kill the enemy soldiers by massed attacks: nothing more, nothing less. Brute force was to battle it out with brute force and the stronger and heavier of the antagonists would win in the end.

In Lloyd George, all the instincts of an agile Celt with a rapier-like mind revolted against such a policy, but there was little he could do about it except plan and wait, watch for his opportunity and cut down the individual soldiers who opposed him upon any occasion when circumstances robbed them of the protection of the command organization. But this Fabian policy would take time to operate – if indeed it operated at all. Perhaps in the end, it would be simply a matter of brute force, when the vast American armies arrived in France and submerged the enemy in a welter of blood and misery.

If they arrived in time.

To the average Briton, either in the trenches or at home in field, office or factory, the news of America's forthcoming help to his own side was received with cool scepticism. 'Forthcoming' was obviously the critical word, and when it became evident that massive armies were not to arrive in Europe by the first boat after President Wilson's epoch-making declaration of war on Germany, any enthusiasm felt by the jaded British public quickly faded. They had come to the conclusion some time before that they had only themselves to depend upon: from what 'the boys' said when they came home on leave it seemed that the French were slippery – if not downright unreliable – and Russia was already on the way out.

There was widespread ignorance and indeed considerable mis-apprehension of things American – only equalled by the average American's mistaken view of European affairs – and most people's idea of their new transatlantic ally was a compound of Ford cars, the Keystone Cops, and soldiers wearing Boy Scout hats. And envy of the health, wealth and carefree spirits of those representatives of their newest ally who had already made an appearance upon the European scene did little, alas, to endear them to the natives.

For by the end of 1917 the drab burdens which war had imposed upon the British at home, had to a great extent damped their natural amiability. They did not doubt that in the end they would win the war – they seemed in fact incapable of envisaging defeat, possibly because a totally irrational atavism told them, obscurely and inaccurately, that they had never lost a war in the past and there would be no necessity to develop the habit now. But they were becoming increasingly bitter at the cost which victory was exacting from them, especially as despite their sacrifices to date, there appeared little sign of fulfilment of the contract.

Because their attention is not so riveted by immediate violence, the morale of those left at home during wartime is always more volatile than that of the men on the fighting fronts, so it is to them that newspaper editors direct their banner headlines and politicians address their oratory. As 1917 faded, the Solicitor-General, Sir Gordon Hewart, K.C., sent to his constituency a motto with which to face the coming year, and it is indicative of the low spirits of his countrymen that they could not devise some means of wrapping it around his neck and hanging him with it. It was 'Let us get on with the war!'

They were well aware of the fact that they had no choice but to 'get on with the war' – but they were doing so in a mood of bitter apathy. They hated it, hated the colourless existence it had brought, hated the hunger, the cold, the loneliness.

The heartbreak and tragedy which it had caused was a factor apart. By now hardly a family in Britain still numbered all its sons among the living, and such is the pressure of popular thought that those who did felt vaguely ashamed of their good fortune. In the first quarter of the war, before the glory died, consolation to those who mourned could be offered (and accepted) in the name of patriotism and sacrifice, but later – during the Somme battle, for instance – when the casualty lists lengthened to include entire divisions virtually destroyed, the system of complete battalions recruited from one locality had plunged whole districts into grief as the result of a single hour's fighting. Fellow-feeling and sympathy might assuage immediate sorrow, but when every other house in a

35

street had received its sombre news, and every street in a town or district, then a shadow settled over it which would not lift while the war lasted. And as the months had passed, the shadows had grown in number, dropping into place like pieces of a tragic jig-saw puzzle.

Time did little to lift this shadow, for it brought increasing hardship. Meat had become more and more difficult to buy, butter almost impossible except for favoured customers, and sugar was already controlled by a rudimentary and not very successful rationing system. Day-long queues stood outside the shops throughout the dank and dreary weeks at the end of 1917, children taking the place of mothers and aged grandparents the place of the children – and only too often the joint vigils would be in vain and the shutters go up on empty shelves. In London and other centres within range of German bombers, the daylight Gotha raids would scatter the queues momentarily – to re-form when the danger was passed with tears and quarrelling over lost places.

Inflation had climbed its dreary spiral ever since the beginning of the war, and as always the economic burden was not shared equally. Business had made huge profits (it had rescued America from a slump to such an extent that there were by now 7,925 more millionaires than in 1914, making 22,696 in all) and protected labour had used the situation to its own advantage so that miners' wages were 91 per cent. above the pre-war level, and munition-workers brought home inflated pay-packets. Any form of entertainment or luxury trade which could remain in business was paying enormous dividends, especially when the leave-trains came in.

With so large a proportion of the nation's manpower dead or in the trenches and so many of the women away in factories or offices doing the men's work, home life was reduced and the children ran riot – undisciplined, uncared for, unhappy. Morality suffered its usual war-time decline, and relief from the long hours, the tensions of separation or the actual desolation of loss was sought in promiscuous love affairs or alcohol. One well-placed Staff officer in London boasted that he had no difficulty in changing his paramour weekly, and that he always insisted that they brought their own champagne. The pattern was doubtless repeated at lower social levels.

To balance this, Evangelism flourished as in the days of the Industrial Revolution – and for much the same reasons – and great was the activity of the Temperance Societies. In *The Times* of January 1st, 1918, the 'Strength of Britain Movement' campaigned assiduously against the beer trade. It was not the war, the movement claimed, which had necessitated the recent introduction of sugar rationing, it was wicked, wanton waste!

'A Thousand Tons a Week are being used in Brewing NOW' its sub-line trumpeted,

> Catch Cold waiting your turn in the queue if you like,
> But DON'T blame it on the WAR.
> IT IS THE BREWER'S FAULT.

There was also an organization devoted to protection of the health and morals of soldiers and sailors on leave, from the activities of pimps and harpies operating in the centres of the big cities; but its efforts were not of much avail against the determination of men intent on enjoying what little life remained to them, before their return to duty.

There was little enjoyment and no luxury available for the solid mass of the middle and lower-middle classes – upon whose stability and fortitude much of Britain's power had been built and still rested. People with small fixed incomes – particularly the elderly – suffered actual hardship and every especially inclement spell drew its death-roll from them. While they lived, they saw their world of security and probity swept away, and perhaps some were not sorry to go with it.

It is indicative of the grinding hardship of the times that the national characteristics of good-humour and rather feckless generosity had gone. Hard up themselves, the British devoured with avidity all reports of peoples worse off than themselves, and newspaper editors with stories of hunger and pestilence abroad sold out their editions: especially, of course, when they retailed such details of the enemy countries. When censorship stripped the columns of hard news, the feature writers fell back upon their own imaginations for gruesome details of desperation within the enemy camp: but they rarely came close to the truth, for they could not picture it. Reality beggared imagination.

The blockade had been strangling Germany ever since the outbreak of war, and the populations of Berlin and Vienna would have welcomed the conditions in which Londoners were living as 1918 began. To them such luxuries as bread, heating and lighting were but nostalgic memories of the halcyon days of 1915. Since then hunger had been a constant condition, and a state of shivering palsy during all but the hottest time of the year was quite normal for almost everybody.

Children and old people suffered terribly. There was just not enough food for growing children, and those of all but the wealthiest and most influential grew up with hardly enough flesh to cover their bones. Vitamin deficiency had already played havoc with their teeth, for which, God knows, there was little enough exercise: a pound of bones for soup was a godsend, meat itself but a distant memory. The boys were in slightly better case than the girls, for they had the hope that if the war lasted long enough they would be drafted into the army – where at least they would be fed before they were butchered.

In winter, the Berlin streets were deep in thawed mud, with queues four deep of exhausted women and children waiting for hours before the shops opened, pressed against each other in order to keep warm; colourless, spiritless, numb with hunger and cold. The pitiful rations of sugar and flour were eked out over the endless days between issues, and even to dream of milk was ridiculous. Ersatz coffee, ersatz soup, ersatz sauce, ersatz soap – there was little for the Berliner to buy not prefaced by the loathed word, and in the minds of all it conjured up the same picture – pebbles, ground to grit. 'It scours the stomach clean, anyway,' was a wry gibe which had lost its savour by 1918. Grandparents and infants scrambled for the indigestible ruins of frozen potatoes.

Almost worse than lack of food was lack of fuel, for the stomach would adapt itself to meagre nourishment, but minds needed distraction from the dreadful reality. In winter after half-past three in the afternoon, there was nothing to do as there was no light to see by: no coal, no gas, no electricity, not even fat for candles. Even children could not sleep for seventeen hours a day, every day, but there was nothing else for them to do except perhaps to listen to stories told by parents or grandparents, too tired and too weak to carry on such genuinely exhausting work for long. So they went to bed in order to keep warm, all the children together irrespective of age or sex, and as parental apathy by now embraced all life, the practice

38

bred a social problem which plagued central Europe for two generations.

Bad conditions breed extremes. In England the mass of the people lived in extreme discomfort while a minority made modest fortunes; in Germany the mass lived perilously near starvation, and the profiteers lived lives of gluttonous luxury. Fantastic fortunes were being made by those who could secure the sub-contracts to main Governmental suppliers or those who could satisfy the demands of soldiers on leave; and Hungary, Rumania, Bulgaria and Austria were plundered to satisfy, in turn, the appetites of the new sybarites.

Early in the New Year there were bread riots in Vienna, and at the end of January a strike in Berlin of startling dimensions. The notices calling the strike were issued in the name of the Executive Committee of the Workers' Councils – a sinister nomenclature now heard for the first time. So certain of firm support were the leaders that they did not issue the strike notices until January 27th, and on January 28th a million workers came out, six hundred thousand of them in Berlin itself. Rioting, pillaging and looting went on for a week during which many people were killed, and then the movement was crushed by the summary arrest of some forty thousand strikers and their families. Among them was Kurt Eisner, who subsequently became President of the short-lived Bavarian Republic.

But the strike was crushed – by the Army, which in effect controlled the Government. For the military leaders in Germany had a power vastly exceeding that of any other faction in the country or among the Central Powers – or for that matter in the whole of Europe. It was, for instance, a scheme bearing the name of the Chief of the General Staff of the Field Army – the Hindenburg Industrial Scheme – under which decisions were taken as to labour allocations to German industry, and indeed what industries were to be allowed to continue functioning. Not that Hindenburg himself took many of the decisions, for the power was wielded by his staff, of whom undoubtedly the most important figure was that of the First Quartermaster-General, Erich Ludendorff.

This large, rather stout, typically Teutonic man was fortunate in being born to serve in the German Army, which had solved the problems posed by elderly and incompetent officers of royal blood who insisted on pressing their claims to high rank. The German General Staff were perfectly willing to allow the titular heads of

39

Army units of corps status and above to hold their positions solely by right of seniority or connection – in fact, they preferred it so. The arrangement gave the formation a figurehead with ample time to spare for the ceremony and external duties to which the public and rank and file had grown accustomed from its important military leaders, without wasting the time of proficient soldiers.

While the scions of royal houses were thus displaying the panoply of war, its business would be directed by their Chiefs-of-Staff – these were the important men, chosen and appointed by the General Staff for their cool heads and professional ability. The antecedents of these officers were not of prime importance, although it is true to say that two-thirds of them prefixed their names with the aristocratic 'von'. But this was no essential qualification, and an officer who combined brains with diligence would earn promotion, be his origins aristocratic, bourgeois or humble. Ludendorff was almost the archetype. In the early days of the war when disaster for the Germans had loomed unexpectedly on the eastern front, he had been hurriedly dispatched thither, collecting *en route* at Hanover – like excess baggage – the elderly von Hindenburg.

Since then the partnership of Hindenburg and Ludendorff had gained immense prestige, although oddly enough there is good reason to believe that on the eastern front where they won their reputation, the Staff practice had been carried another step further and that behind Ludendorff there had been yet another *éminence grise* – a certain Lieutenant-Colonel Max Hoffman.

Be that as it may, when in August 1916 the Hindenburg–Ludendorff combination had been recalled from the eastern front to take command of the entire complex of Kaiserlich and Königlich Armies – in effect, to assume direction of the war effort of the Central Powers – there was no doubt as to whose was to be the guiding brain. Not that of von Hindenburg, dominant, steadfast, oaken personality though he might be.

Ludendorff had realized for some time that between the end of the British 1917 offensive and summer of 1918, Germany must win the war: otherwise the arrival of the American armies would tip the balance against the Central Powers and all their hopes and ambitions be tumbled in the dust. By early November it had become obvious that there was little now to fear in the east, and that a steady drainage away from that front of all first-class fighting material could be commenced.

40

A decision must be forced in the west. On November 11th, 1917, Ludendorff presided at a conference held at Mons to discuss the manner in which this could be brought about. The Kaiser was not present although his headquarters were not far away, nor was the Crown Prince who commanded the group of armies astride the Somme, nor Prince Rupprecht of Bavaria who commanded the northern army group and in whose headquarters the conference took place. Prince Rupprecht did, however, have a short conversation with Ludendorff before the conference began, although upon what subject is not recorded.

At the conference table with Ludendorff were Colonel von der Schulenberg (Chief-of-Staff to the group of armies of the Crown Prince) and General von Kuhl (Chief-of-Staff to the group of armies of Prince Rupprecht of Bavaria). There were also the heads of various sections of the General Staff, including a Lieutenant-Colonel Wetzell and an infantry captain. All points of view were listened to with respect and attention and there appears to have been little attempt by the junior ranks to curry favour of the more senior by subscribing to their opinions.

The main, broad issue first to be decided was whether to launch an attack westwards against the British-held sector of the front, or southwards against the French. The disadvantage of the first was that in the event of the British retreating, they would do so across old battlefields and the desolation and waste intentionally created by the Germans when they retreated to the Siegfried Line (known to the Allies as the Hindenburg Line). This would undoubtedly hamper the attackers and aid the defenders, and the British were likely to prove difficult enough to dislodge from the first line of trenches without giving them the advantage of successive lines in which to fall as they went back.

On the other hand, the French had an almost unlimited space behind them into which they could retreat, and memories of the vast sack which had contained the German armies in 1914 stirred many doubts: even with reinforcements from the Russian front, there was a limit to the length of line the Central Powers could hold, especially with, once again, ever-lengthening lines of communication. A successful onslaught on Verdun might dislodge the eastern hinge of the French Army with advantageous results – and undoubtedly with enormous effect upon French morale and Franco-American

41

co-operation: but as Ludendorff presciently remarked, the British might not feel themselves compelled to send assistance to the French at Verdun, and he would then find himself faced with the necessity of mounting a second large-scale offensive in Flanders.

He eventually summed up at the conclusion of the conference in the following words:

'The situation in Russia and Italy will, as far as can be seen, make it possible to deliver a blow on the Western Front in the New Year. The strength of the two sides will be approximately equal. About thirty-five divisions and one thousand heavy guns can be made available for *one* offensive; a second great simultaneous offensive, say as a diversion, will not be possible.

'Our general situation requires that we should strike at the earliest moment, if possible at the end of February or beginning of March, before the Americans can throw strong forces into the scale.

'We must beat the British.

'The operations must be based on these three conditions.'

There were to be many more conferences, many alternative schemes to be discussed, but in the final analysis it always came back to the belief that as Britain had made herself the dominant partner in the alliance, it was the British Army which must be broken. If that happened, the French would capitulate – but there seemed no reason to believe that a French collapse would persuade the Anglo-Saxons to lay down their arms. Moreover, once the British line broke, their armies would have little room for manœuvre and none for escape: they would quickly find themselves penned against the sea, where they could be annihilated.

So much for the broad strategic outline – its details would be decided upon by Ludendorff at the appropriate time, but none knew better than he that there is more to waging war than drawing large red arrows on maps. For months he had watched the British hurl themselves towards the German trenches, doubtless in attempts to translate into reality other red arrows on other maps. They had failed to burst through and defeat the German armies for a number of reasons, one being that they had been inadequately or wrongly trained, and another that their attacks had been organized and directed upon mistaken lines.

Ludendorff saw no point in learning from his own errors when he could do so from other people's, and he was also well aware of the fact that he had no inexhaustible reserve of manpower upon which to draw. His forces therefore must rely upon tactical skill instead of sheer weight, and brain must be used to defeat brawn. He issued decrees that all troops must undergo special offensive training, and sent for experts to direct it in accordance with a newly issued handbook entitled *The Attack in Trench Warfare*, conceived and written by an extremely able infantryman, Captain Geyer.

The experts and instructors congregated in instructional centres set up behind each army's front, and through them passed all divisions transferred from the east *en route* to their attack positions. Units already in the line were combed for their youngest, fittest and most experienced soldiers (or, more often, weaker elements were weeded out of existing battalions), and formed into Sturmabteilung – Storm Troops: a nomenclature which was to gather for itself a most sinister connotation twenty years later under Hitler.

These Storm Troops were armed with light machine-guns, light trench-mortars and flame-throwers, and their duty was to cross the trench-lines, by-pass centres of hard resistance and machine-gun posts and if possible break through to attack the enemy artillery.

The emphasis was placed on methods of infiltration. Not for Ludendorff's troops the steady advance in line with each man conscious of those to right and left of him: touch with the enemy in front was the desideratum, and the fastest, not the slowest, must set the pace. Nothing must hold the infantry up – if the artillery barrage was 'creeping' too slowly for the leading Storm Troops, then signal methods must be worked out whereby they could be instructed by the infantry to lift forwards. This was in itself a radical innovation, for in previous offensives – especially by the British – the last people to issue orders to the rear support were the fighting troops.

The Storm Troops would be followed by 'battle units' consisting of infantry, machine-gunners, trench-mortar teams, engineers, sections of field artillery and ammunition carriers – and all were to be ready to take over the duties of other sections in case of need. Above all they must be prepared and trained to attack defended positions and repulse counter-attacks with rifle and bayonet, always bearing in mind that no obstacle must hold them up too long: if a defended position would not fall to them as they were then constituted, it was to be left for heavier units behind to deal with. Even tanks were to be allowed virtually free passage through their ranks if any were encountered, although the accompanying infantry must be attacked and annihilated.

Another revolutionary precept for the Western Front, was that reserves should be thrown into the battle where the attack was progressing, not where it was held up. They must flood along the channels already opened and either widen it by mopping up centres of resistance left behind by the advancing Storm Troops, or leapfrog over them if fatigue or wounds had brought them to a halt.

With memories of their own tactics when they retired to the Hindenburg Line, all German troops were expressly warned against booby-traps, poisoned food and drink, and the possibility of suicidal snipers.

All this training needed considerable organization, but having initiated it, the instructors found that the troops needed little pressure to keep them going. It seems that they felt instinctively that such War Games and night exercises as they were called upon to perform had a realism which much of their previous training had lacked – for the British had not held a lien on old-fashioned ideas and elderly instructors. After years of small raids, small offensives, and long periods of static misery, all welcomed an attempt at a decisive offensive.

While his troops were training, Ludendorff and his immediate advisers (among whom was the acute-minded Lieutenant-Colonel Wetzell in his capacity as Head of the Operations Section of the General Staff) had been adapting their ends to their means and coming to certain conclusions as a result.

The first was that they would have more men for the offensive than they had originally thought. On February 9th was signed the Treaty of Brest-Litovsk, by which all hostile action by the Russians ceased, and as this development had been foreseen for some weeks, Ludendorff had already been able to milk away from the eastern front a considerable number of divisions and several thousand ancillary troops. All fit men under thirty-five years of age were rapidly transferred westwards, their places being either left vacant or filled by the elements combed from the Storm Troop battalions. No ranks were spared in this purge, for as an essential part of these preparations a general reserve of officers up to the rank of regimental commander was built up at each West Front Army Headquarters, to cover the anticipated wastage. Neither did rank excuse its bearer from the theory and exercise of the instructional centres.

In addition, by virtue of the Hindenburg Industrial Scheme, Ludendorff recalled 123,000 men from industry to the colours. By the date of the first attack 136,618 officers and 3,438,288 other ranks had been wedged into position on the Western Front. They did so in a hundred and ninety-two divisions, of which sixty-nine were concentrated along the sixty-mile stretch of front between Arras and la Fère. Facing this concentration were thirty-three British divisions, of which ten were as much as fifteen miles from the front line, and two were twenty-five.

This concentration of German troops had been carried out under the strictest possible conditions of secrecy that it had been possible to devise and execute. All important and large-scale troop movements were carried out at night, and the attack divisions had in fact, been kept back until the last possible moment – both in order to rest them and also to conceal the enormous accumulation of troops in the relatively small area. Especially were railheads kept free of daylight congestion, and no troop trains were allowed to draw in unless arrangements had been made for the immediate dispersal of the men.

Special 'Safety Officers' were appointed to watch over and control all means of communication, including censorship of mail and use of the telephone. All officers given any specific details of the attack were required to take an express oath of secrecy – which in view of the terms of their commissions and allegiance to the King-Emperor must have infuriated some of the more stiff-necked – and all maps and papers were kept securely under lock and key unless in use. Special police planes and balloons flew or hovered over the concentration area to ensure that no new tracks were made across open spaces by marching feet, and that all instructions regarding camouflage were meticulously obeyed.

And the military arm across whose activities was drawn the thickest curtain was that of the artillery, for the expert who had been brought across from the eastern front to stage-manage this aspect of the attack was a strong advocate of the tactical value of surprise.

Colonel Bruchmüller had been in charge of the artillery during the attack by General von Hutier's army upon the strongly fortified positions at Riga, and the General had been so impressed that he

45

had earnestly recommended Ludendorff to listen to the advice of this artillery expert. At Riga, Bruchmüller had demonstrated the greater value of gas-shell over high explosive during the hours immediately preceding an infantry attack: for one thing, gas shell left the ground surface virtually intact, for another it poisoned whole areas and in favourable weather conditions would affect reserve gunners brought up almost as much as those originally present when the shells burst.

Above all Bruchmüller insisted upon the value of the short, intense bombardment. The British had bombarded German positions for five days before the Somme battle had opened and for thirteen days before the first assaults of the Passchendaele offensive, with results that were afterwards only too obvious. The ground was impassable and attempts by the troops to cross it gave the German machine-gunners ample time to move into position to mow them down. These bombardments had also given the army commanders full warning of where the blows would fall, and time to concentrate reserves – out of danger but ready for counter-attack.

Before the bombardment could commence, however, Bruchmüller was faced with the problems of getting his guns into position – and this was in many ways more difficult than that of troop movement. Guns have all the blind obstinacy of inanimate matter, as any artilleryman who has manhandled them into position at night will agree, and even when apparently co-operating with their sweating servitors, they still move on wheels which unavoidably leave tracks.

In the end the deployment of the guns was divided into three time-classes, and they were detailed under direction of reconnoitring staff who had carried out all their ground inspection only during the hours of early dawn. Firstly there were the emplacements in which guns would be completely concealed; these were occupied as soon as possible, and either the wheel tracks were obliterated before daylight or some form of camouflage was erected until the traces had disappeared. The second class were those which could be kept in concealment in the neighbourhood of their firing positions, and these too, were brought up at night as soon as possible, and camouflaged in their temporary positions. During the night preceding the attack they would be manhandled into position, each one moving to an exact time schedule as the area was likely to be congested with the traffic of the third class. This was the remainder of the artillery,

46

for which no concealed positions could be found, and they were to be brought up from the rear into pre-surveyed positions and go into action within minutes of arrival.

They would fire, moreover, without the benefit of 'registration' shoots, by which fire upon a target was observed and corrected until it was accurate – thus revealing to the enemy exactly where the fire would fall when the bombardment opened. A system of mathematical prediction of range and bearing had been devised by a Captain Pulkowsky which had already given satisfactory results, although as is usual the world over, there were several men, old and experienced in their profession, to shake their heads dubiously over attractive-sounding theories. The spirits of all troops would be much uplifted if only they could realize that the enemy army has to cope with much the same degree of narrow-mindedness and dull-witted obstinacy as their own. In the end, it all comes down to the mentality of the directing chief.

Ludendorff gave final decisions regarding the direction and scope of the offensive on January 21st, after a tour of the Western Front in company with General von Kuhl and Colonel von der Schulenberg.

He would greatly have liked to attack the Allied line along its northernmost fifty miles – from just south of Armentières up to the coast – in converging attacks on each side of the Ypres Salient which would meet near Hazebrouck and cut the vital north-south railway which fed the armies, then turn north and drive the British into the sea. Two schemes, St. George 1 and St. George 2, had been drawn up by which this might be accomplished, but reluctantly Ludendorff came to the conclusion that they would be too dependent upon the weather. He had no desire to engulf his armies in virtually the same mud as that which had absorbed the force of the British attacks of 1917.

South of this area – along the thirty-mile front covering Béthune and Arras – the British held the heights of the Vimy Ridge in strength, and although the plans Valkyrie and Mars which Ludendorff's indefatigable Staff had produced were very attractive, there was too great a risk that their promise would be thwarted by the sheer tenacity of the British infantry.

But from Arras down past St. Quentin to la Fère ran a long stretch of his own immensely strong and capaciously excavated Hindenburg Line – surely the best place in which to concentrate his

47

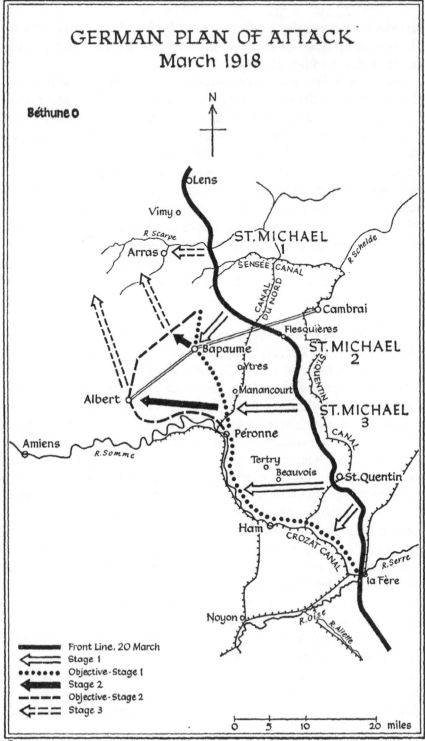

GERMAN PLAN OF ATTACK
March 1918

Béthune O

N

Bethune O

oLens

Vimy o

R Scarpe

Arras o

ST.MICHAEL
1

SENSÉE CANAL

R Schelde

CANAL DU NORD

Cambrai

Flesquières

o Bapaume

ST.MICHAEL
2

o Ytres

ST.QUENTIN

o Manancourt

Albert o

ST.MICHAEL
3

CANAL

Péronne

Amiens

R. Somme

Tertry

Beauvois

St.Quentin

Ham

CROZAT CANAL

R. Serre

la Fère

Noyon o

R. Oise

R. Ailette

▬▬▬	Front Line, 20 March
⬅	Stage 1
••••••	Objective-Stage 1
⬅	Stage 2
– – –	Objective-Stage 2
⬅ = =	Stage 3

0   5   10   20 miles

force and from which to launch his attack – and he had great hopes that the British might rely upon the devastated nature of the ground for its defence, and thus not man it too strongly. In any case, his troops were trained for infiltration, and the maze of trenches, ditches and craters might aid them more than the defenders.

For attacks upon this area, the Staff had produced an overall plan under the code name St. Michael, which was sub-divided into three sections, numbered downwards from the north.

The left flank of the St. Michael 3 attack lay therefore on the banks of the Oise where it flowed through la Fère. As that river flowed on across the lines, it could conveniently continue as the left flank of the attack in that area, and furthermore, four miles on behind the British lines was the Crozat Canal, which bent away north-westwards to connect the Oise with the Somme. This canal would act very conveniently as a line upon which one southern attack group could rest and guard its flank, while the remainder of von Hutier's Eighteenth Army broke the British front on each side of St. Quentin, and flooded forwards until they reached the concave line of the Somme between Ham and Péronne. This would be the flank of the whole offensive, and von Hutier's duty would be to see that no counterattacks broke through to upset the balance of the main weight of the attack, to be borne by General von der Marwitz's Second Army (St. Michael 2) and General von Below's Seventeenth Army (St. Michael 1).

These two armies would drive forwards until they had reached, respectively, Albert and Bapaume, and on that line they would swing north and obtain the decision. They would be aided first by an attack named Mars South by retained right-wing units of von Below's Army against Arras (south of the Scarpe, which would protect its northern flank) and then early in April, by which time the weather should be settled enough to provide the essential firm 'going', by the St. George 1 and St. George 2 attacks in the north.

As Ludendorff knew only too well the vanity of man's proposals and the myriad accidents which can overset them, he also instructed his Staff to draw up plans for offensives along all the rest of the front, from la Fère south and east as far as the eastern flank of the Verdun Salient, naming them, with an odd mixture of religious and classical fervour, Archangel, Achilles, Roland, Hector, Castor and Pollux, from west to east.

49

But the main emphasis should be on Michael, supplemented by Mars to the north – and possibly even by Archangel to the south, although this was an unlikely possibility as the most vital part of the Michael scheme was the smashing in of the British front along the Flesquières Salient, the sweep through Manancourt and Ytres to the Albert–Bapaume line, and the break out to the north. The southern sector around St. Quentin – which Archangel would aid – was only a limited advance to secure the flank of the main attack.

Once the offensive was launched and under way, the British line would start to totter, and when their reserves from the Ypres front were rushed south to contain the attack, then St. Georges 1 and 2 would flatten the Ypres Salient, tear the line away from its anchorage on the sea and roll it up from the north. It would be supported by artillery, trench-mortars and air cover transferred north from the St. Michael's front as soon as circumstances allowed.

One of the factors which may well have persuaded Ludendorff to attack on both sides of St. Quentin and to place his main reliance upon St. Michael, was information which had reached the German Staff during the week before his decision that the British, although protesting that they were already short of men, had agreed to extend their line southwards and relieve the French along a further twenty-five miles of the front. This took the British line down to the village of Barisis, south of la Fère, and meant in effect that with a little extension, the St. Michael 3 attack might strike the point of juncture of the Allied armies. On January 16th, Lieutenant-Colonel Wetzell had received from the Chief-of-Staff of von Hutier's Eighteenth Army, General von Sauberzweig, a letter which contained the following passages:

It may now be accepted that the British have taken over the front of the French III Corps. They will no doubt take over that of the XXXVII Corps up to the Oise, so thàt in future the Oise will be the boundary between the French and the British. (*Not quite correct, but very nearly.*)

The Eighteenth Army will therefore have only British opposite to it. This will make the situation more favourable to us.

The offensive is principally intended to strike the British. They now stand opposite to us on the whole front of the Group of Armies which is to make the offensive. It need not be anticipated that the French will run themselves off their legs and hurry at once to the help of their Entente comrades. They will first wait and see if their own front is not attacked also, and decide to support their ally only when the situation has been quite cleared up. That will not be immediately, as demonstrations to deceive the French will be made by the German Crown Prince's Group.

All in all, therefore, the prospects for the German Spring Offensive seemed excellent, and Ludendorff and his Staff had every right to face the immediate future with hope and confidence.

3. Prospect of Battle

ON December 14th, 1917, there had been issued from Field-Marshal Haig's headquarters a series of instructions with regard to the forthcoming activities of the armies under his command. Somewhat to the surprise but greatly to the relief of those regimental officers who received a copy, the emphasis was for the first time in the war to be placed upon defence. This meant in effect a complete reversal of principle and thought, and a moderate amount of re-training for the troops, almost all of whom had been thoroughly prepared for the Sommes and Arrases of the war, but not many for the glorious retreat at Mons.

During this period of retrenchment, however, their offensive spirit was not to be allowed to wither. It would receive continual nourishment from the series of trench raids carried on during the winter and early spring, some undertaken by a handful of men led by one officer, some mounted on ambitious lines and using the strength of two or three companies. As always with the British, an attempt was made to recapture the atmosphere of school sports, and some divisions instituted a monthly cup for award to the battalion with the greatest success. One point was awarded for identification of opposing enemy units by articles taken from dead bodies, two points were awarded for each live prisoner captured, three for each enemy machine-gun or trench-mortar brought in.

On the night of February 10th/11th, men of the Australian 3rd Division mounted a raid on the German-held village of Warneton. Possibly because their Divisional Commander, Major-General Sir John Monash, possessed one of the few 'Big Business' type of brains among the Allied commanders, his officers and men too, thought in large-scale terms: one hundred and ninety-five men under nine officers took part in this raid, and they had the support of well-organized artillery and strategically placed covering fire.

The River Lys crossed the lines at Warneton, and to the south it flooded almost the whole of no-man's land and the trenches each side of it. But to the north, the trenches were continuous and strongly held, and in the area of the proposed raid some two hundred and fifty yards apart. The raid was to be made upon a frontage of nearly five hundred yards, between the northern edge of the flooded Lys and the remains of the Armentières–Warneton railway line. A road once bisected this front, running eastwards from the centre of the Australian positions, and the vague lines of its embankments were still perceptible, piercing the enemy line and continuing to the ruins of the village some two hundred and fifty yards behind.

The night was warm, with promise of rain and no moon, and just after nine o'clock the leading groups of Australians crept out into the shell-holes in front of their positions and began to work their way forwards to the edge of their own wire: Bangalore torpedoes had previously been laid in selected positions, each with a length of fuse leading back towards the raiders.

At ten o'clock, a heavy barrage opened up on the enemy front line, the fuses were fired and the charges blown, cutting the necessary gaps in the wire. The width of the trench-mortar and artillery barrage had been extended well north of the railway line in order to deceive the enemy, and to heighten the deception, plywood figures of crouching men had been fixed into position in that part of no-man's land as well. Small parties lying in shell-holes operated these figures by controlling wires: they lay under a horizontal tapestry of machine-gun and rifle bullets and it was not long before the wooden figures were split to pieces by bullets or blown apart by grenades.

In the meantime, however, the raiding parties had worked their way through their own wire (one party each side of the road) and were searching for gaps in the enemy's defences. The party on the left found them easily enough and went through into the enemy trenches, but the right-hand party ran into trouble due to the fact that some enemy troops, instead of sheltering from the barrage in their dug-outs, had thought it wiser to avoid it altogether by moving out into the shell-holes in front of their own lines. As the right-hand party of Australians searched for gaps in the wire they were thus sniped at from these positions, and also machine-gunned from a nest set out from the enemy line on their own right flank. The Australians went to ground, pulled the pins from their grenades, and endeavoured to bomb their way forwards.

Then the left-hand party already clearing the front enemy positions realized the situation on their right, charged along the trench and attacked the enemy snipers from behind, thus allowing the men trapped in the open to swarm through a gap they had themselves blown in the wire. There was a brief, vicious hand-to-hand struggle over the shell-holes and then the second party were in the enemy positions.

The raiders spread out and began penetration of the communication trenches. Danger of mistaken identity during the confusion was minimal because, apparently, of the phrases used by the Australians as they fought, and the separate parties linked up time and time again in the web of trenches behind the front position. Prisoners were dispatched overland (many were killed by their own machine-gunners), a nest of dug-outs on the left flank was blown in, but a concrete multiple machine-gun nest in the second line on the right proved invincible.

After half an hour, the withdrawal began and the tumult rose to a height. Both Australian and German artillery and trench-mortar batteries were in action now, each trying to block the movement of the troops: the Australians wished to stop German reinforcements re-occupying their own trenches so they shelled the village and its communication lines, the Germans endeavoured to stop the return of the raiders by dropping a curtain of fire into no-man's land.

Through this inferno the raiders and their prisoners made their separate, precarious ways. Very lights and star shells lit the scene with garish intensity, trench-mortar and minenwerfer bombs exploded violently in clouds of earth and the horrid debris of battle, machine-guns laced the darkness with glowing tracer.

Shortly after eleven o'clock the Australians began to pour back over the lips of their own trenches, chalk-faced beneath their cocoa-butter or burnt-cork camouflage, panting, arid with thirst, many bloodstained. They had lost two officers and eight men killed, twenty-nine men had been wounded and nine men of the 37th Battalion were missing. They brought back with them thirty-three prisoners who were immediately hurried off to divisional head-quarters for questioning, and claims to the effect that whilst in the enemy trenches they had killed just over a hundred of the original occupants. This information was not regarded as particularly important, and indeed was received with a certain amount of scepticism.

But the information obtained from the prisoners was considered of consequence, especially when it reached GHQ – for it added to an accumulation of evidence which suggested that the expected enemy attack would fall on the northern half of the British line. Five days later at a conference of army commanders held at Doullens, the Commander-in-Chief mentioned that in view of the presence of important coal-mines around Béthune, it might well be that the main enemy thrust would be in that direction. However, it was too early to say for certain.

Sir Douglas Haig had, in fact, a number of rather pressing problems on his mind at the time, the most important of which was that it looked distinctly possible that he would shortly lose his chief henchman and support in London, Sir William Robertson, the Chief of the Imperial General Staff. From what Sir Douglas could deduce from reports, it seemed that Robertson had been manœuvred into a situation by the 'frocks' in which he would be reduced to a mere cypher – one moreover, in the politicians' hands, instead of in Haig's.

As soon as the conference ended therefore, the Commander-in-Chief motored to Beaurepaire Château, had lunch, and went at once to Boulogne, where a destroyer waited to take him across the Channel. By 6.30 p.m. he was in London.

Calm, immaculate and apparently imperturbable, the figure of Sir Douglas Haig will present an enigma to historians for generations to come.

At the moment he was concerned with the loss of yet another of the men who had surrounded and supported him since his appointment as Commander-in-Chief of the British Armies on the Western Front. His Chief Intelligence Officer, Brigadier-General Charteris, had been taken from him in December, he had been forced to change his Chief-of-Staff the following month, and now it looked as though he was to lose his spokesman in London.

There was also the problem presented by the formation of the Versailles Inter-Allied Supreme War Council during the previous November, with as the British military representative the very officer who had incurred Haig's most intense dislike and distrust, Sir Henry Wilson. At first this Council had been relatively harmless, as it had been invested with purely advisory capacities – but at the end of January, by what Haig regarded as a piece of typical chicanery, Lloyd George and the French Premier Clemenceau had put their heads together and decided to give the Council executive powers. They had, moreover, requested that Haig should provide several divisions from his already exiguous forces in order to set up a general reserve; this reserve to be moved and employed by order of the Council. This meant in effect to put them at the disposal of the French representative, General Foch, at whose command General Wilson had always leapt like a lap-dog.

Only a private agreement which Haig had already reached with the French Commander-in-Chief, General Pétain, for mutual support in emergency (for Pétain objected to the Council's suggestions just as strongly as Haig did) avoided compliance with the thoroughly objectionable scheme. It would have made General Foch virtual Supreme Commander of the Allied Forces, and Haig saw no reason to believe that British troops would fight any more successfully under French direction than they had already done under his own.

So far as Pétain was concerned, Haig got along with him very well, appreciating his cold manner, his dignity, his firmness, his lucidity. Relations between GHQ and the French CQG had never been more cordial, and Haig's eventual but reluctant agreement to lengthen the British front an extra twenty-five miles down past la Fère, had sealed the concord.

In London, Sir Douglas found that he had arrived too late. Sir William Robertson had refused to continue as CIGS in view of certain restrictions of power which were to be placed on that post, and he had also refused to take Sir Henry Wilson's position on the Versailles Council. Robertson was, in fact, to be placed on half pay the following Monday, pending relegation to a home command.

Sir Henry Wilson had been recalled from Versailles and was to take Robertson's place in London.

Haig returned to France during the following week, after meetings with the Secretary of State for War, Lord Derby, with Sir Henry Wilson, already installed in his offices as Chief of the Imperial General Staff, with Mr. Bonar Law, the Leader of the Conservatives in the House of Commons, and with the Prime Minister at Downing Street, about which he recorded acidly in the diary: 'The PM's house reminds me of summer lodgings at the seaside – a sort of maid-of-all work opened the door to us.'

One gathers an impression from the diary of long, courteous conversations, in which everyone stated his own point of view and then listened with interest to the others'.

But there seems to have been little concrete agreement and one cannot help wondering upon what grounds Haig wrote on Tuesday, February 19th: 'I think I can fairly claim, as the result of my visit to London, that a generally saner view is now taken of the so-called military crisis, and the risk of a quarrel between "civilian and soldier" (which last Saturday seemed imminent) has been avoided.'

For the military crisis was still building up, and Lloyd George was still of the opinion that the Allied Armies would operate better under the command of one Supreme Commander, as long as it wasn't Haig.

During the next few weeks, as the intelligence reports flooding into GHQ were interpreted, analysed, disregarded or emphasized according to the intuitions and preconceived ideas of their readers, a picture of the imminent German offensive began to form in the minds of those who were to direct the defence against it. Less than three weeks before it was launched, this picture was not inaccurate, although there was evidently some lack of important detail, for on March 2nd Haig wrote in his diary:

The usual statement on the position of the enemy was made by my Intelligence Officer (Cox). He gave reasons why we think the enemy is preparing to attack on the fronts of our Third and Fifth Armies. I em-phasized the necessity for being ready as soon as possible to meet a big hostile offensive of prolonged duration. I also told Army Commanders that I was very pleased at all I had seen on the fronts of the three Armies which I had recently visited. Plans were sound and thorough, and much work had already been done. I was only afraid that the enemy would find our front so very strong that he will hesitate to commit his Army to the attack with the almost certainty of losing very heavily.

These fears might have been set at rest by a closer examination of the defences.

The front to be held by the Allies was some four hundred and forty-five miles long from the sea to Switzerland. The *northernmost* eighteen miles – from the sea past Dixmude to the banks of a small

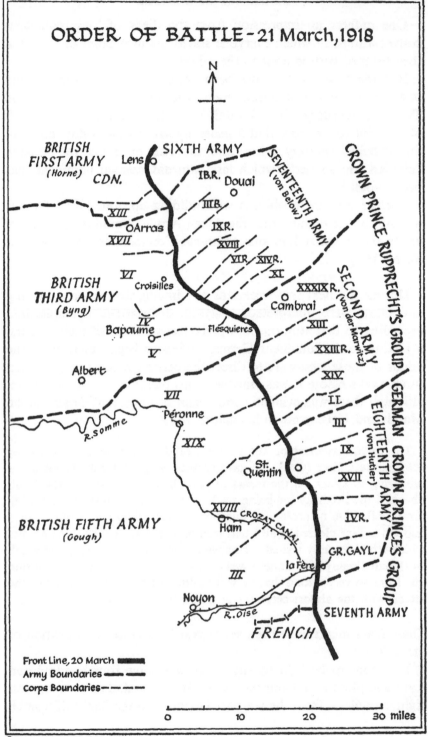

ORDER OF BATTLE – 21 March, 1918

N

BRITISH
FIRST ARMY
(Horne) CDN.

Lens

SIXTH ARMY

I B.R. Douai

III R.

IX R.

SEVENTEENTH ARMY (von Below)

CROWN PRINCE RUPPRECHT'S GROUP

XIII

O Arras

XVII

XVIII

VI R. XIV R.

XI

BRITISH
THIRD ARMY
(Byng)

VI Croisilles

IV

Bapaume

V

Albert

VII

XXXIX R.

Cambrai

XIII

XXIII R.

XIV

SECOND ARMY (von der Marwitz)

Flesquières

Péronne

R. Somme

XIX

II

III

IX

XVII

St.
Quentin

EIGHTEENTH ARMY (von Hutier)

GERMAN CROWN PRINCE'S GROUP

BRITISH FIFTH ARMY
(Gough)

XVIII
Ham

CROZAT CANAL

IV R.

GR. GAYL.

III

la Fère

Noyon

R. Oise

SEVENTH ARMY

FRENCH

Front Line, 20 March ▬▬▬▬
Army Boundaries ▬ ▬ ▬
Corps Boundaries ▬ ▬ ▬

0   10   20   30 miles

© CASSELL & CO. LTD. 1962

stream called the Coverbeek – were held by the single cavalry division and the twelve infantry divisions of the Belgian Army under nominal direction of their King, who rarely strayed more than ten miles from their front. Although it would invariably act in concert with the British on its right flank, it did not form an integral part of Haig's command.

The *southern* one hundred and fifty miles of the front, from the St. Mihiel Salient to the Swiss border, was of secondary importance. Guarded by the immensely strong fortress positions built by the French and by the inaccessible Vosges country, it had never been seriously menaced by an offensive on the part of the Central Powers – which justified the British contention that they held as great a length of the really important section of the line, in proportion to their strength, as did the French.

It was this central section that was under threat, and by the middle of March the armies of the British and the French were holding themselves ready to withstand an attack anywhere along the line of entrenchments two hundred and seventy miles long between the Coverbeek and the St. Mihiel Salient, of which the British held one hundred and twenty-five miles and the French one hundred and fifty.

The British sector was held by four armies.

From the Belgian right flank on the Coverbeek, around the blood-drenched profile of the Ypres Salient to just north of Armentières, lay the twelve divisions of the Second Army – all breathing heartfelt sighs of relief at the news of the promised return to them of their beloved commander, General Sir Herbert Plumer. This was the army – though they were unaware of it – which would face the St. George 1 and 2 attacks.

From Armentières, along the dominant features of the Lorette and Vimy Ridges for thirty-three miles as far as the village of Gavrelle, just north of Arras, lay the First Army under General Sir Henry Horne. This army covered the Béthune coalfields and had been strengthened because of that. It comprised fourteen divisions, including two Portuguese divisions and the Canadian Corps. Here were concentrated 1,450 guns and howitzers, which together with the advantages of the ground were considered enough to beat off any strength which the enemy could accumulate opposite it: its northern half faced the southern section of Ludendorff's St. George 1 scheme, its southern half the whole of Valkyrie.

The fourteen divisions of General Sir Julian Byng's Third Army held the next twenty-eight miles – to face Mars, Michael 1 and the northern half of Michael 2 – from Arras down to the Welsh Ridge on the southern face of the Flesquières Salient.

And the remaining forty-two miles of the British front – from Gouzeaucourt down past la Fère to Barisis – was the responsibility of the twelve infantry and three cavalry divisions of General Sir Hubert Gough's Fifth Army. Nearly ten of these forty-two miles were, however, partially guarded by the Oise where it flooded into a wide, marshy valley south of la Fère.

Eight divisions were held in GHQ Reserve.

Each infantry division was composed of nine battalions, and owing to such factors as leave, sickness and overdue reinforcements, each battalion could be considered to muster an average of only five hundred rifles. Obviously, some divisions of each army must be held in reserve inside the army area (as apart from GHQ Reserve) and the line divisions were in fact so disposed that some 36,000 rifles were spread out along twenty miles to face the Michael 1 and 2 attacks, while 31,000 rifles, along twenty-eight miles, faced the southern flank of von Hutier's Eighteenth Army, on its Michael 3 sweep to the Crozat Canal and the Somme.

This in theory, gave one man to each yard along the defences of the northern sector, and one man to each five feet along the southern – but it would be an extremely foolhardy commander who placed his entire force in one thin line in the front trenches, quite apart from the fact that the Commander-in-Chief had expressly forbidden it. Defence in depth was the suggested technique – troops in the forward positions fighting until they were overwhelmed in an attempt to check the first onslaught, the main mass waiting farther back in the 'Battle Zone' to absorb the remaining momentum of the offensive and to launch (it was hoped) the decisive counterattacks.

As the depth of this Battle Zone was to be, in places, as much as four thousand yards and there was envisaged yet a further 'Rear Zone' behind that, it will be seen that there would be considerably less than one man to every five feet along any line facing the Michael attacks. Four manned lines, for instance – one forward, two in the Battle Zone and one in the Rear Zone – would give an average of one man to every twenty feet, which can hardly be called excessive, and although defensive fortification would help to economize man-power to a great extent, there was a point beyond which it would no longer be effective. No machine-gun, however efficient, will hold up the enemy unless there is a machine-gunner behind it. The men of the Fifth Army were thus likely to find themselves thinly dispersed – especially in view of the novel tactics which von Hutier's Army intended to employ.

From Barisis on southwards and eastwards as far as the beginning of the Verdun Salient, were the Sixth, Fifth and Fourth French Armies, together making up the Groupe d'Armées du Nord under General Franchet d'Esperey. They held, in all, a front of seventy miles, while the whole of the Verdun Salient itself was occupied by the French Second Army. The French First Army held the southern flank of the St. Mihiel Salient, the Eighth the next thirty miles to the northern end of the Vosges, and the remaining seventy miles down to the Swiss frontier were held by the Seventh Army.

These last four armies made up the Groupe d'Armées de l'Est under General de Castlenau, both groups being part of the command of the French Commander-in-Chief, General Henri Philippe Benoni Omer Joseph Pétain, the possessor of probably the most lucid – and certainly the most realistically inclined – mind among the Allied commanders.

It would be a mistake, however, to consider Pétain a defeatist: he had every intention of ensuring that the Allies defeated the Central Powers, but not at an inflated price. The smallest possible price was, in Pétain's economical mind, the correct one to pay for purchases. If Britain or possibly America cared to act extravagantly, that was their own business (although he regretted to watch waste of any sort) but so far as his own country was concerned, Pétain was determined that no more of her blood should be poured out than was absolutely necessary for victory. France had, in his opinion, already paid out enough, and Britain had paid out so much of late that she was seriously weakened (not that this was any business of Pétain's except in so far as it affected the total Allied effort). Therefore, to any man of logic and common sense, it was obvious that the correct strategy now to follow was to remain strictly upon the defensive, and to await the build-up of the American armies, which could then bear the burden of the remainder of the war. 'I await the tanks and the Americans!' he told his troops, to their immense relief.

To be fair to Pétain, it is probably true to say that so far as he was concerned, the American armies could also have all the immediate glory of victory, as well as its weight. Reserve, self-discipline and self-effacement are the indicative words in any description of Pétain, and he had sufficient faith in the future to believe that France's contribution to victory would be recognized by history, irrespective of who led the celebratory parades.

But that was something in the far future. More immediately he believed that in the coming German offensive, Ludendorff's main attack would be against his own Fourth Army in the country east of Rheims (the organizers of Ludendorff's Roland scheme would have been flattered) and despite what the British believed, Pétain was to remain for a long time convinced that the Champagne country would be the scene of the greatest battle.

As the French had behind this front – unlike the British behind theirs – ample room for withdrawal and manœuvre so long as they left a shield for Paris on their left flank, Pétain could arrange to keep a larger proportion of his troops in reserve than Haig could possibly have afforded. Of a grand total of ninety-nine divisions, he placed sixty in the line, retaining fifteen behind the Vosges front (he entertained suspicions that the Germans might try to force a passage through Switzerland, thus ending the war as they had begun it with a violation of neutrality), twenty divisions behind the central front spread between Soissons and Bar le Duc, and in accordance with his verbal agreement with Sir Douglas Haig, four divisions available to aid the British.

Two of these last divisions were deployed just west of Soissons, and two up in the northern sector of the front, behind the Belgian Army.

There remained the Americans – who could undoubtedly contribute an extra reserve of strength behind the French front, if only their Commander-in-Chief could be persuaded to throw them into the battle. Four large-size American divisions had so far arrived in France, and General Pershing had set up his headquarters at Chaumont, some sixty miles south of the point of the St. Mihiel Salient. The men of his command were undergoing training in the surrounding countryside interspersed with spells in the quiet sectors of the line, during which they were commanded by French officers while their own officers acted as observers.

These divisions were the 1st Division, a regular division made up to strength with a small proportion of war-time volunteers (of whom one had already been killed during the first American brush with the enemy), the 2nd Division, composed of both United States Marines and regular infantry, the 26th 'Yankee' Division, which had won the race to be the first National Guard division to be sent overseas – the men were from New England and had all been spare-time volunteer soldiers after much the same fashion as the British territorials – and the 42nd 'Rainbow' Division of National Guardsmen, drawn from every State in the Union. Each division consisted of one field artillery and two infantry brigades, which with supply and repair units made up to a total strength of nine hundred and seventy-nine officers and 28,050 men.

There were thus some 116,000 American soldiers in France, and it is not surprising that their Commander-in-Chief had to guard them jealously against the designs of the military and political heads of the other Allied nations, for they were very fine-looking troops indeed. They were young, they were fit, they were enthusiastic. Their bodies were not scarred by year-old wounds, neither had their nerves been stretched beyond endurance by never-ending months of mud, blood and a troglodyte existence. As a result, General Pershing was able to insist at this time upon a standard of smartness and discipline to which the French had never aspired except with regular élite regiments, and which the British had been forced to abandon in all but the Guards Division and a few battalions of some of their more famous and old-established regiments.

Human nature being what it is, the French and the British were jealous of the Americans – with the jealousy which all men who had been through Verdun and Passchendaele felt for those who had not, with the jealousy of all men aged and embittered before their time by the chaos and disaster of battle, for those who still looked forward to the fray with eager confidence.

And if the Tommy and the Poilu were jealous of the Doughboy, the British and French Staffs were envious of the American Command. They were basically envious of the fact that America still had such men as these left, for when Pershing referred to his divisions as 'the best damn divisions in any army' it was no aid to his popularity that he may well have been right. His army in 1918 was composed of elements similar to those of the German Student Divisions which had perished in the 'Kindermord' of October 1914, of the divisions which held the flower of British manhood and were slaughtered on the Somme, and of those of the pride of French audacity which had been trodden into the plains of Verdun and Champagne. These had all been magnificent fighting armies, for in addition to physical attributes of note, the men comprising them had possessed those two inestimable military virtues – in the eyes of the Staffs – innocence and hope.

Now General Pershing's army was the only one to possess those priceless gifts in abundance; no bitter memories of muddle and waste would hold his men back, no distrust of high-level strategy weaken their resolution.

They had in fact, already given evidence of this, for American Engineers had been engaged in work behind the British line since the end of 1917, and Edmund Blunden speaks of them as 'men of splendid but risky ease of mind'. Their trench raids too, carried out by battalions training in the French sector, were pressed home with an eagerness and an élan which had been missing from the Western Front since late 1916, and one lately carried out by men of the Rainbow Division had even been distinguished by the presence of the Divisional Chief-of-Staff, Colonel Douglas MacArthur, wearing a turtle-necked sweater and an overseas cap, for he disdained the use of a steel helmet.

On another raid, hand-to-hand fighting developed in the pitch-black corner of a deep German trench, in the course of which an American corporal and a heavy-weight German grappled with each other at too close a range for either to use a weapon. A second American hovered on the skirts of the fray endeavouring to bayonet the enemy, his bafflement eventually expressed by the plaintive inquiry: 'Homer, for Pete's sake which is you?'

Such concern for another indicated a generosity of spirit which past events had ground out of most other troops – and generosity is closely linked with the spirits of self-sacrifice and trust. No wonder the American divisions were objects of envy.

But despite the most urgent pleas from Allied commanders, Pershing refused to yield up any of his fighting troops for incorporation into other armies – either as individual infantrymen fed into under-strength British battalions, or as battalions to fight in the line under British or French command.

His intention was to build an American Army and then to direct it in battle; in co-operation with those of his Allies, certainly, but as a separate and distinct component of the total force. In this he had the legal warrant contained in the first part of the fifth paragraph of his official instructions, received by him from the American Secretary for War, Mr. Newton D. Baker, which read:

> In military operations against the Imperial German Government you are directed to co-operate with the forces of the other countries employed against that enemy; but in so doing the underlying idea must be kept in view that the forces of the United States are a separate and distinct component of the combined forces, the identity of which must be preserved. This fundamental rule is subject to such minor exceptions in particular circumstances as your judgement may approve. The action is confided to you and you will exercise full discretion in determining the manner of co-operation.

This was the part of his instructions which General Pershing staunchly upheld at many a formal and informal discussion of the developing military situation. He also stubbornly countered the attempts by the voracious (and increasingly worried) Command Staffs of his allies, to nullify the effects of this part of his instructions by political manœuvre or administrative adjustment.

He assured President Wilson and Secretary Baker, for instance, that the imminent danger was by no means so great as Lloyd George and Clemenceau would have them believe, adroitly pointing out that if the British were as short as they claimed of men along their section of the front, they could hardly afford to keep so many army units abroad in such places as Palestine and India. He had also been gratuitously provided with one excellent argument against the amalgamation of American with British units, by the ever-helpful Marshal Joffre. Even inside the British Army, the Marshal pointed out, the Canadians and Australians, and even the Scots and the Irish, were kept together in their own corps and divisions.

And when Sir William Robertson (still CIGS at that time) stated that Britain would be willing to forgo shiploads of essential supplies in order to bring over one hundred and fifty American infantry battalions, *without* their administrative divisional 'tails', Pershing suggested that the same space could better be used to bring over complete divisions.

65

There was of course, no reason why Pershing should have courted popularity with his allies. He was convinced – rightly – that the armed strength under his command would exercise the decisive force on the field of battle, but he also seems to have believed that it would be able to do so even in the event of a collapse of the British or French armies. When at a crucial phase of the battle to come he was asked by an indignant and vociferous Foch whether he was prepared to risk the French being driven back behind the Loire, Pershing answered crisply and unequivocally 'Yes!'. – and his certainty that the Americans would still be able to retrieve the situation would have been admirable in less precarious circumstances.

Few people are sufficiently objective in their view of their own condition to be able to appreciate when their commendable determination passes over the peak of increasing value and slides down the other side into stubborn obstinacy. To expect such objectivity of 'Black Jack' Pershing seems on the face of it like hoping for gold from granite, for there had been little occasion in his life of action and ambition for the development of powers of self-examination. To European eyes, Pershing appears as the embodiment of the American military tradition – although from the perspective of the 'sixties one must wonder whether he was not, in fact, its originator.

He had been born in 1860 of poor parents in what were then the frontier lands of Missouri, and his life presents the popular picture of the rise to fame and fortune of the possessor of aggressive pertinacity in the land of opportunity. He was very much a self-made man. When young, he had supported himself by teaching at a children's school whilst taking a law course at the Normal School at Kirksville, but a competitive examination for entrance to West Point offered and in due course gave to him the opportunity of a career in which he would be fed and clothed whilst being trained. He passed out high on the list and by 1887 was riding as an officer with the United States Cavalry against the Apaches. Three years later he was in charge of Indian Scouts during the crushing of the Sioux rising.

Later, he served in Cuba and there attracted the attention of Theodore Roosevelt, who wrote: 'I have been in many fights, but Captain Pershing is the coolest man under fire I ever saw in my life.' This was a most fortunate impression to make upon one who was soon to have the political power to aid the careers of promising officers, although some years were to elapse before it bore fruit. In the meantime, Pershing went to the Philippines where he occupied his spare time studying the ways of the savage Moros to such good effect that when an emergency arose he was called upon to take a general's role, and to act as administrator of the district in which lay the Moro country.

During all this time, his reputation had been growing as a man of stubborn determination, physically tough, morally of indestructible fibre. He went straight for anything he wanted, regardless of physical, social or military barriers: slackness in the ranks (there was never insubordination) he had in certain circumstances cured with his fists, and when on one much publicized occasion he queued up with the men for beans and coffee, it is fair to surmise that it was because he was hungry and not for any notions of democracy – a concept for which he cannot be said to have shown much more than lip service. His nickname 'Black Jack' was a reluctant tribute to his aspect of soldierly implacability.

He accompanied the Japanese forces as observer during the Russo–Japanese War, and then Roosevelt, impatient with Congress, used a singular power which had been granted to him for the creation of brigadier-generals, and Pershing suddenly found himself promoted over the heads of eight hundred and sixty-two of his seniors. It was as well that he had by now become impervious to unpopularity.

He was commanding a brigade in San Francisco in 1916 and was thus favourably positioned when trouble flared up on the Mexican border as a result of the activities of Pancho Villa. By 1917, owing to the death of the original holder of the command, Pershing was the Major-General in control of the only American troops engaged in hostilities and thus the only ones to be prominent in the eyes of public or politicians. He was also – to his personal tragedy, but to his professional advantage – the widower of the daughter of the Chairman of the Senate Committee on Military Affairs, and possibly as a result of this had received from him on the morning of May 3rd, 1917, the following telegram:

'Wire me today whether and how much you speak, read, and write French' – to which he made a suitable reply which he was later to admit was 'rather optimistic'. But, he added with delightful candour, it seemed 'justified by the possibilities to be implied.'

There were, in fact, four generals whose names were considered for command of the first American forces to be sent to Europe, but two of these were found to be in doubtful health for such an important and probably arduous task, and the third, Major-General Leonard Wood, had given no indication during his military career that he appreciated advice, help or control from civilian politicians. These therefore chose Pershing, who had shown a quite unexpected ability in reconciling political and military expediencies whilst in command in Mexico.

From America's point of view it is probable that no better choice could have been made. Pershing's appearance and manner, for one thing, was the direct antithesis of the European picture of the American soldier, who it was fully expected would be reckless, braggart and extravagant. Haig immediately appreciated Pershing's qualities, and wrote in his diary after their first meeting: 'I was much struck with his quiet, gentlemanly bearing – so unusual for an American', adding later: 'The ADC is a fire-eater, and longs for the fray' – a remark concerning a Captain Patton, whose spirit apparently was not to be affected by the passage of time.

If the French were impressed, however, they avoided showing it. Perhaps they were disappointed that the American Commander-in-Chief gave early indication that he would prove intractable to their somewhat exigent demands, or perhaps they felt that neither he nor his officers showed the correct degree of appreciation of or subservience to their own military experience and superiority. It finally became necessary for General Pétain to issue a broadsheet to the French Staffs to the effect that 'the Americans are a proud and sensitive people who will not tolerate the patronizing attitude commonly displayed towards them.'

Despite their differences in the military field, however, the three Allied Commanders-in-Chief, Haig, Pétain and Pershing, maintained excellent relations, all thoroughly misunderstanding the others' points of view without being particularly conscious of any basic divergencies, and appreciating their personal qualities. Reserve, autocracy and martial determination distinguished all three, for they were cast in virtually the same mould, and it is noteworthy that later biographers of two of them each made the same claim for their subjects – that they were the possessors of the most imposing chins in Europe. It is curious how rarely military biographers point with pride to the physiognomy of intellect in those they portray.

This then, was the man who commanded the American forces in Europe as the immense threat of Ludendorff's offensive grew ever larger before the alarmed eyes of the Intelligence Staffs of the British and French Commands. They could only hope that if their danger became acute, General Pershing would give a wider interpretation to his official instructions than he had shown any likelihood of doing so far, and possibly even to pay specific attention to the end of that paragraph whose beginning he had so far invariably invoked. For the paragraph concluded: 'But, until the forces of the United States are in your judgement sufficiently strong to warrant operations as an independent command, it is understood that you will co-operate as a component of whatever army you may be assigned to by the French Government.'

Not that this was likely to be of much assistance to the British. There was very little that was going to be of much assistance to the British, other than their own fortitude. In front of the Michael attacks, the men of the right wing of the Third Army and the whole of Sir Hubert Gough's Fifth Army, had been valiantly endeavouring to carve a coherent defensive system into the devastated waste intentionally created by the Germans in 1917, when they retreated to the Hindenburg Line. In places this was proving far more difficult than Ludendorff could have hoped for, even in his most optimistic moments, especially in the St. Quentin area and southwards along the stretch recently taken over from the French.

The chief problem was one of transport. Every necessity of life itself, plus those for holding the line whilst trying to build sound defensive positions behind it, had to be brought forward for miles across a flat but cratered surface, at night. There was by early March a labour force of nearly forty-eight thousand men available behind the Fifth Army front, in addition to the men of the army, but so difficult was the problem of transport that the greater part of this force was necessarily employed laying roads and railways leading up to the proposed Rear Zone (the Green Line) while the defences of the Battle Zone were finally undertaken largely by the men who would have to fight in them – and there were just not enough of them to carry out this Herculean task in the time available.

Every building, every tree and natural barricade had been methodically flattened by the enemy, so there was nothing in the area to assist or afford a short cut in the construction of the defences. Villages had been reduced to the foundations of their buildings – which invariably lay across the best line for the trenches – trees and orchards had been cut down so that their trunks were just high enough to obstruct fields of vision and fire without offering the slightest cover. What trenches remained had crumbled and were half-full of debris – inchoate, isolated and incomplete. Only where wire belts were not wanted, it seemed, had any ever been constructed solidly enough to withstand the passage of time.

Across this desert of apparently wilful unhelpfulness had by early March been laid the outlines – they would never be much more – of the defensive Battle Zone. There were wire belts with no trenches behind them, half-finished switch lines with no wire, lengths of trench working towards each other but not yet connected.

In view of the obvious impossibility of building and manning continuous trench systems, it had been decided to form a series of wired-in redoubts (the 'Blob' system as it was derisively named by those whose military development had not passed the 'thin red line' stage), all in theory with mutually supporting fields of fire. But even with the consequent economy of labour that this would yield, it had been calculated that for the defences behind the Fifth Army front nearly three hundred miles of trench with appropriate wire belts would be needed, and that it would take five hundred men two to three months to bury the essential telephone wires alone. 'No amount of labour – nothing short of a fairy wand – could have prepared all those defences in a few weeks.' So wrote Sir Hubert Gough in after years.

But the effort was made, for the men knew that their lives would depend almost solely upon their own endeavours. By now, everyone sensed the approaching battle. Almost every night, the enemy raided the front trenches and took from the Fifth Army one or two prisoners; and every day it became more and more dangerous to loiter anywhere in the open, as the enemy shell-fire – although never continuous – grew increasingly active. By the middle of March, the men were feeling the strain of the back-breaking manual labour combined with accumulating sleeplessness.

Their condition was not eased by the fact that their commander, Sir Hubert Gough, did not enjoy a lucky reputation.

He was, like Haig, a cavalryman. Like the Commander-in-Chief he was also a man of immense determination; he was charming, ebullient, and psychologically inclined and fitted for the attack, and one gathers the impression from his writings that he viewed the preparations for defence with glum reluctance. By himself he would have made a popular commander, for his manner was gay and friendly and he felt a genuine sympathy for the plight of his troops, to which that tiny percentage which came into personal contact with him responded with affection; but he had in the past retained about him a Staff which had made itself bitterly disliked and with whom many of the fighting officers were not even on speaking terms. His command had also suffered such severe casualties – sometimes through sheer misfortunes, but at others through crass administrative inefficiency – that many men feared and hated to be appointed to the Fifth Army.

Some of his Staff had in fact been recently removed to other spheres of action (at Haig's instigation) but as a result of the new faces at Army Headquarters, the troops merely felt that their destinies were now controlled by devils they did not know.

As the days went by and the offensive loomed nearer, Gough did as much as it was humanly possible to do to dispel the results of past misfortunes; but he was himself faced with gigantic problems, and could thus spare little time for meeting and heartening his troops. This was unfortunate, for all men before battle like to feel that the apparent arbiter of their destiny is at least somewhere in the neighbourhood.

A week previous to the attack, it became evident that it would fall on March 21st. Evidence suggesting that Gough's Fifth Army would have to bear the brunt of the attack had so accumulated that Haig had reluctantly – for he was suspicious of a feint here – sent three more divisions to the Fifth Army area; but only under the condition that they were held in reserve in places specified by his Staff. One of these divisions was fifteen miles behind the front and another twenty-five miles – this in circumstances where it was doubtful if they could move forward much quicker than ten miles in twenty-four hours – and on the evening of March 19th, Gough rang up GHQ to request that he be allowed to move them some eight miles nearer to the enemy.

For his pains, he was read a lecture upon the conduct of military operations by Haig's Chief-of-Staff, Sir Herbert Lawrence, and specifically forbidden to move a man; it was also suggested that Gough had been both unwise and temeritous in moving his own reserves nearer to the front during the previous week, without seeking guidance from the speaker – a grim-visaged man, two stages junior to Gough in rank, who had only held his post for two months and who now – to quote the General – 'purred on the telephone like a damned pussy-cat.' But however soft his voice, the Chief-of-Staff's insistence that the reserve divisions remained where he ordered them was unyielding.

It had been raining on and off during that day and the hopes of Gough's Intelligence Staff had risen as a result, although in view of their insistence nine months before that the bucketing downpours then persisting should not affect the advance of really determined troops, this spirit of optimism over a few warm showers seems unreasonable. Perhaps it was due to a real need for a crumb of comfort, for there was little to be found elsewhere. Every hour brought them evidence of the almost inconceivable detail with which the German offensive had been planned, and of the massing of men and arms along the short length of front.

Prisoners recently taken had revealed that assault troops in the forward positions had been there for ten days while others moved up close behind them, but food and a moderate degree of comfort had been so excellently organized that there was no drop in morale. For weeks past, ammunition had been hauled into position and was now piled in mountains around the guns. A German trench-mortar section which had deserted *en bloc* (it had just been transferred from the Italian Front, and its members were frankly appalled by the extent of the preparations and the holocaust it foreshadowed) supplied details which gave a clear and fairly accurate picture of divisions lying one behind another to an unprecedented depth, of vast accumulations of rations, ammunition, bridging materials and the thousand other essentials of war. Three German armies – the Eighteenth, the Second and the Seventeenth – were wedged into position along an infinitesimal front, their forty-two divisions having all been brought up to full strength with fit, eager troops, well-trained and confident. A large proportion of them, moreover, would be fighting over ground they already knew, either from the Somme battles or as a result of having taken part in the retreat to the Hindenburg Line.

So there was little for the British Intelligence Staffs to do but to issue carefully and noncommittally phrased warnings, and pray for a renewal of the torrential rains in which they had watched their own hopes founder nine months previously. But the following morning (of Wednesday, March 20th) was damp with white fog, not sodden with cloudbursts, and although later there was a little more rain, it was only heavy enough to mix with the dry and powdery earth surface, to form a thin slick over everything.

There was no deep mud.

The troops in the British front line had little need of the Intelligence warnings that an attack was coming. They had lain in forward listening posts too long and counted the number of German raids on their lines during the last weeks too accurately to have any doubts on the subject. The date was the only detail of which they were uncertain and they were prepared to accept the Staff's forecast, as no observations of their own denied it.

They waited in their positions during that last day, cold, contemptuous, isolated from all the world except themselves – and Brother Hun across the silent, shattered earth.

During the afternoon, they either volunteered or drew lots for the various obviously suicidal tasks, and in due course as evening fell (it was raining softly again) some of them moved along the front trench to the saps, and out towards the isolated forward posts. Each man carried a Very pistol: when he fired his green flare he would be signalling his own death or defeat, and those behind could expect the enemy in ten minutes or less. As the last man reached the post, the sap trench was blocked with knife-rests and wire entanglements behind him; if there was an officer or senior NCO in the forward post, he usually occupied the rearmost position in order to block the retreat of any whose nerve, in the face of an inescapable destiny, should fail.

During the early part of the night it was not completely dark; faint stars shone mistily through light clouds, and the rain ceased. From in front came still the never-ending rumbles of transport, an occasional stammer of machine-gun fire, the boom and crash of an isolated German battery firing a few rounds in order to give the impression that all was as usual, that tonight would end as all others had – with stand-to, and rum, and tea, and early morning 'hate'.

It is doubtful whether many were deceived: only the young, the prisoners of hope.

Just before midnight it was noticed that the flares from the enemy lines were not quite so bright, that the crack of explosion was losing its edge. Cloud cover was solidifying and closing down; mist was rising. By two o'clock visibility all along the front had been reduced to a few yards, fog was thickening and nothing could be seen of enemy activity except occasionally a silvered glare in the whiteness above, refraction from a flare which had soared above its ceiling.

In a hundred isolated posts pushed out in front of twenty miles of trench, men watched the increasing pearly density with emotions ranging from a sickly and unfounded hope that it might cloak them from the wrath to come, to cold anger. There was little enough religious feeling left in these men after four years of war, but there were many who questioned that night whether the motto 'Gott mit Uns' on German belt buckles, might not after all have some basis in fact. That Jerry could conjure weather to defeat British attacks had been a wry, half-accepted belief for many months. Now it appeared that Ludendorff could order conditions for his own attack.

So that no element might be missing from their condition, platoon officers in the section opposite St. Quentin received telephoned instructions from Headquarters to the effect that in view of information just brought in from a raid, all gas cylinders in their trenches were to be turned on. The gas mixed thickly with the fog, remained static, and caused considerable discomfort to those in its immediate vicinity – and German units in St. Quentin twice complained of the unpleasant smell.

At 3.30 a.m. British artillery began sporadic bombardment of trench and road junctions behind the enemy lines in the hope of catching troop concentrations and traffic jams, and a few shells came back over in reply. But beyond this, the enemy line was silent – and owing to the fog, invisible. But the British infantry knew it was there, and as they lay in their shallow ditches or leaned against their parapets, they listened for the thunder that all were sure was coming.

They said their prayers, or they swore softly to themselves as they wiped the condensation from the metal parts of their weapons, or they kept silent, each in his own solitude of hope or despair, of fear or disregard, of acceptance or bitterness.

And they waited for the battle to start.

4. Peal of Ordnance: St. Quentin

JUST before five o'clock on the morning of Thursday, March 21st, began the most concentrated artillery bombardment the world had ever known. Nearly six thousand German guns opened fire almost simultaneously along a forty-mile front between the Sensée river and the Oise, and when the two thousand five hundred guns of the British artillery answered, the additional noise was hardly noticeable even to the men who fired them.

Tons of steel and high explosive fell with shattering force upon the forward positions and the Battle Zone. As the men crouched deafened and dazed in their trenches or staggered drunkenly towards control points, the ground rocked and heaved under them, the surrounding fog coiled and twisted, then sweetened suddenly with the sinister taint of lethal and lachrymatory gas. Shocked, cursing with anger yet sick with fear, those who survived the first few seconds pulled on their gas masks and listened despite themselves for the sound of their own deaths rushing near.

In the Battle Zone, gun positions, battery and brigade headquarters, telephone exchanges and road junctions collapsed or split apart under the weight and volume of fire. Ammunition dumps blew up in towering mushrooms of flame and destruction, the laboriously laid signal wires were ripped apart, and cannon were pounded into unrecognizable masses of bloodstained metal – some before they had fired their first rounds. For forty miles the eastern horizon was a line of leaping red flame, with a dulled reflection beneath the sheet of fog which covered the British positions.

Soon a pattern emerged. Trench-mortars only were bombarding the front trenches and after twenty minutes their fire slackened – but never ceased. The guns plastered the Battle Zone and were to do so for two hours. Heavy shells hurtled overhead and crashed to earth amid the camps, the artillery horse-lines, the billets and casualty clearing stations of the rear areas; howitzers and the lighter

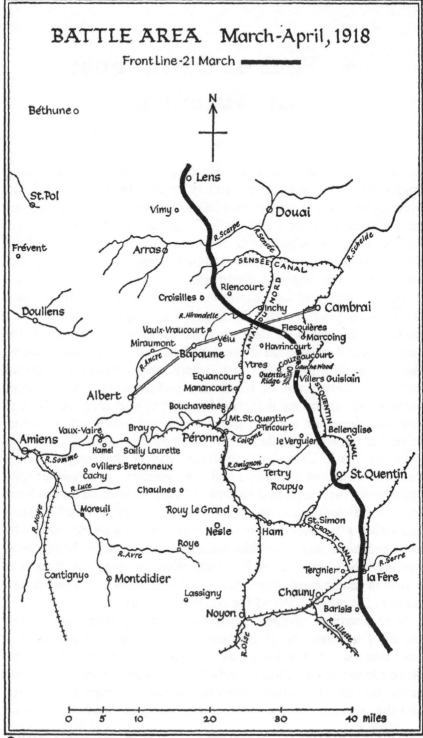

BATTLE AREA March-April, 1918

Front Line - 21 March ▬▬▬

N

Béthune o

St.Pol o

Frévent o

Doullens o

o Lens

Vimy o

Arras o

o Douai

R.Scarpe

R.Sensée

R.Schelde

SENSÉE CANAL

Croisilles o

Riencourt o

o Inchy

o Cambrai

R.Hirondelle

Vaulx-Vraucourt o

o Vélu

Flesquières o

o Marcoing

Miraumont o

Havrincourt o

R.Ancre

Bapaume o

Ytres o

Couzeaucourt o

Gauche Wood

Equancourt o

Quentin Ridge

Villers Guislain o

Manancourt o

Albert o

Bouchavesnes o

Mt.St.Quentin o

Vaux-Vaire o

Bray o

Tincourt o

Bellenglise o

Amiens o

Hamel o

Sailly Laurette

Péronne o

R.Cologne

le Verguier o

R.Somme

o Villers-Bretonneux

Cachy o

R.Omignon

Tertry o

R.Luce

Chaulnes o

Roupy o

o St.Quentin

Moreuil o

Rouy le Grand o

R.Noye

Nesle o

Ham o

St.Simon o

CROZAT CANAL

R.Serre

Cantigny o

o Montdidier

Roye o

R.Avre

Tergnier o

o la Fère

Lassigny o

Chauny o

Noyon o

Barisis o

R.Oise

R.Ailette

CANAL DU NORD

ST.QUENTIN CANAL

0   5   10   20   30   40 miles

© CASSELL & CO. LTD. 1962

field-guns pounded the redoubts, the wireless and power-buzzer installations, the communication trenches. It was evident that the attackers had marked down their targets with considerable accuracy.

And everywhere gas drenched wide areas, and lines of coughing, vomiting and blinded men congregated at the aid posts.

At times the fire grew so intense that the very laws of nature seemed in abeyance. The air vibrated with shock, black layers danced in the fog, fixed objects flickered to and fro, and in the light of mounting flame and fire the mist became a crimson, yellow-shot effervescence. The thunder and crash of explosion became a norm which was heard no longer, as senses numbed and violence and horror increased.

Then, after fifty minutes, the barrage abruptly shifted to the front line and the known infantry positions were systematically swept for ten minutes. Trenches caved in, machine-gun posts were obliterated, wire belts blown apart, men blown to fragments.

Ten minutes later the main weight of fire was switched back on to the Battle Zone and once again the destruction of communication and control centres began, the systematic gassing of artillery and reserve formations. This continued until 6.40 a.m., then it slackened as one third of the German howitzers and field-guns fired again in turn upon the British front-line infantry – registering now, for the wrath to come.

By now daylight was growing, dimming the brilliance of the shell-bursts, whitening the scenes of desolation – but adding little to their visible areas for the fog was still dense. In front, the British lay in the remains of their trenches or in shell-holes, desperately watching for signs of enemy movement, shivering with shock, with anticipation, with dreadful tension. At isolated places along the front, German infantry appeared out of the smoke, and bitter hand-to-hand fighting took place, generally in no-man's-land with the bombardment as fitting backcloth. But these attacks were exceptional – mostly the infantry of both armies lay waiting with mingled hope and terror for the moment of mass assault.

And those British who could still distinguish phenomena beyond the radius of their own immediate danger realized that the main weight of the barrage, which had fallen behind them up to now, was gradually concentrating along the forward edge of the Battle Zone and creeping back across the intermediate area towards them.

It was all done systematically, accurately, and inexorably. By 8.20 a.m. all German guns with the exception of the long-range and counter-bombardment batteries were firing on the British front-line infantry positions on the entire length of the Fifth Army front north of the Oise, and along that part of the Third Army front which extended from the northern flank of the Flesquières Salient up to the Sensée river. The Salient itself was at this time almost an oasis of peace within the holocaust – for Ludendorff's plan was to pinch it out, not to annihilate it.

For eighty minutes this bombardment on the forward positions continued – murderous, remorseless, devastating, rising to a climax at 9.35 a.m. when every trench-mortar along the German line came into massed action again and German engineers added to the uproar by firing the charges they had laid in the tattered remnants of the British wire.

And at 9.40 a.m., the German infantry rose to their feet and stormed forward.

The main assault troops moved fast as they had been trained to do. Generally they raced ahead with their rifles slung – relying for effect upon ample supplies of the stick-bombs they all carried, and upon the light machine-guns and flame-throwers which accompanied each section. Aided by the fog, they passed quickly through the forward positions, evading the known isolated posts and redoubts, jumping across the trenches when they came to them, finding their way by compass and memory of well-conned maps or often of the ground itself when they had fought across it before. Behind them, the second and third attack waves mopped up – sometimes by merely directing dazed and bleeding prisoners to the rear, sometimes completing the havoc of the guns with bayonet and rifle butt. Where organized resistance remained, they encircled it, but if its reduction proved too difficult or too lengthy, the task was handed over to the follow-up divisions and the artillery. Then the attack waves followed the Storm Troops on into the Battle Zone.

Their fortunes on the Fifth Army front varied inversely with their distance from the Oise, and the resultant density of the concealing fog; for it was in the valley of this river that the fog was thickest and so the slowest to disperse. It did not do so here until the early afternoon, and by this time the Storm Troops had fought their way under its cloak deep into the Battle Zone, and in one place south of St. Quentin were practically through it.

Around St. Quentin, however, and to the north, the British were holding on to the forward edge of the Battle Zone for some miles. This was in part due to the earlier clearing of the fog which allowed the emplaced machine-guns to fire upon the advancing enemy before they were actually close enough to bayonet the crews, and in part to the tenacity of the front-line battalions, some of whom were still fighting in forward redoubts and were to continue to do so until early evening. Some idea of their ordeal may be gathered from the fact that of the eight battalions in the front line of XVIII Corps, only fifty men survived to retire to the Battle Zone (and half of them quickly became casualties there) and no indication of the fate of two battalions of the King's Royal Rifle Corps was found until months later, when a few survivors were found recovering from their wounds in German hospitals. But this happened everywhere along the fronts, especially where bombardment had sealed the avenues of escape or the exhortations by the Staff to fight on to the last man and the last bullet had been obeyed perhaps too slavishly.

Fortunately this did not happen everywhere, for some of the front-line commanders were quick to realize that the enemy were following methods of attack similar to those they had themselves been urging upon the Staff for several years. With all the communications to the rear now cut, these men gathered together what forces remained to them, and either struck overland in a series of vicious, desperate flank attacks against the German waves, or raced back through the winding communication trenches towards the strong-points of the Battle Zone. Often they came across the deserted or annihilated remains of their own battalion or brigade headquarters; sometimes they avenged the deaths of their commanders in bloody hand-to-hand clashes with the overtaken Storm Troops.

Further north still, up towards the Flesquières Salient and the point of juncture of the Fifth and Third Armies, some penetration of the Battle Zone had occurred where the fog had persisted in dense pockets in the Omignon valley. Two miles north of the valley, however, a redoubt had been formed around the ruins of a village named Le Verguier and into it had retreated the survivors of the 3rd Rifle Brigade and the 8th Queens, who had been holding forward positions during the bombardment. The survivors had, moreover, brought their Lewis guns back with them, and when, shortly after their arrival between 10.30 and 11 a.m., the sun broke through the mist and dispersed it, they saw in front of them and well within their fields of fire, German troops swarming like ants from a disturbed nest across towards the Battle Zone. Few of the Germans reached it. Once visibility was granted to Fifth Army defenders, no training or tactics by the attackers availed: they were mown down in hundreds by troops with vivid and lacerated memories of the morning's carnage, and no mercy for those who had thought to benefit from it.

From this position northwards, the British were fighting in trenches which had been their own responsibility for a considerably longer period than those to the south. They were better dug, better sited and better protected – and this was as well, for here was delivered the main Michael 2 attack of the German Second Army under General von der Marwitz. It was designed to cut deep across the line south of the Flesquières Salient, join hands with the Michael 1 attack smashing down from the north – thus cutting off the British divisions facing Cambrai and Marcoing as a first objective – then to sweep westwards to Péronne and Bapaume preparatory to the wheel up through Albert to the north.

Immediately south of the Salient, Scottish and South African divisions clung to the forward edge of the Battle Zone from morning till night with grim determination. They had been forced back out of Gauche Wood by a combination of bombardment and infiltration, but possibly the wider horizons of the Springboks' birthplace had given them a more natural appreciation of country and manœuvre: attacked from the rear, they had retreated rapidly from a position obviously soon to become untenable to a redoubt on the heights of Quentin Ridge. From there they were not dislodged – indeed early attempts by the enemy to storm the redoubt proved so costly to them that the assault waves, true to their training, quickly turned elsewhere to probe for easier penetration.

But not to the Flesquières Salient. Here, the Royal Naval Division – composed originally of seamen for whom no ships were immediately available, but since established as a permanent division – and their immediate neighbours of the southern corps of the Third Army had beaten off early morning attacks, and then been subjected to a heavy bombardment of mustard gas shells which caused them many casualties and extreme discomfort for those who survived. But no main attacks smashed through the positions of the Forward Zone – although the outposts were withdrawn – and for the whole of the first day the Salient formed the hinge upon which the British front to the south slowly turned, as it was pressed back at its farther edge in the Oise valley, opposite la Fère. So in the late afternoon, the Hawke, the Drake and the Royal Marine Battalions were still holding the support trenches of the front line and listening with awe and some bewilderment to the sounds of gigantic conflict on each side. It was not until midnight that some inkling of the situations there reached them, and they received orders to retire to their Intermediate Zone and hold themselves in readiness for further and speedy withdrawal to their Battle Zone in case of necessity.

For immediately to the north, von Below's Storm Troops of the Michael 1 offensive had smashed through the front of the 51st Highland Division on each side of the main Cambrai–Bapaume road, encircled the main redoubts and reached the rear edge of the Battle Zone. In the afternoon their support divisions swept up with artillery which blasted the centres of resistance over open sights, while additional assault sections mopped up with their light machine-guns and flame-throwers. Small parties of Seaforth and Gordon Highlanders, of the Argyll and Sutherland, and the Black Watch, bitterly defended isolated positions; but they had suffered severely in the opening bombardment and the German infantry fought with a fierce determination which won them an ever-growing control of the Battle Zone.

In the centre of the Third Army front, too, Storm Troops reached the last line of the Battle Zone, shouldering their way forward on an ever-widening front. Here most of all their tactics paid, for the corps commanders of the British Third Army had been tempted by the strength of their own forward defensive positions into packing them too tightly with their troops. There had been, for instance, twenty-one battalions in the front line on the ten miles across which Michael 1 had been delivered (against eleven battalions on a similar length of the Fifth Army front) – and although this offered in theory an immensely strong protective casing to the corps areas, in practice it had merely provided densely packed targets for the German bombardment.

In the forward posts and the front line, the slaughter during the

81

opening hours of the offensive had been horrific. Entire platoons had been wiped out in seconds, men had been killed by the flying fragments of their friends' bodies, buried in collapsing trenches, trodden to death by those seeking room to dodge their own. And not only had there been more troops compressed into the Forward Zone, but the reserve battalions had been held far back, and there were relatively few battalions holding the main Battle Zone.

Once the Storm Troops broke through the corps fronts, they therefore faced a far easier task than their compatriots to the south. Still infiltrating past centres of resistance, they struck deep into the Battle Zone, while behind them their support waves tore open gaps in the blood-soaked forward positions, and widened them to let through the full flood of the German Seventeenth Army.

Even these troops still followed the same tactics of by-passing resistance and working around behind it. Time after time during the day's fighting, Third Army runners dispatched to battalion or divisional headquarters found them already in German hands, gun-crews were attacked from the rear and fought hand-to-hand with enemy infantry under the barrels of their own guns. During that afternoon – for the first time for many months – artillery duels took place between batteries which could see each other.

As the few battalions in the Battle Zone were outflanked or pressed back by the weight of enemy attack, a number of unlikely place-holders found themselves forced to learn again the arts of infanteering which they had fondly hoped they had put behind them. Mess waiters, cooks, quartermasters and office clerks fought – and fought well, too – to beat off the German attack upon the last line of the Battle Zone; a Special Duties Gas Unit of the Royal Engineers literally raced a platoon of Storm Troops across open ground for possession of an unoccupied section of trench, and the instructors and pupils of a Divisional Bombing School aided a counter-attack in the Hirondelle valley, during which legend recounts that a pupil was heard remarking aggrievedly to an NCO, 'I thought you told us yesterday that so long as we did as you said, we wouldn't come to no harm on this course?'

On the ridge above the Sensée valley, Lieutenant-Colonel Deneys Reitz – who had ridden with Boer Commandos against the British sixteen years before – was now commanding a battalion of the Royal Scots Fusiliers. Despite their casualties during the bombardment, despite the fact that he himself was twice badly gassed, the battalion held the crest through the entire day and lent support to the battalion on their left front, to such effect that between them they formed the left flank of the British defence. There was no encroachment north of them, and Arras was therefore never – during the first day – in danger.

As dusk fell, the fighting died. Each side licked its wounds and made what preparations it could for the morrow. For the German army commanders it was mostly a question of moving up their reserves and endeavouring to ensure that they were in the most advantageous positions for the next stage of the attack: for the British commanders, it was a question of discovering what they had left, for there were virtually no reserves available.

Gough telephoned GHQ and was answered with sympathetic reassurance by the soft voice of the Chief-of-Staff. To Gough's assertion that the Fifth Army had done magnificently to hold the enemy along the front of the Battle Zone, with the exception of two breaches in the valleys of the Cologne and the Omignon and the wider and more serious penetration south of St. Quentin and in the Oise valley, Lawrence answered with enthusiastic agreement and the suggestion that they would certainly do even better tomorrow. But when Gough pointed out that there was always the possibility that the Germans instead might do better tomorrow, he was assured that after the severe losses the enemy had suffered that day, they would be far too busy clearing the battlefield and treating their wounded, even to consider another attempt at an advance.

'I found it difficult', Sir Hubert wrote later, 'to get the full gravity of the situation understood.'

He persevered however, and in due course obtained permission to withdraw his severely mauled right flank back during the night behind the protection of the Crozat Canal, and also to reinforce it with some units from the 2nd Cavalry Division. The left flank of this withdrawal would be connected along the line of the St. Quentin Canal with the troops still in the Battle Zone. He also made adjustments to buttress the flanks of the two breaches in the more northern valleys and he was forced to order the reluctant retreat of the South African Brigade in order to conform with the withdrawal to their Intermediate Zone of the divisions in the Flesquières Salient.

For the success of the Michael 1 attacks on the Third Army had undoubtedly rendered necessary the partial evacuation of the Salient – and from midnight on the men of the Royal Naval Division slowly filtered back through their communication trenches, full of puzzled anger and frustration over a situation which has bedevilled so many soldiers in so many wars. They had fought hard and held their positions all day while the battle had raged: now it was over they were retreating. 'It was enough,' as they bitterly remarked to each other, 'to make you wish you hadn't volunteered to go to sea.'

Other – sometimes almost incredible – movements of troops took place during that night.

Under cover of night, along the whole length of the line won that day by the Germans, parties of British infantry crept out from shell-holes, from dug-outs and sections of blown-in trenches, to begin filtering back towards their own lines. Platoons – or their survivors – sections, individual men, all moving secretively and intently across the cratered surface, listening for guttural voices, for the grate of the sentry's rifle on the parapet, for the smooth click of the cocking-handle. Sometimes they were caught or killed, sometimes they had to fight their way through enemy positions – preferably with bayonet or club – more often they avoided them. Sometimes, inevitably, they completed their journeys only to be shot by their own compatriots holding the foremost British positions, and taut with expectancy for the renewal of attack.

In several places the British artillerymen returned to the guns they had abandoned during the day, connected up the gun limbers, and dragged the guns out. One such episode took place near Velu:

I had given strict orders as to silence, and from now on all instructions were given in whispers and every effort was made to keep the horses and limbers clear of anything that might make a noise. In silence I led three teams forward to the three right guns ... and in almost complete quiet we limbered them up and then moved back about fifty yards. There I had to leave them whilst Ogilvie and I took teams to the other two guns 400 yards away from the main positions over the hill to the left. ... Yet I hated to leave them where they were, for every moment I expected a burst of machine-gun fire or shelling, and to either of these they would be entirely exposed. But during the hour we were in the position everything remained wrapped in complete silence, which was made even more intense by the deadening effect of the heavy mist; no gun-fire; no rifle-fire; all was as peaceful as a night on Salisbury Plain, and it was in very strange contrast to the tremendous noises of the day just past.

When dawn came there was another thick mist to blind the machine-gunners of the defenders, and to cloak the movements and intentions of those Storm Troops who had survived the ordeal of the first day.

After hearing the official report of the progress of his armies on the opening day of the offensive, the Kaiser ordered an immediate award of the Iron Cross with Golden Rays to von Hindenburg. As the last occasion of this award had been to Blücher in 1814, it can be seen that the All Highest took a sanguine view of the results of the battle: but it does not seem that his enthusiasm was shared by any of his more responsible officers. Ludendorff maintained an aloof silence, von Kuhl contented himself with the observation that British obstinacy was proving, for the moment, a most useful ally. They both watched the lines on the Staff maps of the northern area with peculiar intentness, and despite news of success elsewhere, became more and more concerned at the lack of progress of the Michael 1 attack against the suddenly solidifying front of the British Third Army.

For von Below's Seventeenth Army, after its successes of the first day, on the second ran into the apparently impenetrable wall of the Third Army reserve battalions. Nothing the German infantry could do availed, for they could not retrieve a partial failure on the part of their artillery. Whereas in the previous day's bombardment the German gunners had known exactly where the British front line lay in relation to their own guns and were thus not inconvenienced by the fog, on the morning of March 22nd they lacked this know-ledge, and until the fog lifted were firing by guesswork. Often their guesses were based on sound surmise, but the confidence of certainty was missing and thus the targets could not be pin-pointed. When the mists dispersed (before 10 a.m., along the whole of the Third Army Front) the Storm Troops therefore found themselves attacking the well-entrenched positions of the rear line of the Battle Zone, still strongly held by troops whose morale had not been shaken nor their ranks decimated by pulverizing bombardment.

All day long the battle raged, from the positions north of the

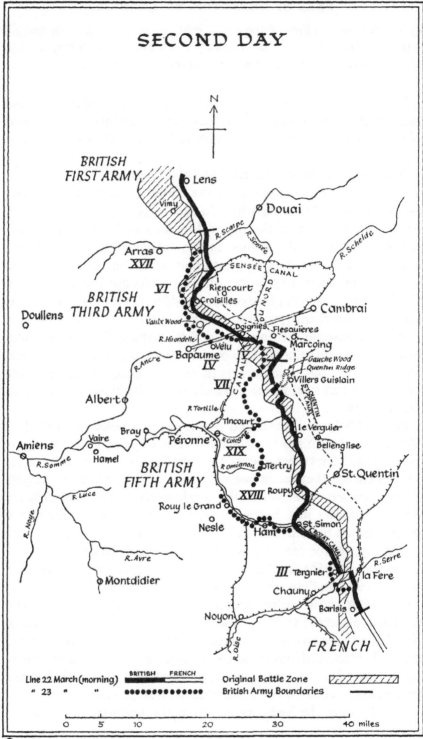

SECOND DAY

N

BRITISH
FIRST ARMY

o Lens

Vimy

o Douai

R. Scarpe

R. Sensée

R. Schelde

Arras o

XVII

SENSEE CANAL

BRITISH
THIRD ARMY

Doullens
o

VI

Riencourt

Croisilles

Cambrai

Vaulx Wood

R. Hirondelle

Doignies

Flesquières

Marcoing

Ovélu

Bapaume

IV

Gauche Wood

Quentin Ridge

V

CANAL DU NORD

Villers Guislain

R. Ancre

VII

Albert o

R. Tortille

Tincourt

le Verguier

CANAL

Bray

Vaire

Péronne

R. Cologne

XIX

Bellenglise

Amiens

Hamel

R. Somme

BRITISH
FIFTH ARMY

R. Omignon

Tertry

St. Quentin

R. Luce

XVIII

Roupy

ST. QUENTIN CANAL

Rouy le Grand

R. Nogue

Nesle

Ham

St. Simon

R. Avre

CROZAT CANAL

R. Serre

III Tergnier

la Fère

Montdidier o

Chauny o

Barisis o

Noyon o

R. Oise

FRENCH

Line 22 March (morning)   BRITISH   FRENCH   Original Battle Zone
  " 23   "   "   British Army Boundaries

0   5   10   20   30   40 miles

© CASSELL & CO. LTD. 1962

Sensée where Lieutenant-Colonel Reitz's battalion still held the ridge, southwards in a twelve-mile sweep to the Cambrai–Bapaume road and the Flesquières Salient beyond. It was as though the Arras defences above and the Salient below were iron spikes driven into the ground, anchoring at each end a flexible and slightly elastic cable: and Michael 1 could not break it. As so often before, rifle and machine-gun dominated the field, and all the valour and sacrifice of the attackers was to little effect against entrenched defenders.

It was not, however, entirely in vain. Soon after 3 p.m., there was an enormous massing of German attack waves in Vaulx Wood and along the Hirondelle valley, which culminated in a crushing attack on the British holding the ruins of Vraucourt. Every mound of rubble, every ditch and every shell-hole became the scene of epic battle, and the ground between was carpeted with grey-uniformed bodies – and still the attack was pressed. British reinforcement battalions digging defence lines further back 'downed tools' and moved up in support – but now they were moving above ground into a position partly held by the enemy, and inevitably their ranks were quickly thinned. The original occupants of the village were driven back by sheer weight of numbers and by 6.30 p.m. the Germans were in sole possession. Thus an indentation was made in the line, necessitating withdrawal on either flank.

And by direct orders from Ludendorff, the drive along the Cambrai –Bapaume road was intensified and the northern haunch of the Flesquières Salient eroded even further, regardless of cost. Early in the afternoon it became obvious that the whole of the Third Army's V Corps, including the Royal Naval Division, must come back deep into their Battle Zone: the southern anchor-point was shifting under the inexorable pressure.

South of the Salient, the situation was much more serious for the British.

As a result of the withdrawal behind the Crozat Canal during the night, the length of the Fifth Army front had been increased by some five miles, and owing to their casualties during the previous day it was all extremely thinly held. Moreover, with the sometimes total loss of battalions holding the front line when the offensive began went a large number of Lewis and heavy machine-guns, whose loss was to be keenly felt during the days which followed.

On the right flank, the Crozat Canal offered some protection, but its vapours also contributed to the fog in the Oise valley which blindfolded the defenders. Under its cover, von Hutier's Storm Troops moved up close to the east bank of the canal and as soon as the fog lifted, without waiting for support from their artillery, they laid down a short and furious barrage from trench-mortars and machine-guns. By noon they had crossed the canal on the debris of an inefficiently destroyed road bridge in the extreme south, and were fighting through the remains of the village of Tergnier against troops whose confidence was wilting under many rude shocks. During the morning a British subaltern went mad and tried to shoot the horses of a battery of artillery taking up new positions under the impression that they were Uhlans, twice a London battalion had reason to believe it was being shelled by its own artillery, and as more and more Germans poured over the canal and into Tergnier something very close to panic seized the hard-pressed and harassed British infantry. They were eventually rallied on a line some mile and a half in the rear, their flank bending back to the canal north of yet another village which had fallen into enemy hands as a result of only partial demolition of a bridge.

By evening, therefore, the whole line of the Crozat Canal was in danger of being turned from the south, and its tired defenders cannot have been much heartened by a message which reached them from General Gough, reading: 'In the event of serious hostile attack, corps will fight rearguard actions back to the forward line of the Rear Zone (Green Line) and if necessary to the rear line of Rear Zone.'

They were already behind the first, and whatever the illusions of their army commander the troops knew quite well that in their area at least, the second was nothing more than a line drawn on a map.

But it was to the north of the Crozat Canal that utter disaster threatened, for the troops which had yesterday fought their way back out of the shambles of the Forward Zone were finding that the defences even of the Battle Zone were either unmanned or non-existent. They had, moreover, received little training in the techniques of steady and controlled retreat – this as a matter of Staff policy ('It is undesirable to train troops for retirement, as such a movement is not envisaged and it would affect troops' aggressive spirit adversely.') Once withdrawal began, therefore, they quickly lost contact with units on either side and became isolated in belief if not in fact, often with ruinous consequences. They had lived and fought in line for almost the whole of their military experience, and the new conditions were a psychological shock to the vast majority.

At Roupy, for instance, a battalion of the Green Howards were holding a redoubt, but the second-in-command was in grievous uncertainty as to the tactical situation:

Again the morning was thickly misty. Our own artillery fire was desultory and useless. Under cover of the mist, the enemy massed in battle formation, and the third attack commenced about 7 a.m. We only heard a babel in the mist. Now our artillery was firing short among our men in the redoubt. About ten o'clock the enemy penetrated our left flank, presumably in the gap between us and the battalion on our left. . . . Machine-gun fire began to harass us from that direction, somewhere in the ruins of the village. We never heard from the battalion on our right, and a runner I sent there did not return.

Altogether, they were attacked seven times during the day, and the onslaught at four o'clock was obviously intended to be conclusive.

We fired like maniacs. Every round of ammunition had been distributed. The Lewis-guns jammed; rifle-bolts grew stiff and unworkable with the expansion of heat. . . . In the height of this attack, while my heart was heavy with anxiety, I received a message from brigade. Surely reinforcements were coming to our aid? Or was I at length given permission to withdraw? Neither: it was a rhetorical appeal to hold on to the last man.

It was an appeal which fell, fortunately for the Green Howards, on ears which became in time deafened by the clamour of the attack.

Another hour passed. The enemy pressed on relentlessly with a determined, insidious energy, reckless of cost. Our position was now appallingly precarious. I therefore resolved to act independently, as perhaps I should have done hours earlier. I ordered the organization of a withdrawal. This message dispatched, I lay on my belly in the grass and watched through my field glasses every minute trickling of the enemy's progress. Gradually they made way round the rim of the redoubt, bombing along

89

the traverses. And now we only held it as lips might touch the rim of a saucer. I could see the heads of my men, very dense and in a little space. And on either side, incredibly active, gathered the grey helmets of the Boches. It was like a long bow-string along the horizon, and our diminished forces the arrow to be shot into a void. A great many hostile machine-guns had now been brought up, and the plain was sprayed with hissing bullets. They impinged and spluttered about the little pit in which I crouched.

I saw men crawl out of the trenches, and lie flat on the parados, still firing at the enemy. Then, after a little while, the arrow was launched. I saw a piteous band of men rise from the ground, and run rapidly towards me. A great shout went up from the Germans: a cry of mingled triumph and horror. 'Halt Englisch!' they cried, and for a moment were too amazed to fire; as though aghast at the folly of men who could plunge into such a storm of death. But the first silent gasp of horror expended, then broke the crackling storm. I don't remember in the whole war an intenser taste of hell.

My men came along spreading rapidly to a line of some two hundred yards length, but bunched here and there. On the left . . . the enemy rushed out to cut them off. Along the line men were falling swiftly as the bullets hit them. Each second they fell, now one crumpling up, now two or three at once. I saw men stop to pick up their wounded mates, and as they carried them along, themselves get hit and fall with their inert burdens. Now they were near me, so I rushed out of my pit and ran with them to the line of trenches some three hundred yards behind.

It seemed to take a long time to race across those few hundred yards. My heart beat nervously, and I felt infinitely weary. The bullets hissed about me, and I thought: then this is the moment of death. But I had no emotions. I remembered having read how in battle men are hit, and never feel the hurt till later, and I wondered if I had yet been hit.

Then I reached the line. I stood petrified, enormously aghast. The trench had not been dug, and no reinforcements occupied it. It was as we had passed it on the morning of the 21st, the sods dug off the surface, leaving an immaculately patterned mock trench.

Such bitter disillusionments occurred a hundred times along the tenuous front held by the XVIII and XIX Corps of the Fifth Army, and as the day wore on, the battalions – now down to company or even platoon strength – retreated further and further, reaching out blindly all the time for contacts on either side. With the weight of the attack, the disruption of communication systems and the chaos of unrehearsed – virtually unimagined – retreat, disappeared all form of organization or command at higher than battalion and often company level. Enemy aircraft hovered over the men as they hurriedly dug temporary defences, their menace often enough to cause abandonment of the positions even before enemy guns sent over their high explosive to cause tired flesh to shudder, strained nerves to twist. The contact flares used by the Storm Troops had a similar effect, rising and falling often in lines curved around the defenders, like horseshoes with their points miles to the rear. As confidence evaporated, discipline weakened and sometimes naked force was used to strengthen it again. Groups of fleeing men were rounded up by military police and herded into isolated and improvised redoubts, already held by men kept in position by officers with drawn revolvers standing behind them.

This was not always necessary and many posts were held to the last with utmost gallantry – but nothing could serve to halt the enemy advance, and points of resistance had only the effectiveness of high patches of sand in front of the incoming tide. By dusk the entire Battle Zone of the Fifth Army had been lost, and during the night the remnants of three army corps – the XVIII, the XIX and the XII – fell wearily and tragically back to what derisory defences their commanders could devise for them. In the south, the XVIII Corps had lost the line of the St. Quentin Canal and gone right back behind the Somme, with the exception of a tiny bridgehead around Ham: in the centre, a yawning invitation to the enemy stretched for four miles up to the Omignon valley, and from there a thinly-held, forlorn horseshoe curved around to the Cologne valley. Here lay an exposed flank pointing towards the enemy, for the valley was occupied for nearly two miles as far forward as Tincourt, where the survivors of the 6th Connaught Rangers – the headquarters company and thirty-four riflemen – under command of their sole remaining officer, held the southern extremity of the VII Corps Green Line.

I must say I had hoped to find some fresh troops there, but there were none. Indeed the trench was practically empty ... [wrote Lieutenant-Colonel Feilding]. I made my Headquarters for the night in an exceedingly comfortable three-roomed hut in Tincourt Wood, formerly the abode of an officer of the Divisional Staff, whose Headquarters had been here until the proximity of the enemy during the last two days had driven them further back.

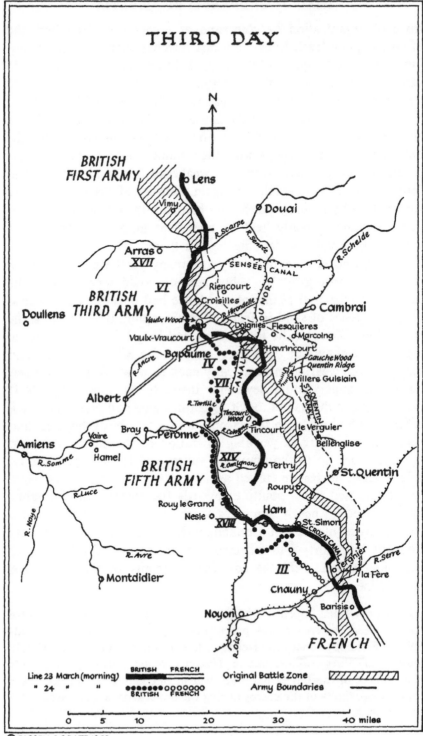

THIRD DAY

N

BRITISH
FIRST ARMY

o Lens

Vimy

o Douai

R. Scarpe

R. Sensée

R. Schelde

Arras o
XVII

BRITISH
THIRD ARMY

VI

SENSÉE CANAL

Riencourt

Croisilles

R. Hirondelle

CANAL DU NORD

o Cambrai

Doullens
o

Vaulx Wood

Doignies Flesquières

o Marcoing

Vaulx-Vraucourt

Havrincourt

Gauche Wood
Quentin Ridge

R. Ancre

Bapaume

IV

IV

o Villers Guislain

VII

CANAL

Albert
o

R. Tortille

ST. QUENTIN CANAL

Tincourt
Wood

Amiens
o

R. Somme

Vaire
o

Bray o

Péronne

R. Cologne

o
Tincourt

le Verguier
o

Hamel
o

BRITISH
FIFTH ARMY

XIV

R. Omignon

Bellenglise

o Tertry

St.Quentin

R. Luce

Roupy o

R. Noye

Rouy le Grand

XVIII

Ham

St.Simon

CROZAT CANAL

Nesle o

R. Avre

III

Terghier

R. Serre

Montdidier
o

Chauny o

la Fère
o

Noyon o

Barisis o

R. Oise

FRENCH

Line 23 March (morning) — BRITISH ——— FRENCH

" 24 " " •••••• oooooo
BRITISH FRENCH

Original Battle Zone ///////
Army Boundaries ———

0   5   10   20   30   40 miles

© CASSELL & CO. LTD. 1962.

Having in my mind the heroic exhortations which had of late been coming so unsparingly, addressed to us in the front line from this wood, I confess I was not prepared for the aspect of sudden abandonment which the hut presented.

Its appearance suggested that some sudden and deadly cataclysm had overcome the occupant while he was having his breakfast, the remains of which, together with one or two half-finished cups of tea, still littered the table. The walls were hung with bookshelves and maps (of which latter I have annexed a useful specimen): the floor had a carpet: expensive oil lamps, crockery, and a profusion of knick-knacks lay about: but there was no sign of any effort having been made to save these treasures, so rapid, apparently, had been the owner's exit. Lastly, and to our great satisfaction, there were two camp beds and a mattress of the softest down.

Think of the exhausting hours through which we had passed, and you will understand that I shall not easily forget that night's rest, the only pity being that we did not get enough of it, and that the few hours we did have were spasmodic and disturbed.

And from Tincourt, the Green Line – held everywhere in similar insubstantiality – covered the front of VII Corps up to the edge of the Fifth Army area, where it met the flank of the Third Army's V Corps, still jutting forward into the Battle Zone of the Flesquières Salient, and increasingly sensitive to threats of encirclement.

All through the next day – Saturday, March 23rd – the pressure continued, and under it the defences crumbled, the Fifth Army slowly but surely disintegrated. Reeling with weakness and fatigue, the troops fought until they were killed or retreated until they dropped unconscious – and inevitably contact with the army to the north was lost.

At 7 a.m. on Sunday, March 24th, the six battalion commanders of the Royal Naval Division – in the absence of any form of direction from higher command – decided that their position had become untenable, and that in order to avoid capture or annihilation, they must withdraw.

The Flesquières Salient was evacuated: the iron spike wrenched from the ground.

The Great Retreat had begun.

*   *   *

In accordance with the agreement for mutual support which had

93

been made between the two Commanders-in-Chief (thus avoiding the necessity of complying with the directive of the Versailles Council to place a reserve force under General Foch), on the evening of March 21st Pétain had ordered the three divisions of the French V Corps to be ready to move, and a few hours later he instructed them to begin concentration in the Noyon area, some twelve to fifteen miles behind Gough's right flank. This reinforcement was delayed for a few hours upon receipt of a courteous note from Haig thanking the French for their offer but intimating that it would not be necessary, but was expedited and indeed doubled shortly afterwards in response to a second message from Haig dispatched after his realization that the southern corps of the Fifth Army was being pressed right back to the line of the Somme.

By March 23rd, six French divisions – which had been considered the limit of assistance Haig might need – were moving into position, but although this aid was prompt, it was ineffective for a reason which had not been foreseen or even imagined. The speed given to von Hutier's advance by the new tactics, plus the enormous advantages conferred upon the Germans by the fog, had wrecked all estimates of time and movement, which had not unnaturally been geared to the elephantine cadence of previous experience.

As the first French divisions came up, they therefore found themselves – instead of manning or digging positions in rear – first swamped by groups of shaken, unco-ordinated, bitter and sometimes panic-stricken British troops retreating through them, and then themselves subjected to the same fierce and incomprehensible form of attack which had caused this near-rout. As the British right flank swung back like the edge of an opening door, the last three French divisions to be sent were flung into the gap so hastily that they were compelled to leave their artillery behind, and rush their infantry and cavalry forward with only the ammunition which each man could carry. It was extremely fortunate for them that, for the moment, von Hutier was only interested in smashing back the British, and had as yet no designs for a breakout to the south – through the gap between the edge of the door and its original jamb. And as the door opened further, more troops were needed: late on March 23rd, Pétain ordered yet another six divisions into the breach.

But if the French managed by superhuman efforts to close the gap, they never managed to get around behind Gough's fast-disintegrating army in order to support it – to act as door-stop. This essential function, as Ludendorff and his advisers had shrewdly divined, would have to be performed by British troops brought down from the north – and they obviously could not arrive for some days.

All day long on Sunday, March 24th, the respective Commanders-in-Chief listened to the reports coming in and watched their maps. With the anchor-point in the Flesquières Salient gone, the line of the British retreat straightened, hinging in the north now from the defences in front of Arras and Vimy Ridge: as the remnants of the Fifth Army went back and back, the right flank of the Third Army stretched out and backwards too, groping for contact with their sorely-pressed neighbours. By evening General Pétain's cold and logical mind had forced him to certain conclusions and he set out for Dury to meet Sir Douglas Haig and place these before him.

They met at 11 p.m.

'Pétain struck me as very much upset, almost unbalanced and most anxious,' Haig later wrote in his diary. 'I explained my plans ... and asked him to concentrate as large a force as possible about Amiens astride the Somme to co-operate on my right [sic]. He said he expected every moment to be attacked in Champagne and he did not believe that the main German blow had yet been delivered.

'He said he would give Fayolle [who was to command all British and French troops south of the Somme] all his available troops. He also told me that he had seen the latter today at Montdidier where the French Reserves are now collecting and had directed him in the event of the German advance being pressed still further, to fall back south-westwards towards Beauvais in order to cover Paris.'

What Pétain had also said, in justification of his attitude, was, 'If you withdraw your hand in proportion as I'm stretching out mine towards you, contact between our two armies will be broken in the end; your army then risks being cornered in open country, while I shall be reduced to covering Paris.'

One cannot feel that this was an unreasonable picture of the developing situation, but in Sir Douglas Haig's view the continuity of the Allied line was sacrosanct, and Pétain's proposal would break it. This spelled the end of the private arrangement for mutual assistance which, in all fairness, was never envisaged to bear such an enormous strain as that to which it was now subject. It also

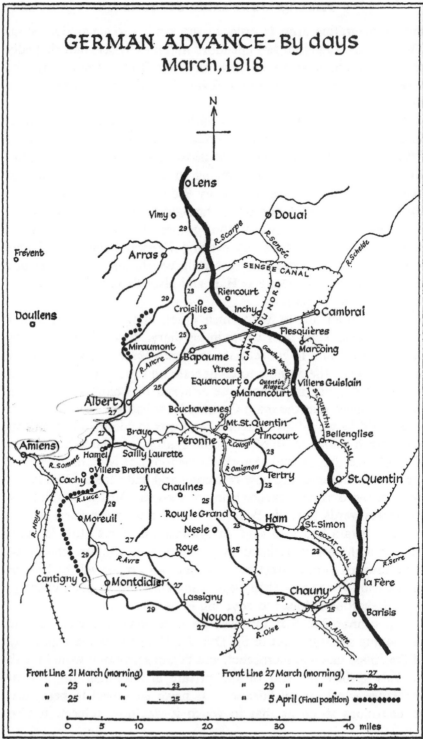

GERMAN ADVANCE— By days
March, 1918

N

Lens

Vimy
29
Douai

Frévent

Arras
23

R.Scarpe
R.Sensée
R.Scheldt

SENSÉE CANAL

Riencourt
23
Croisilles
Inchy
Cambrai

Doullens

29
25
23

Flesquières
Marcoing

Miraumont
R.Ancre
Bapaume
Ytres
Equancourt
Quentin Ridge
Manancourt
Villers Guislain

25
23

Gauche Wood Qr

CANAL DU NORD

Albert
27
Bouchavesnes
Mt.St.Quentin
Tincourt
Bellenglise

27
Bray
Péronne
R.Cologne
23

ST.QUENTIN CANAL

Amiens
27
Hamel
Sailly Laurette
R.Omignon
Tertry
23

R.Somme
Villers Bretonneux
Chaulnes
23

Cachy
R.Luce
27
25

29
Rouy le Grand
Ham
St.Simon

Moreuil
Nesle
23

R.Noye
27
Roye
25
23

CROZAT CANAL

29
R.Avre
25

R.Serre

Cantigny
Montdidier
27
Chauny
la Fère

Lassigny
25
25
23
Barisis

29
Noyon
27

R.Oise
R.Ailette

Front Line 21 March (morning) ▬▬▬▬▬   Front Line 27 March (morning) ――――・27

   " 23 "   "   ――――23   " 29 "   "   ――――29

   " 25 "   "   ――――25   "   5 April (Final position) ●●●●●●●●●

0   5   10   20   30   40 miles

opened Haig's eyes to certain benefits which could accrue to his command under a scheme which he had long spurned: if in the past he had seen little point in a Supreme Command which held British divisions in reserve to assist the French, he could now well appreciate the advantages of one which held French divisions in reserve to assist him. Bidding Pétain a rather cold farewell, he hurried back to GHQ and sent urgent signals to London requesting the immediate presence of Lord Milner (a member of the War Cabinet) and his own military *bête noire*, the CIGS, Sir Henry Wilson.

So far as the former was concerned, Haig had been anticipated, for Lloyd George had already dispatched Milner to France during that afternoon, feeling that in such critical hours he should have a representative on the scene of action. Milner, however, was at that moment *en route* for Versailles (having called at GHQ during Haig's absence) for consultation with the British representative on the Council, Sir Henry Rawlinson, and later with the French Premier, Clemenceau.

Sir Henry Wilson, the Chief of the Imperial General Staff, arrived at Haig's headquarters at 11 a.m. the following day (Monday, March 25th), to listen with sympathy to the Commander-in-Chief's troubles and with great interest to his suggestions. Beneath his charming and affable exterior, there must have been a certain element of sardonic satisfaction, for after many months in partial eclipse, it seemed as though Sir Henry's star might be in the ascendant again, much as a result of Haig's own actions. And in this Sir Henry could rejoice, despite the catastrophe which brought it about. During the late afternoon, he joined Milner and Rawlinson at Versailles, and in the evening arrangements were finalized for a joint Anglo-French Conference to take place the following day.

To Doullens, during the morning of Tuesday, March 26th, came the key figures of the Entente Cordiale, with the sole exception of the British Prime Minister. The first to arrive were the army commanders – the 'Robber Barons' as they were referred to by members of Haig's Staff. From the north came the beloved Plumer, his hair whitened by the strain of almost continual command in the Ypres Salient, his cherubic pink face and absurd little pot belly giving him the flagrantly unfair appearance of a Colonel Blimp caricature. From Béthune and the threatened but still unmenaced coalfields came General Horne – a man of oak, uncommunicative, dour but obedient – and from Arras came General Sir Julian Byng, commander of the Third Army, scion of a noble house, implacable, and looking as always as though he had been carved from polished ivory.

Only Gough was not present – and as excuse for his absence it could be argued either that as his army no longer existed he had no right to be there, or that he was too busy collecting its remnants into some form of organized retreat to be able to spare the time. (In the opinion of Sir Herbert Plumer, this last condition ought also to have applied to Byng. 'Ought to be with his army,' he muttered to his Chief-of-Staff. 'Doesn't matter for you and me, as we're not engaged.')

From these men, a worried but still undaunted Sir Douglas Haig demanded fullest support (Plumer had immediately offered twelve of his fourteen divisions in exchange for exhausted ones), and above all, no retreat; the line of their armies must be held where it was, until such time as the Commander-in-Chief could arrange for French divisions to come up in support. In particular, the right flank of Byng's Third Army must anchor itself in front of Bray-sur-Somme, ten miles south of Albert and, incidentally, some twenty-five miles behind the front line as it had existed on the morning of March 21st. To this end, the 4th and 5th Australian Divisions and the New Zealand Division were already hurrying south. (As Haig was speaking, some of them were passing through Albert.) Above all, the vital road and rail junction of Amiens, sixteen miles behind the latest known position of the front, must be covered.

Before he had time to go into further details, the Commander-in-Chief was informed that several other important personages had arrived for conference with him, and as one of them was the French President M. Poincaré, and another the French Premier, it might be as well not to keep them waiting any longer. As Haig hurried down the steps of the Town Hall, in which the conference was being held, a French general nudged Clemenceau and whispered, 'There's a man who will be obliged to capitulate in the open field within a fortnight, and we'll be very lucky if we're not obliged to do the same.'

Whoever this French general was, it is quite certain that it was not that indomitable and fiery prophet of the offensive, Ferdinand

Foch, Chief of the French General Staff and their representative on the Versailles Council, who was also present and whose hour was about to strike.

Nobody had been a more ardent believer in the 'Spirit of the Offensive' doctrine to win immortal glory for France than Foch. As he had been for years before the war an instructor at the Ecole de Guerre, he had been in a position to preach this doctrine to many minds, since rendered sceptical by bitter experience – and the aphorisms with which he had instructed and imbued a generation of French soldiers had thus been subject to some caustic reappraisal. One such was 'Any increase in fire-power will aid the offensive' – which must have caused bewilderment to many a young officer caught in the open during an attack and lying flat beneath traversing machine-gun fire; another was 'Success justifies anything' – a creed which in an earlier war had led Napoleon to St. Helena, and in a later one, was to submerge Hitler and the entire German Nation into overwhelming disaster.

On the other hand, Foch's argument 'A battle won is a battle we will not acknowledge to be lost', has a ring of fundamental truth. Moreover, in the circumstances existing on March 26th, 1918, it was a maxim which offered hope – which at that moment was at a premium. There were thus many speculative glances cast at the short, portly figure of the ebullient general as he stumped into the Town Hall after his President and his Premier.

Lord Milner and Sir Henry Wilson had been the last to arrive – almost as Haig came down the steps to greet Poincaré, and as Milner had not seen Haig during the previous day, he asked time for a short private discussion with the British army commanders before the beginning of the joint conference. It did not take long as – for one reason or another – almost all those present in Doullens Town Hall had come to virtually the same conclusions.

At 12.30 p.m., the Anglo-French conference opened with M. Poincaré in the chair, and a flat inquiry from Clemenceau as to whether Haig intended to defend Amiens or to continue falling back, possibly even to the Channel ports. He was reassured on this point. Haig stated firmly that he could, and would, hold on north of the Somme, although south of the Somme he could do little – in any case, Fifth Army troops there had already been placed under French Command. This statement received immediate qualification from

Pétain who interjected bleakly, 'Very little of it remains, and in strict truth we may say that this army no longer exists.' At this, Haig quickly finished his résumé of British intentions and inquired pertinently what the French were doing.

They were doing, under Pétain's direction, considerably more than could reasonably have seemed possible in the light of his previous reports upon French preparedness. Rather like a bankrupt reluctantly admitting that he could, if necessary, drive away from court in a new Rolls Royce large enough to carry the Lord Chancellor and the whole of the Supreme Court, Pétain revealed that he had thinned out the eastern sector of his front to such an extent that he was now able to concentrate *twenty-four* divisions in the threatened area. However, he quickly added, any optimism which might rise in his hearers' hearts as a result of this announcement should be strictly controlled, as 'in such a situation one ought not to hug delusions, but to face realities and, consequently, not to hide that these divisions would take some time to arrive on the scene, moving at the rate of two a day.'

According to the account of the French Minister of Munitions, M. Loucheur, Pétain also added that it was evident that everything must be done to defend Amiens – at which Foch, who had listened so far with an obviously fast-increasing irritation, burst out, 'We must fight in front of Amiens, we must fight where we are now. As we have not been able to stop the Germans on the Somme, we must not now retire a single inch!'

The silence which followed this *cri de coeur* was apparently broken by Haig saying, with deceptive humility, 'If General Foch will consent to give me his advice, I will gladly follow it' – an unlikely remark for him to make, except that support for its utterance can be found in the events of the next few minutes.

Milner and Clemenceau immediately retired for a brief talk to one corner of the room, feeling – as did everyone – that the moment of decision had arrived. They returned with the basis for a proposal which, after putting it to the meeting, Clemenceau then drafted, to read: 'General Foch is appointed by the British and French Governments to co-ordinate the action of the British and French Armies around Amiens. To this end, he will come to an understanding with the two Generals-in-Chief, who are requested to furnish him with all necessary information.'

100

To the surprise of all – with the possible exception of Pétain – this did not go far enough for Haig. With what bore a strong, but fallacious, resemblance to a magnanimous gesture, he announced that this was too narrow a brief for Foch and too limited a power. Foch should, he suggested, be placed in control of the Allied Armies as a whole, 'from the Alps to the North Sea' – and while Clemenceau hastily amended the draft and Foch saw at last before his eyes the realization of his fondest dreams, the atmosphere in the room changed smoothly from one of chilled despondency to one of warm and mutual admiration. French pride was at last to be assuaged by the apparent surrender of the independence of the British forces – a long-sought victory as satisfying to them as any over the Germans, and few, if any, among them remembered that Haig was a Lowland Scot with all the prudence and practicality of the breed. For undoubtedly, he seemed most likely to profit from the bargain.

In the situation which then existed, reserves could only flow one way – to support the British line – and the greater the extension of Foch's power, the greater therefore the number of reserve divisions he would be able to contribute to Haig's command. For the tactical command of the troops in battle would remain with Haig in the north and Pétain in the south – where the reserves must come from. Moreover, when Clemenceau read out the draft amended by the substitution of the words 'on the Western Front' for 'around Amiens', Haig came forward with yet another suggestion – that the term 'British and French Armies' should be removed and 'Allied Armies' written in its place; and as neither General Pershing nor the King of the Belgians was present to object, the suggestion was put into effect.

Those who believe that Sir Douglas Haig lacked shrewdness or subtlety would do well to ponder this episode.

The meeting then broke up, and the French departed amid protestations of esteem; but the British, according to their Chief of the Imperial General Staff, remained for a little longer to ponder over the last piece of business on their agenda. Somebody, obviously, must be responsible for the unfortunate events of the last few days, and somebody's head must roll. As Sir Hubert Gough was not embarrassing them with his presence and as in any case his army had ceased to exist, Sir Henry Wilson suggested that it might be a good thing for him to be sent home, and when an army was formed to take the place of the one whose shattered remnants were still desperately clinging together to form a screen in front of von Hutier's victorious but now thinning ranks, who better to command it than Wilson's old friend and fellow infantryman, Sir Henry Rawlinson, now at Versailles? In any case, some employment must now be found for Rawly, as his present position as British representative on the Versailles Council would be rendered superfluous by these newly-concluded arrangements.

Although Haig protested that Gough had dealt with a difficult situation very well, it was apparent that he did not intend to contest the issue vigorously, so if the matter was not wholly agreed there and then, Sir Henry Wilson could at least feel that he had won his point. He had, in fact, won several points that day, for Foch had been his idol for many years, the French Army had always in his opinion, been superior to the British: and Rawlinson would be delighted to re-assume control of an army in the field.

Moreover, Wilson had disliked Gough ever since their violent disagreement in 1914 over the Curragh incident.

There was in fact, rather more reason for the spirit of optimism with which the Doullens Conference concluded, than is at first sight apparent or could indeed have been known to its participants; especially as one of the first items of news to be given to Sir Douglas Haig as he left the Town Hall, was that despite his emphatic instructions, Bray-sur-Somme had already fallen, the corps holding the Albert–Bray line was falling back across the River Ancre, and German troops were already fighting in Albert.

The truth was, however, that despite the apparently inexorable advance of the German Army up to that time, the troops themselves were beginning to tire and lose spirit. The dogged resistance of most of the British units – especially at the beginning – had thinned the German ranks, the first ardour of the attack had evaporated, and they were not yet clear of a devastation for which they were themselves responsible, but which complicated their supply problems a millionfold. As an illustration of their difficulties, Binding's diary entry as early as March 23rd reads:

We are glad if ration-carts and field-kitchens can get up to us at night; then men and horses feed for the next twenty-four hours at one sitting . . .

We have reached the zone in which all wells and streams have been wrecked and the water for the attacking troops has to be brought up in watercarts. That applies to the men. The horses have to wait until we cross the canal at Moislaines-Nurlu ... the devastation is immeasurable.

Three days later, he wrote:

We have now spent two nights in the crater-field of the old Somme Battle. No desert of salt is more desolate. Last night we slept in a hole in the crumbly, chalky soil, and froze properly. ... Yesterday I was looking for Bouchavesnes, which used to be quite a large place. There was nothing but a board nailed to a low post with the inscription in English 'This was Bouchavesnes'.

All the resources of today's mechanization would have been barely sufficient to solve the logistics problem which faced the German Command as their troops fought their way into Albert – and they had to depend for transport of supplies solely upon man-power, carts drawn by dogs and horses, of which the horses at least were in poor condition. British prisoners taken on the first day recorded that even the German cavalry looked 'like a collection of old cab-horses' – and of the dead animals which littered the battlefield, as many had collapsed from exhaustion as had been killed by bullets or shell-fire.

The men were evidently in better state than their horses, for the hope of victory and the excitement of battle kept them going, but even the flame of exaltation needs fuel for burning, and with its curtailment the flame burns low: by the seventh morning of the attack the German troops were very tired and very hungry. During that day (March 27th) there were several occasions when the British retired at a slow walk – for exhaustion was affecting them, too – and the Germans followed at a distance of a few hundred yards at the same pace, halting when they halted, making no attempt to force them on. Gaps in the British line gave the attackers peace to sleep, not opportunities to exploit.

But the factor which affected the advance more vitally than any other was the untimely appearance of an uncertainty – amounting almost to vacillation – in the mind of the German High Command. Ludendorff's original intention had been to smash through onto the Bapaume–Albert line with the Michael 1 and 2 attacks, then to swing north and roll up the British line. This was the scheme decided

103

upon after the tour of the front on January 21st, but even before the attacks began he allowed the outlines of an alternative scheme to disseminate amongst the Staff, whereby the Michael attacks pressed forward directly, serving primarily to draw British strength down from the north, while the St. George attacks on each side of Ypres performed the breakthrough. These would then swing *south* and roll up the British line.

It is doubtless an excellent rule in life to have alternative schemes for the attainment of any object, but in such a situation it is a fundamental necessity to be completely clear in mind which plan is being pursued at each particular moment. It does not seem that this essential condition existed throughout the German Staff. Very soon after the promulgation of Ludendorff's original plan, the German Crown Prince – who commanded the army group containing the forces for the Michael 3 attack (but not those for Michael 1 or 2) – put forward, upon von Hutier's suggestion, the proposal that the Eighteenth Army, instead of merely holding the eastern banks of the Crozat Canal and the Somme, should cross the waterways and advance beyond – but to an unspecified distance.

As a result of this, the Kaiser's Operation Order for the Offensive contained the following sentences: '... The Eighteenth Army will seize the passages over the Somme and the canal by rapid forward movement. The Eighteenth Army will also be prepared to extend its right wing as far as Péronne' – and upon this directive Prince Rupprecht of Bavaria (commanding the forces delivering the other Michael attacks) based the relevant part of his own orders, and the Second Army's battle plan.

The Eighteenth Army commander, von Hutier, however, issued his own operation order, containing no reference whatsoever to a movement towards Péronne on the part of his own command, but only of westward and south-westward advances, in order either to attack French reserves moving up against the flank of the Michael 2 attack, or to press the British farther back.

And Ludendorff apparently made no attempt to clarify the situation during the week which remained before the offensive began; according to the Crown Prince, von Hutier's intentions were specifically passed to Main Headquarters 'but the latter declined to express any definite opinion on the matter for the time being.'

It would seem, therefore, that there was a certain amount of indecision in Ludendorff's mind, which can hardly have been dismissed by the events of the opening days of the offensive, for until March 24th the main weight of his attack was either held fast in the Arras–Flesquières loop, or blocked on the line immediately south of the Salient, whilst his southern section, which had been intended for a virtually subsidiary duty, forged ahead with ever-growing impetus. During all of March 22nd and 23rd, Ludendorff's armies made no appreciable progress against Sir Julian Byng's Third Army, for the iron spike of the V Corps remained immovable. Ludendorff was thus faced with a situation whereby if he arrested the victorious course of the Eighteenth Army in order to conserve the planned shape of his offensive, he would not only kill the sole impetus his armies possessed, but also present to the watching world the picture of the much-vaunted German Spring Offensive apparently brought to a premature halt.

As a routine preliminary to the attack, Ludendorff had discussed with his chief assistants, von Kuhl and von der Schulenberg, the tactics to be followed in the event of a rapid and decisive victory even greater than that for which they planned, resulting in a complete rupture of the British line and emergence into open country beyond. The decision taken was that in such a case, the Seventeenth Army (Michael 1) would swing north-west on St. Pol and drive the British into the sea, the Second Army (Michael 2) would drive on westward to Amiens and thus separate the British from the French, while the Eighteenth Army would swing south-westwards and defeat the French.

In sum – having *converged* in order to effect a breakthrough, it was intended then to *diverge* in order to exploit it: a concept with which few would disagree, so long as the breakthrough was successful and complete.

To von Kuhl's dismay, however, orders directing a very similar series of divergent thrusts to those outlined above, were issued by Ludendorff to his armies at 9.30 a.m. on March 23rd, and at a conference in the afternoon they were confirmed. Only the virtual impossibility of obedience to these orders prevented a dispersal of force before an unbroken line – for the Seventeenth Army remained penned in the loop until the following day, the Second Army could do no more than press hard against the right flank of the British

105

Third Army and the doughty South Africans (the middle of the door), while rightly or wrongly, the Crown Prince and von Hutier ignored their instructions to turn on the French and instead drove due westward against the British – against the outer stile of the door.

It could well be argued therefore, that the spectacular success which seemed to be attending German arms (and by March 26th, the day of the Doullens Conference, they had won more territorial gains on the Western Front in four days than the Allies had in three years) had been achieved in spite of the High Command, and not as a result of Ludendorff's genius.

Nevertheless, his train of thought can be seen to have travelled along not illogical lines. From the beginning his strength had been massed in the north, and when the door swung open – and continued to open – the temptation to use it to break the hinge opposite and thus to tear loose the entire structure, must have been very great. Moreover, there was little else he could do with this concentration of power, for the logistic problems attendant upon the withdrawal of some of its divisions and their dispatch as reinforcements to von Hutier thirty-five miles away, were insoluble. It took, for instance, thirty trains to transport one German division – where trains ran.

As day succeeded day with no change in the strategic pattern, therefore, the temptation grew ever greater – so great indeed that Ludendorff decided that one final and immense effort must be made to break the *impasse*. On the morning of March 28th – in direct contradiction to his own doctrine of reinforcing success and not failure – he shifted the centre of gravity of his offensive even further north, and launched the Mars attack against Arras.

It failed – for three principal reasons.

Seven of Ludendorff's reserve divisions had already been drawn as though by a vacuum to the support of the Eighteenth Army – the greatly enlarged front which von Hutier's success opened necessitated this – and the intended hammer-blow against Arras could therefore not be sufficiently strengthened. Thus only thirteen German divisions made the initial attack on six British divisions – British divisions moreover, of high morale, defending well-dug and well-wired positions with determination and skill, and who unbeknown to the Germans had retired from their forward positions to

106

the security of their Battle Zone. Thus the opening artillery bombardment, so far as it was directed against the infantry positions, crashed down upon empty trenches.

And there was no fog.

All day long the German infantry attacked with vigour and dash, but they were fought to a standstill – inevitably – by entrenched defenders firing emplaced machine-guns in perfect visibility. Line after line of Storm Troops and picked infantry were mown down, and those only wounded by the bullets rarely survived the shell-fire of the defensive barrages laid down by the British artillery when they had recovered from the effects of the gas-shells with which, as before, the German bombardment had opened. Nowhere was the British line pierced – and the Mars attack was called off that evening: as the light died, so did the hopes of the German Staff.

It was, however, necessary to have something more to show for the immense effort of the March offensive than what have been so aptly called by Sir Winston Churchill 'the Dead Sea fruits of the mightiest military conception and the most terrific onslaught which the annals of war record.' Despite the area of the ground wrested from the Allies, no centre of strategic or even tactical value had yet been won; only the vast, ghoulish graveyard of previous battles.

That evening the commanders of the Second and Eighteenth Armies received the following directive: 'Amiens is now the objective; to secure that place all the efforts of this and the following days will be directed; the attacks near Montdidier and eastward of that town are only diversions designed to delay enemy forces.'

This was really little more than an acknowledgement that von Hutier and von der Marwitz could continue with their non-observance of Ludendorff's directive of the 23rd – but even so its intention was too late. In addition to the exhaustion of the German troops and the enormous difficulties of supplying them across the wasted areas, yet another subtle but insidious factor was coming into play against the Germans: the British blockade was, in fact, having an unlooked for effect upon the field of battle. In his diary for March 28th, Rudolf Binding wrote:

Today the advance of our infantry suddenly stopped near Albert. Nobody could understand why. Our airmen had reported no enemy between Albert and Amiens. . . . Our way seemed entirely clear. I jumped into a car with orders to find out what was causing the stoppage in front.

As soon as I got near the town I began to see curious sights. Strange figures, which looked very little like soldiers, and certainly showed no sign of advancing, were making their way back out of the town. There were men driving cows before them on a line; others who carried a hen under one arm and a box of notepaper under the other. Men carrying a bottle of wine under their arm and another one open in their hand. Men who had torn a silk drawing-room curtain from off its rod and were dragging it to the rear as a useful bit of loot. More men with writing paper and coloured notebooks. Evidently they had found it desirable to sack a stationer's shop. Men dressed up in comic disguise. Men with top hats on their heads. Men staggering. Men who could hardly walk.

Three and a half years of grim austerity had led to this. As the front of the German advance crept out of the battle area into the line of villages which had until a few days before been inhabited by civilians – grown rich most of them, on commerce of one sort or another with English troops – it seemed to the Germans that they had stumbled into an Aladdin's Cave. All were affected – officers and men, rich and poor alike, for the wealth of Prussia had been unable to buy during the last years the booty which now lay around for plunder. Binding himself writes, almost with hysteria, of 'smearing our boots with lovely English boot-polish'; of a captured officer 'excellently – one can almost say wonderfully – dressed and equipped ... with his short khaki overcoat on his arm, in breeches of the best cut and magnificent high lace-boots. .... The sight of all this English cloth and leather made me more conscious than ever of the shortcomings of my own outfit, and I felt an inward temptation to call out to him, "Kindly undress at once," for a desire for English equipment, with tunic, breeches, and boots, had arisen in me, shameless and patent.'

And together with this understandable but uncontrollable lust for the trivial comforts and luxuries which had been so long denied them, drunkenness now combined to check the German armies. This too, is understandable, for fear and battle dries the moisture from a soldier's body quicker than the desert sun – and after a week living on scummy water from the bottoms of shell-holes foul with cordite and decomposition, the troops found themselves in deserted villages whose houses still held wine-stocked cellars. That tiny percentage of officers and men present who had also accompanied the

108

first triumphant sweep to the Marne in 1914 must have felt many ominous stirrings of memory: then, too, supplies had failed, and only plundered alcohol had kept the armies moving during those last few days, before the disillusioning and mortifying repulse.

During March 29th, only a tiny advance was made by the Crown Prince's army group – the flattening of a derisory salient south of Villers-Bretonneux – but on the 30th, as a result of much activity on the part of the Feldpolizei and the supply columns, a heavier attack was launched on a twenty-five mile front curving from the Somme at Sailly Laurette to Montdidier. It crept forward for an average advance of two miles, then died in exhaustion and inanition. *Faute de mieux* a rest was ordered, and inevitably trenches were dug, defensive positions were formed – and from them on April 4th, when the last despairing effort was made to reach Amiens, tired, ill-equipped and now unenthusiastic troops climbed out into the open and advanced with customary but useless gallantry against defenders who had also been given time to rest, time to dig, time to reinforce.

Moreuil fell, the German waves lapped the outskirts of Villers-Bretonneux, but Amiens was never seriously threatened, for with retreat the defenders' lines of communication and supply had shortened, their task been made easier – and the four days' respite had given the defensive crust time to harden.

In all, the German March offensive launched by the three armies of the Michael attacks had won from the Allies in fifteen days some twelve hundred square miles of territory, vast quantities of stores, over ninety thousand prisoners and over a thousand guns: it had also presented the victors with nearly fifty extra miles of front to hold, none of which would ever be as strongly fortified, as defensible, or even as comfortable as the Hindenburg Line from which it had started. The remorseless logic of the battles of the Western Front had inevitably applied.

There is little doubt that with the failure of the Mars attack, Ludendorff realized that his dream of a breakthrough in the southern half of the British front was fast vanishing – but there were still the other schemes produced for him by the Staffs, notably the St. George attacks, which might serve to sap the Allies' strength and thus prolong his period of opportunity. His original objections to the St. George offensive no longer applied, as March had been exceptionally dry and it was considered probable that the ground had dried out, so even while some members of his entourage were composing that last exhortation to the exhausted divisions to capture Amiens, others were putting into effect the administration to withdraw from them the battering train of heavy artillery and trench-mortars, and transfer it to the north.

However, by April 1st, investigations had revealed the unwelcome fact that only eleven fresh divisions would be available to reinforce those holding the line in Flanders, and these would obviously be inadequate to crush in both sides of the Ypres Salient. St. George 2, therefore, on the northern flank, was perforce abandoned, and even St. George 1 severely curtailed – so much so that as the front of the attack could now only stretch from La Bassée to Armentières (twelve miles) instead of from Lens to Ypres (thirty miles), even its code-name was changed. With wry humour, Lieutenant-Colonel Wetzell, whose original insistence it had been that the only potentially decisive thrust against the British must be towards Hazebrouck via Armentières and Bailleul, agreed that a more fitting title for the attack as now envisaged would be 'Georgette.'

It remained to be seen whether the female of the species would be more deadly than the male.

5. Clash of Arms:
The Lys

WHILE the German General Staff busied itself with the organization of this second act of their offensive, the Allies – severely shaken but thankfully aware of the passing of the most immediate peril – held a series of rapid and salutary post-mortems and then quickly passed the necessary military and civic measures to put their findings into effect. Sir Hubert Gough, for instance, was summarily dismissed from command of the Fifth Army, with only a vague promise of a Court of Inquiry at which he might be allowed to challenge the justice of this action – a promise which in the event was never kept. The British Government also found it necessary to rescind its promise to the public not to send boys less than eighteen years old overseas, and were then forced seriously to consider the advisability of introducing compulsory military service into Ireland, about which on March 29th Haig entered the ineffable comment in his diary: 'The King said he was opposed to forcing conscription upon Ireland. I strongly pressed the contrary view not only in order to get men but for the good of Ireland.'

There was also a need to strengthen further General Foch's position, for the decision at the Doullens Conference had not proved entirely satisfactory. Another conference was held at Beauvais on April 3rd, attended this time by Lloyd George, and also by the American Generals Pershing and Bliss, at which it was agreed that if Foch was to have the responsibility of ensuring inter-Allied co-operation, it would be as well if he also possessed a comparable authority. The Doullens agreement was therefore superseded by the following:

General Foch is charged by the British, French and American Governments with the co-ordination of the action of the Allied Armies on the Western Front. To this end all powers necessary to secure effective realization are conferred on him. The British, French and American

111

Governments for this purpose entrust to General Foch the strategic direction of military operations. The Commanders-in-Chief of the British, French and American Armies have full control of the tactical employment of their forces. Each Commander-in-Chief will have the right of appeal to his Government if in his opinion the safety of his Army is compromised by any order received from General Foch.

This apparently satisfied Foch, and if the present-day reader wonders what might have been happening while the various generals appealed to their respective Governments, his scepticism is possibly due to the frenetic pace of life today. Whether Haig was satisfied or not is difficult to determine, for although he agreed, he did so in a statement in which he also affirmed that this new arrangement did not in any way alter his attitude towards Foch, or to Pétain. There is however, a note of vexation about some of his diary entries for the day of the Conference, at odds with his usual magisterial acceptance of life's tribulations: 'Generals Bliss and Pershing were also at the Conference. 120,000 American Infantry are to arrive monthly for four months – 480,000. I hope the Yankees will not disappoint us in this. They have seldom done anything yet which they have promised.

'The P.M. looked as if he had been thoroughly frightened, and he seemed still in a funk. ... L.G. is a fatiguing companion in a motor. He talks and argues so! And he appears to me to be a thorough impostor.'

It seems only fair to add to this, however, that there were other observers present whose recollections do not agree with the Field-Marshal's. The present Lord Hankey, for instance, records nothing of any apparent failure of nerve on the part of the Prime Minister, although he did think that the soft-voiced Sir Herbert Lawrence lacked confidence, and that Haig failed to inspire it in those around him; while a Regular Army colonel present later stated categorically that whereas Lloyd George kept up a confident front, Haig appeared white and shaken.

The most hopeful factor of the entire conference was the presence at it of the two American generals – for the American Army was at last definitely committed to action, although it would be some weeks before its divisions would come into the line.

March 28th had sounded the knell of Ludendorff's hopes to a far greater extent than he knew. As the tattoo of fire around Arras died down at the end of the Mars attack and von Kuhl and von der Schulenberg issued instructions for the initiation of what was to become Georgette, a portentous scene was enacted at Foch's Headquarters at Clermont. According to the official French report upon the episode, a large car drew up amid clouds of dust and from it emerged the splendid and immaculate figure of General Pershing, who immediately delivered himself of the following unlikely declamation:

'I come to tell you that the American people will esteem it a great honour that our troops should take part in the present battle. I ask it in my name and theirs. There is at the moment no other question than that of fighting. Infantry, artillery, aeroplanes, tanks, all that we have is yours. Dispose of us as you wish. Other forces will soon come, as numerous as is necessary. The American people will be proud to take part in the greatest and finest battle in history.'

This is grossly unfair to Pershing. He would not only have scorned such verbal histrionics, but he was also only too well aware of the fact that no American aeroplanes had as yet arrived in France, and neither had any artillery or tanks. In the event – though Pershing was not to know this at the time – none ever did, and the Americans finished the war fighting with British and French guns and French tanks; but at this date it seems impossible to find out exactly what Pershing did say upon that momentous occasion. It is likely that his words approximated more closely to those of General Bliss than to the French communiqué.

General Bliss had said: 'We've come over here to get ourselves killed; if you want to use us, what are you waiting for?'

Despite its mordant note, few speeches have ever afforded greater relief. Munitions for the front were ready and to hand – so much so that the losses of material were easily replaced from British reserve stock – but only America could replace the lost legions; and as a token payment, within a week American engineers assisting the construction of defence lines threw aside their shovels and joined a mixed force of riflemen quelling the last dying spasms of the German attempt to reach Amiens.

Problems of man-power, of course, were the most urgent in

demand of all those facing Haig during the early days of April. Many divisions, especially those of the original front line south of St. Quentin, had been virtually wiped out, and even those held in reserve had suffered severe losses during the desperate attempts to hold together an extended and disintegrating line. There were, however, unexpected exceptions to the general rules, usually when some spirit of sturdy independence had kept the units compact in the face of violent attack from in front, or stupid direction from behind. The 51st Highland Division, for instance, had held together despite its ordeal on the northern flank of the Flesquières Salient, as had the 9th Division of Scots and South Africans on the south. Incredibly, the 61st Division which had stood opposite St. Quentin was still in existence as a fighting force, although reduced to less than one tenth of its rifle strength.

But all these divisions were decimated, and not only that, their few survivors were exhausted by the physical and nervous strain of the long retreat.

So as the battle in the south died away and fresh divisions came down to relieve them, they were withdrawn, sent north and their units brought up sometimes to as much as three-quarters of their established strength with nineteen-year-old boys, forty-five-year-old men, or seasoned soldiers almost recovered from their last wounds. Rheumatism often slowed down the pace of their training marches, but necessity knowing no laws, these divisions were very soon either again in the front line or in close reserve.

By April 5th, the 25th, the 19th and the 9th Divisions – all of which had been closely involved in the holding of the Flesquières Salient – had been formed into the IX Corps and put into the line on the right flank of Plumer's army to hold the front from the Ypres–Comines Canal down to the River Lys, just east of Armentières. This was the junction of Plumer's Second Army and Sir Henry Horne's First Army – the army which held the heights of Vimy Ridge with the Canadian Corps in great strength, as shield against the threat which Haig still considered the most dangerous – that to the Béthune coalfields.

In these circumstances, it was obvious that Horne's centre could not be weakened, but in a spirit of commendable co-operation he announced that he was prepared to house weak divisions on his left flank, in the sector which GHQ – and he – considered safe, between La Bassée and his northern boundary, the Lys at Armentières. This northernmost position was thus filled by the XV Corps, consisting of the re-formed 40th and 34th Divisions – the former recovering from the battle for Bapaume and the latter from the strain of clinging valiantly to the hinge of the door just south of Arras – while seven other divisions late of the Third or Fifth Armies occupied the flat basin of the Lys valley behind, 'convalescing' after their recent mauling.

South of this sector, at Givenchy on the La Bassée Canal, lay the 55th Division – Territorials from West Lancashire and immensely proud of the fact – and this division had not been concerned with the fighting at St. Quentin and the Somme. It formed, therefore, the northern bastion of the fortifications to defend Béthune, and south of this point there should be no weakness.

But between the 55th Division and the two battle-worn divisions of the XV Corps was a very weak front indeed, about which Sir Henry Horne had been perturbed for some time. It was held at the beginning of April by the 1st and 2nd Portuguese Divisions, who had been there far too long. The Portuguese Corps had in fact been due for relief before the onset of the St. Quentin battle, but events since then had clearly necessitated their retention in the line; they were by now very tired, and somewhat disgruntled.

They had good cause to be.

As Britain's oldest ally, Portugal had offered help – as she was to do again in 1939 – within weeks of the declaration of war, but she did not actually enter it until 1916 and if it had then taken some time for the fitting out, training and dispatch of her two divisions to the Western Front, this did not detract from the worth of a fine traditional gesture. Unfortunately, since the dispatch of the two Portuguese Divisions, the Government which sent them had fallen and been replaced by one whose attitude to the war was negative, and to Allied co-operation, hostile.

Moreover, a large percentage of the corps' officers were in sympathy with this new Government – and utterly out of sympathy with both the peasant class from which their troops were drawn and conditions of life on the Western Front. They took extended leaves at home (the troops were allowed none) and one brigadier exercised his command entirely from Paris where he was a popular and well-known figure.

THE BATTLE
OF THE LYS,
April 1918

MILES

0   5   10

evening 9 April
"   10   "
"   19   "
"   29   "

Ridges

On April 2nd, Sir Henry Horne decided that the Portuguese must be relieved, so the 50th Northumbrian Division was instructed to begin moving up immediately in order to carry out the relief of the Portuguese 2nd Division on April 9th. On April 5th, the Portuguese 1st Division had been withdrawn, but as no one was ordered forward to occupy the vacated trenches, their compatriots extended themselves northwards to do so for the remaining four days.

But on April 7th and 8th Armentières to the north and the area around Lens to the south were deluged by mustard gas barrages, and at 3 a.m. on the morning of the 9th – the day of the proposed relief – an intense bombardment from almost the whole of Ludendorff's 'battering train' fell on the stretch of front between. Shortly after 8 a.m., nine full-strength German divisions attacked – once again through a thick mist – and the main weight of the attack fell upon the Portuguese sector.

Pausing only long enough to remove their boots, the troops fled – and several of them expedited their passage to the rear by commandeering the bicycles of the British 11th Cyclist Battalion, who rushed up to hold the gap.

The remainder of the morning was a wild confusion of attack and counterattack, advance and retreat, as every available British unit was hastily flung into the breach, but by the evening the German attack had stormed directly forward for six miles as far as the banks of the River Lawe, behind which the Highlanders of the 51st Division now waited in grim anticipation for the next morning's battle.

On the southern flank of this penetration the British 55th Division still held Givenchy against the weight of the Prussian IV Corps, and its flank battalion had covered the gap left by the Portuguese by a skilful extension back to Festubert. Between Festubert and the Highlanders lay the 55th's reserve brigade, together with the aggrieved survivors of the 11th Cyclist Battalion and the dismounted troopers of a squadron of King Edward's Horse, the natural antipathy between cavalrymen and cyclists having been temporarily submerged by an acute and shared aversion for all foreigners.

On the northern side, Yorkshire units of the 50th Division held the village of Estaires, while the newly reconstituted 40th Division was bent in a tight semi-circle around the southern outskirts of Armentières and the small town of Erquinghem, defending itself from furious attack by the Saxon XIX Corps, intent on crossing the Lys and striking up towards Bailleul. By 3 p.m. Saxon units were on the northern bank of the river Lys at Bac St. Maur, thrusting north-wards and beating off frantic attempts by the British divisions holding Estaires and Erquinghem to link up and stabilize the line. The fighting here was as fierce and intense as at any time or place during the entire war, for the Saxons had a specific role to fulfil, a specific target to reach – and by a certain time.

For only half of Georgette had as yet been delivered, and upon the progress of the Saxon Corps depended not only the launching of the second half but to a great extent the success of the entire offen-sive. Ludendorff's plan was double-pronged.

The Flanders plain east of Ypres is so flat that any slight rise – there is none really deserving the description hill – possesses a military value far greater than its height would suggest. It was, for instance, for the possession of the series of ridges, all less than fifty feet high, which curved around the ruined city of Ypres, that the British had poured away a generation's lifeblood during the previous three years; but south and west of Ypres, the ridge continues for fifteen miles in a series of small mounds, at the eastern end of which stands Mont Kemmel and at the western end the Mont des Cats. These two are as much as three hundred feet high.

If Ludendorff could win possession of these hills, his troops would dominate the country to both north and south, and so force a withdrawal not only to behind Hazebrouck and the vital railway which was his original objective, but also from the Ypres Salient: the objective of the two St. George attacks might thus be gained solely by Georgette.

To the south of this ridge, the Lys winds slowly as though along the bottom of a shallow dish. The valley had not so far been greatly – or at any rate, violently – disturbed by the war. Armentières for instance, although closer to the line than the ruined ruins of Ypres, was still inhabited by civilians, though many had left as a result of the mustard gas bombardment of the previous two days. Small villages with cottages still intact stood along the Lys banks, and the woods around had not yet been reduced to pale phalanxes of splintered spars.

A little to the north of centre of the dish stand the two towns of Armentières and Erquinghem, both on the Lys. From the Wyt-schaete Ridge on the northern edge of the dish, Plumer's line came down in a slight westward curve of which that afternoon the Saxon Corps had bent the southern end backwards into a hook around the two towns – and to the north of them, facing Plumer's line, waited the northern half of Georgette, consisting of the German Fourth Army under General Sixt von Arnim. Thus if the Saxons could reach around behind Armentières and Erquinghem on the southern side, and if von Arnim's troops could break the British line to the north of the town and thrust forward to Neuve Eglise and Messines, not only would the two central towns be pinched out, but the conjoint force would be admirably placed for an attack on Mont Kemmel and the commanding ridge.

Thick fog filled the entire dish the following morning (of April 10th), thus giving to the South Africans, the Scots and the Midlanders of the newly constituted IX Corps at least the illusion of familiarity: they were used to being attacked in such conditions by now, and from experience had distilled a few safeguards. Forward posts were left booby-trapped but unmanned, reserve battalions stationed whenever possible behind the junctions of brigades, reserve brigades where possible behind the junctions of divisions: when the men heard the sound of action behind them, they retired – and on the morning of April 10th they could have done so more efficiently and more quickly had they not been sometimes delayed by the sense of duty of some of their youngest and newest officers, straight from school, keen and naïve.

The fog cleared at about midday, by which time the lower slopes of the Wytschaete Ridge had been occupied by the enemy – to their considerable discomfort and danger as the Scots of the 9th Division still held the crest – Messines had fallen and von Arnim's Storm Troops were working methodically towards the village of Ploegsteert. During the afternoon a brigade of South Africans retook Messines in a series of vicious street battles but could not advance beyond without exposing their flanks, Ploegsteert fell into German hands, and with a sense of realism which augured well for the future, the 34th Division – which had so far not been attacked – withdrew from Armentières to the northern bank of the Lys. They thus avoided encirclement and retained contact with the 40th Division – still holding the Saxons along the line of the Bailleul–Armentières railway as far as the village of Steenwerke. Reinforcements had arrived during the night to block the Saxons, and the line thereafter curved back to Estaires (where the 50th Division had fought doggedly all day in a series of grim, closely-fought battles), and from there on around past Lestrem to Festubert and Givenchy.

Georgette was gaining ground for the Germans, but at a high cost – and the British troops in Armentières were not to be cut off.

It would be ludicrous to suggest that the British troops were enjoying themselves in any way whatsoever – yet there is an unusual note of satisfaction in the accounts written of this prolonged, and in some cases almost Thermopolean battle by those who took part in it. The anger, frustration and hopelessness which gripped the troops after the Somme and Passchendaele offensives, are missing. Now the lives which were lost were paid for in full by the enemy.

In the past, the experienced soldiers of these battered British divisions had repeatedly charged forward against protected rifle and machine-gun positions and seen thousands of their compatriots die for futile and derisory gains: now they were behind the guns, and the temptation to sit tight until all the ammunition was gone and it was too late to retire was so great that some succumbed. But not many, and as day followed day during that crucial fortnight in April, and Ludendorff fed in more and more divisions – but never fast enough – the British line fell methodically back, never breaking, always exacting an extortionate price for every yard of ground.

But of course, there is a price to be paid even for retirement, and reinforcements were needed not only to replace casualties but also to hold the greater length of the curving line: and the only divisions available were those still coming up for a rest after their ordeals on the Somme. On April 11th the 31st Division arrived from the south and went straight into action behind the left flank of the Highlanders – now falling wearily back from the River Lawe – and the following day, Deneys Reitz's division, the 9th, and the 61st from St. Quentin came up in time to support the Highlanders' right flank and the 55th's reserve brigade with its attached cyclists and cavalrymen, now tightly stretched out between Festubert and Hinges.

Now, at last, Béthune's coalfields were in real danger – but indirectly and from the north, not directly from the west where the Canadians still waited, numerous, well-fortified and with ample artillery; but unattacked.

Nevertheless, it was felt that Sir Henry Horne's responsibilities were too great in the centre of his front for him to be able to handle satisfactorily the fracas on his left flank, so command of the battle area down to its southern border was taken over by Plumer, whose army as a result stretched in a gigantic reversed S from the Belgian right flank on the Coverbeek Stream north of Ypres, right around the Ypres Salient through Poelcappelle to the Passchendaele Ridge of fearful memory, back across Wytschaete Ridge, and around in the first twelve miles of the bottom curve of the reversed S as far as Merville.

This transfer of command occurred at noon on April 12th – the third day of the battle – when on new instructions from Ludendorff, who had at last realized that success could only be won in Flanders by a maximum effort, the most powerful German drive to date was launched on the approaches to Bailleul. When Plumer surveyed the new extension to his command, even that great-hearted man must have wondered whether the demands of duty might not be sometimes too high, for the supply of human putty with which to stop innumerable breaches was running short.

More cyclist battalions, pioneers, and every available man from local instruction centres and reinforcement camps had now been drawn into the battle, but still the German attack persisted, still the German battle units pressed forward. On the 13th, the battle raged all along the line from Wytschaete to Merville with unparalleled fury, the only relief to the hard-pressed British being the arrival – four hours late because of congestion on the railways – of the Australian 1st Division, who immediately joined the 4th Guards Brigade to form an impenetrable protective shield between a collapsing sector of the front and Hazebrouck.

Thus the original objective of the Georgette offensive was screened, but by this time either Ludendorff's vacillation was becoming chronic, or perhaps he was exhibiting an unusual elasticity of mind: the Mont Kemmel–Mont des Cats ridge was now the prime target, and as General Sixt von Arnim's Fourth Army was making slow progress at an almost prohibitive cost, the general suggested to the High Command that a dislodgement of the British on this *southern* face of the Ypres Salient – which is what his army's front had become – might be accelerated by an attack on the *northern* face. In other words, that a modified form of St. George 2 should be launched.

With a celerity which from the German point of view was surely

121

ominous, Ludendorff agreed, and the Staff instructions were quickly issued, reserve divisions moved up into the Houthulst Forest and the necessary artillery and trench-mortars transferred yet further north. This indeed could have been the decisive stroke, for Plumer's line was by now stretched to its limit and his attention and all his available reserves were concentrated in the battle area to the south.

But in the event, the British were saved by a combination of their own peril and the sound common sense of their Commander and his Chief-of-Staff, 'Tim' Harington. In order to provide the essential reinforcement for the sagging line in the Lys valley, they decided to shorten their line around Ypres; so during the night of April 15th/16th, with what must have been infinite and heart-breaking reluctance, Plumer superintended the voluntary relinquishment of all the ground won at a cost of some quarter of a million casualties less than a year before.

Back from Houthulst and Poelcappelle, from Passchendaele itself, from Broodseinde and Polygon Wood, the troops wound their silent way through the communication trenches threading the grave-yard of unnumbered friends. By morning they held a line closer in places to Ypres than that from which the armies had started out on that ill-fated morning, eight and a half months before, to fight and die for a few yards of worthless ground, a few feet of elevation from which it had been found impossible to dominate the enemy because of the price paid for it.

Whatever the bitterness of the withdrawal, however, it released strength to buttress for a while the defence of the line from Wytschaete to Meteren. More important, it completely upset the balance of the St. George 2 attack which must now, in order to reach the retrenched British line, advance down the open face of the deserted ridge, dragging its artillery across two miles of churned mud. Baulked, it turned the following day as though in pique against the long-static and well-fortified Belgian line at Merckem, where it was thoroughly repulsed: it is doubtful whether it would have served any valuable strategical end had it succeeded.

And now the battle of the Lys began to show the same signs of stagnation as those which had heralded the halting of the Michael offensive. Although the attacking troops still made progress – and Bailleul fell into their hands as a smoking ruin on April 15th – they were tired, their supplies were arriving late and inadequate, while all the time the defence grew stronger as its supply lines shortened. In the entry for April 17th, the official German history of the battle records:

The attacking waves were cut down by furious machine-gun fire. The enemy had a continuous main line with an outpost line consisting of short lengths of trench in front of it, and the whole of the intervening ground was covered by unerring machine-gun flanking fire, which made progress impossible. The foremost waves were compelled to return to their jumping-off places suffering severe losses. There they lay the whole day under the heaviest fire.

Once more the defensive crust had been given time and opportunity to harden, and the chance of a breakthrough appeared to have been lost. The following day violent but totally unsuccessful German attacks were launched southwards against the sector still held by the left flank of Sir Henry Horne's army, but on April 19th a lull descended on the entire front.

French divisions now came up to take over the line between Meteren and Wytschaete (two of them had been in the area since the 14th), the 28th Infanterie assuming responsibility for Mont Kemmel although it would not appear that they devoted much time or labour to improving the rather sketchy defence lines, hastily thrown up by the British under fire.

During all this time a less sanguinary but equally bitter battle was being fought out, miles to the rear and at long range, between the occupants of various chilly but impressive châteaux. Foch had hardly waited for the dispersal of the participants of the Beauvais Conference before issuing his first directive, which opened:

The enemy is now held up from Arras to the Oise. On this front he can resume the offensive (a) with ease north of the Somme, and particularly in the region of Arras, thanks to the numerous railways at his disposal; (b) with greater difficulty on the south, where the railways he has captured are less numerous, are in bad order, and lie partly within the range of our guns.

This must have been gratifying to Sir Douglas Haig, whose fears for Arras thus received support, but it is unlikely that the rest of the missive was read with much enthusiasm, for it continued:

123

As soon as possible a double French offensive in the Montdidier region with the object of clearing the St. Just–Amiens railway [should be mounted] and a British offensive eastward astride the Somme, between the Luce and the Ancre, with the object of disengaging Amiens. ... It would be of the greatest advantage if these two offensives, whose directions fortunately harmonize, could be carried out simultaneously. The Commanders-in-Chief are therefore requested to be good enough to notify the date on which they judge it possible to undertake these operations; it is important that they start with the least possible delay.

Haig promptly countered with the announcement that he had firm grounds for believing that the drive across the Vimy Ridge to Béthune which Foch feared, was imminent, coupling it with a request that he should have 'without delay' four French divisions either as direct reinforcement, or to relieve more British divisions in the south with which to counter this threat. Pétain remained passive, but dispatched one of his subordinates to Clemenceau with the suggestion that as a new form of warfare seemed to have developed since March 21st, it would be as well to wait until the poilus were trained in it, and better still to wait for the Americans. A degree of stalemate thus resulted.

Then on April 9th, Georgette effectively dispelled all thoughts of an Allied offensive but gave Haig an excellent opportunity to press Foch – who was visiting him at GHQ at Montreuil – for the French divisions for which, after all, Haig had bartered strategic command of his armies. To his intense disgust, Foch clung perversely to his belief that Haig had been right in his earlier announcement of the imminent threat to Arras, and refused point-blank to reinforce the front behind Armentières and the Lys.

'I found Foch most selfish and obstinate,' Haig entered in his diary that evening. 'I wonder if he is afraid to trust French divisions in the battlefront. ... Henry Wilson did not help us at all in our negotiations with Foch. His sympathies almost seem to be with the French.'

It must have been very provoking.

The following day Foch received from Haig a note couched in official phrasing to the effect that he feared he would be unable to mount the British offensive astride the Somme mentioned in the Directive of April 3rd – to which Foch replied with courteous understanding, nevertheless impressing upon Sir Douglas that 'it is as essential to maintain completely the existing front in Flanders as that in the region of Arras.'

By the time Haig received this message, thirty miles of his front from Givenchy to Wytschaete had been stove in, and the enemy were on the Lawe, six miles back; but despite this, it became quite obvious that the British would have to rely, at least for the time being, solely upon their own resources – and these were very slim. As reports of bitter fighting reached headquarters and as the thin line fell back before the onslaught, Haig – who if inarticulate in speech was remarkably lucid on paper – composed what has come to be accepted as one of the historic calls to action of our time, and issued it as an Order of the Day which ended:

There is no other course open to us but to fight it out. Every position must be held to the last man. There must be no retirement. With our backs to the wall and believing in the justice of our cause each one must fight on to the end. The safety of our homes and the freedom of mankind alike depend upon the conduct of each one of us at this critical moment.

When these inspiring words reached the British public through the medium of the press, popular enthusiasm knew no bounds, and the message kindled a firm determination among the Staffs and the rear echelons to resist the enemy to the last infantryman. Vera Brittain, serving as a nurse in a Base Hospital, has recorded the wonderful spiritual effect of this stirring appeal among the medical staff, and so, unfortunately for legend, has the medical officer of a battalion of the Royal Welsh Fusiliers, actually engaged in the fighting.

'What bloody wall?' inquired a weary and indignant Fusilier – and the answer was obscene, bitter – and extremely libellous.

Haig should really have known better: as a soldier himself he shared the military dislike of other people's prose.

Foch in the meantime had not been idle. He issued orders for the dispatch of a cavalry corps to St. Omer, and also instructions as to how the battle of the Lys should be fought, which seem, however, never to have reached Plumer, for the pattern of the conflict remained unchanged.

But however he occupied his time, Foch remained adamant that

French reserves must be husbanded for his offensive schemes. No pleas, no threats, no reports of danger or disaster would move him, and at a conference held at Abbeville on April 14th he refused point-blank to allow any reliefs of the divisions fighting the Lys battle: 'the operation would immobilize the relieving troops and those being relieved during the time required for the operation, and this at the very moment when the size of the Allied reserve is barely sufficient.'

His invariable comment upon every aspect of the military situation, however dire, was 'Bon!', until at last Haig's patience wore thin and he slapped the table and retorted, 'Ce n'est pas bon du tout!'

There was yet another reason for annoyance on Haig's part that day, for Foch, even after Beauvais, had required further recognition of his authority. That morning, Clemenceau had received from Lloyd George, and later from the American General Bliss, agreement that Foch should be entitled to style himself 'Commander-in-Chief of the Allied Armies in France' – and if this title ever became more than nominal, Haig stood in real danger of being hoist with his own petard.

Two days after the Abbeville conference, Foch decided that the situation in Flanders was perhaps after all more critical than he had recognized, and after issuing orders to Pétain to 'prepare to move a French division direct to Flanders', he travelled up to Plumer's headquarters at Blondecques to appraise events for himself.

There followed two days of furious argument during which Foch vehemently denied the necessity, value or even possibility of supporting the British – now fighting desperately to hold the vital east–west ridge – or of the protection which might be obtained by the operation of an alternative scheme to open floodgates and allow the sea to inundate the northern stretch of the front, thus releasing the Belgian Army (whose King, incidentally, had flatly refused to recognize Foch's authority) for action further south.

Then on April 19th the lull descended on the battlefront and with a Gallic gesture of sweet reasonableness Foch produced three French divisions – brought up by rail and motor lorry from the south – and put them into the line in place of five British divisions which had been severely mauled in both the recent crises. These British divisions – the 50th, the 8th, the 21st, the 25th and later the 19th – were transferred south to a quiet section of the French front along the

126

Chemin-des-Dames, where it was confidently believed that they would enjoy ample facilities for rest and recovery.

If Foch, with little apparent grounds for it, had been throughout the crisis incurably and infuriatingly optimistic as to its final outcome, Ludendorff on the other side of the line had been growing increasingly depressed. Despite the gains in territory, booty and prisoners – vast in comparison with those of any previous Allied offensive on the Western Front – he had nevertheless failed to attain the type of sweeping victory which had attended his efforts on the Eastern Front. St. Quentin had produced no flash of triumph, no undeniable strategic benefit such as had Tannenberg: instead, his depleted armies were extended in a longer front, bent around in a dangerous salient.

Now the same appeared to be happening in the north.

And for the apparent stagnation into which his two offensives had fallen, Ludendorff could not at first sight blame his luck. Extraordinary good fortune had attended him at the outset of both his main enterprises – Nature having gratuitously provided his spearheads with cloaks of invisibility under which to advance. On the Somme it could, of course, be claimed that fortune gave him his greatest gain where he had least desired it – in the south instead of in the north – but this did not apply to the Georgette offensive, for here his main drive had fallen directly upon the Portuguese with results which should in theory have been conclusive.

Yet once again his armies were held in a dangerous loop, nearly twice as long as the line from which they had started, exposed in hastily erected fortifications to increasingly heavy artillery fire, and without having yet gained any worthwhile objectives.

Amiens in the south, and both Hazebrouck and the Mont Kemmel–Mont des Cats ridge in the north, remained tantalisingly just beyond his grasp; in the circumstances – for he still had divisions under his command which had not been so far engaged in this, his supreme effort to win victory for his Kaiser and his Fatherland – he can have had little choice in his own mind but to make one further attempt in each sector, to win some form of solid benefit with which to crown his hitherto barren victories.

He appears to have drawn, however, certain conclusions from the results of the last month's fighting, in the light of which the type of orders issued to his subordinates suffered some modification. His original directives and his scheme of training – especially for the Storm Troops – had laid down the precept that the most important contact for them to maintain was with the enemy in front. This had led von Hutier's troops to Montdidier in seven days, and those of General von Quast commanding the southern half of Georgette, to the River Lawe in one. However gratifying these advances may have at first sight appeared to be, they had surprised the German General Staff: and Ludendorff, who already thoroughly appreciated the supreme value of an unpleasant surprise when it is sprung upon the enemy, was driven to the conclusion that in some circumstances a pleasant surprise could be just as fatal when sprung upon oneself.

There must therefore be no surprises for the German General Staff, pleasant or unpleasant, in these two last and, he hoped, culminating strokes; and in order to avoid them, he placed strict limits upon the advances of his troops.

In the south, Amiens only was to be the objective, whilst from the Lys basin the attacks should be limited to the villages of Givenchy and Festubert on the southern flank (Béthune could wait), and the capture of Mont Kemmel on the northern.

Thus during the last three nights of the week-long lull which had fallen on the Lys valley at dusk on April 19th, an increase in the muffled tramp of marching men and the creak and rumble of gun-limbers and transport was heard again as the reserves moved up. At 3.30 a.m. on April 25th, the French division holding Mont Kemmel, together with the fronts of the British 9th Division to their left and the flank brigade of the 21st Division at Wytschaete, were all subjected to the type of intense high-explosive and gas bombardment to which the British were becoming accustomed (so far as flesh and blood can become accustomed to manifestations of violent death and destruction), but which to the French was something of a novelty. Shortly after 6 a.m., the first Storm Troop attack was launched, and as early as 7 a.m. the French were streaming to the rear, leaving some of their compatriots beleaguered on the top of the hill together with the crews of a few British trench-mortar batteries which had, unfortunately for themselves, been loaned to the French.

Except for these isolated groups, which held out until the evening,

Mont Kemmel was in German hands by 10 a.m., and Anglo-French relations, which had not been markedly cordial of late, were further strained.

To the east of Mont Kemmel – on the left of the vacated French positions – stood the British 9th Division, upon whose right brigade had fallen the main weight of the German attack. The attack had, in fact, been planned in the form of a hook to take the hill indirectly from the east, but with the unlooked-for success of the frontal attack, four German divisions (two of them fresh) swept straight across the British brigade, not a man of which escaped death or capture, and were then carried on by their own momentum beyond the set limit of their advance.

They hit first a Highland Brigade in reserve, and then a South African Brigade which came across in support, and during the remainder of the afternoon these two brigades gradually absorbed the attack impetus by conducting a dogged retirement to Vierstraat. Here the Germans were held.

Throughout the afternoon, the South Africans had managed all the time to retain contact with the 21st Division on their left who were employing exactly the same Fabian tactics, in a withdrawal from their original positions at Wytschaete to a line between Voormezeele and Hill 60. On the right of the Highlanders, however, where had stood the unfortunate French, yawned a four-mile gap from Vierstraat to a point west of Mont Kemmel where the other French divisions put into the line by Foch still stood, apparently awaiting the infantry attacks which, they felt, should have followed their share of the early morning bombardment.

They waited all day, but the attacks never developed: so from shortly after 10 a.m. until late in the evening, when the British 25th Division arrived from reserve (with orders to retake Mont Kemmel), there had existed in front of the victorious Germans on the hill a gap through which they might have poured. It was fortunate for the Allies that Ludendorff had restricted his objective and that his troops had been satisfied merely to gain it for him – for there had been virtually nothing to stop them from advancing along main roads to the Mont des Cats and thus taking the vital east–west ridge from the rear.

All next day the battle raged, from north of Bailleul to Zillebeke, the Allies striving to recapture their lost ground and the German troops, given now the fresh objective of Poperinghe by their Army Commander Prince Rupprecht of Bavaria, trying to create again the opportunity they had lost by default. No success attended either side, but during that night, more Allied reserves were created for the battle by yet another shortening of the line around the Ypres Salient, under Plumer's direction.

And as these reserves were poured like cement into the Allied line, the line hardened and set, and nothing the enemy could do could break it thereafter. Neither the ponderous and fearful weight of Ludendorff's battering train nor the undoubted valour of his troops could avail, though on the last day of the battle, April 29th, the German Fourth Army mounted yet another onslaught between Dranoutre and Voormezeele which used up all the reserves of men and ammunition which Ludendorff – agonizingly conscious once again of opportunities let slip – had been able to feed up to the front. They gained a slight and temporary success north of the village of Locre, which they then held for a few hours before being driven out by the French from whom they had taken it; but against the British front they made not the slightest impression. The crust had been given time to form.

It had also been given time to form, even before this second stage of the battle of the Lys, on the southern flank – and no attempts to take either Givenchy or Festubert from the British met with any success.

At 10 p.m. on the evening of April 29th, therefore, in agreement with the Chiefs-of-Staff of the Groups concerned, Ludendorff ordered the cessation of the attack, and in the words of von Kuhl:

The whole 'Georgette' operation was finished. The Fourth and Sixth Armies had exhausted their offensive powers. ... The attack had not penetrated to the decisive heights of Cassel and the Mont des Cats, the possession of which would have compelled the evacuation of the Ypres Salient and the Yser position. No great strategic movement had become possible, and the Channel ports had not been reached. The second great offensive had not brought about the hoped-for decision.

If Ludendorff was depressed at the beginning of April, he must have been near despair at the end.

The end of Georgette was anticipated surprisingly closely by the last spasms of the Michael offensive – for on the day before the successful attack on Mont Kemmel, there had been launched a final attempt to redeem the hollow triumphs in the south.

At dawn on April 24th, after a virtual armistice of nineteen days, von der Marwitz's Second Army began an attack by elements of nine divisions on a three-mile front between the small town of Villers-Bretonneux and the River Luce. In view of the time which had elapsed since the cessation of the previous fighting in the area, it had been obvious to both Ludendorff and von der Marwitz that the attempt would stand no chance of worthwhile success unless it held some element of surprise, comparable with the methods of infantry attacks employed on March 21st.

In this case the surprise was to be provided by tanks.

Despite Ludendorff's undeniable mastery in the field of tactics, he had remained blind to the value of armoured vehicles on the field of battle until a surprisingly late date. Their appearance on the Somme during September 1916 had come as a complete surprise to him, and it was a stroke of good fortune for the Allies that despite that hasty revelation to the enemy of their new war-winning weapon, Ludendorff had failed to appreciate its significance.

It was not, in fact, until the spring of 1917 that the Central Powers began the manufacture of tanks, by which time the British were producing their Mark IV model, and the French their Schneider CA3. To modern eyes these first tanks appear rudimentary in the extreme. The British Mark IV, for instance, was rhombic in longitudinal section and moved on caterpillar tracks which clattered and banged around the entire peripheries of both its vertical sides. It weighed thirty-one tons, and its 125-h.p. engine could move it along at a maximum speed of 3·7 m.p.h. on level ground. Four men were required to drive it and four more to man its guns, of which one model, the 'Male', carried two short 6-pounders and four Hotchkiss machine-guns, while the 'Female' carried six machine-guns.

The first German tank, the A.7.V., was not quite so heavy, but carried (in conditions of acute discomfort) a total crew of eighteen, packed into a space of less than twenty-four feet by eight. Its armour enclosed its tracks like a carapace, and having sprung tracks and two 150-h.p. engines, its speed over flat ground was as high as 8 m.p.h. – although if this speed was long maintained, the temperature inside could rise to as high as 140° Fahrenheit, thus quickly exhausting the crews.

On April 24th, thirteen of these fearful-looking mastodons rumbled gigantically out of the fog (for Nature was once more aiding Ludendorff) at the head of the German attack – three to the north of Villers-Bretonneux and ten to the south – and in the words of the British Official History, 'Wherever tanks appeared the British line was broken.'

This was hardly surprising as no anti-tank weapons had yet been designed by the British, let alone issued to troops properly trained to use them, and it should also be remembered that when British tanks had first attacked élite German divisions in 1916, panic had touched even their stalwart hearts. On this occasion, however, aid for the defenders was at hand. Three tanks of the 1st Battalion of the British Tank Corps were lying up in the Bois de l'Abbé just west of Villers-Bretonneux, and although some of the crews were suffering from the effects of the gas bombardment with which the German attack had been preceded, the section started up their engines and drove their unwieldly vehicles out of the woods to engage in the first tank versus tank battle of history.

Typically, it began with disaster for the British.

The first two tanks to debouch from the woods were Female Mark IVs, armed only with machine-guns which made little impression upon the 30-millimetre armour of the first German tank to be sighted. On the other hand, the captured Russian Sokol 57-millimetre gun of the German tank, holed the armour of the British tanks, causing the two Females to withdraw sedately into the concealing shadows of the wood.

As they did so, the 6-pounder gun of the only Male Mark IV tank present came into action, its shell smashing against the side of the German tank with such devastating effect upon those inside that the German tank commander, endeavouring to avoid a repetition, ran his vehicle aslant on to a steep bank and overturned it. Two more German tanks now arrived on the scene, but were so fiercely engaged by the British tank that the crew of one incontinently deserted their vehicle and bolted back into Villers-Bretonneux (by now completely in German hands) while the other turned cumbrously on its tracks and followed them, its superior speed taking it quickly out of danger.

Of the other ten German tanks which advanced to the attack that morning, the three on the north of the town returned to their assembly point having secured as complete a success as could be envisaged at that time and place; of those on the south of the town one fell into a shell-hole (from which it was afterwards salvaged by the French), two developed engine trouble and one, coming under heavy infantry machine-gun fire, was abandoned by its crew and fell into British hands. Thus ended the first tank battle, and it was appropriate that the triumphant Male Mark IV had been No. 1 Tank of No. 1 Section, A Company, 1st Battalion, Tank Corps.

Other British tanks had also been in action that morning – as a result, moreover, of happy co-operation between the two latest arms of warfare.

Shortly after 10 a.m., by which time Villers-Bretonneux was almost entirely in German hands, a British reconnaissance aircraft spotted two enemy battalions converging on the small village of Cachy, just south of the Bois de l'Abbé, in which had sheltered the three Mark IVs. Three miles away were leaguered seven British Whippet tanks – far lighter in design than the Mark IVs and speedier, for they were intended not so much to smash a breach in a defended line as to exploit it afterwards – and by a stroke of good fortune, the pilot of the reconnaissance aircraft saw them and dropped a scrawled note revealing the presence of the enemy troops.

At 10.20 a.m., the two enemy battalions, who had by this time foregathered in a sheltering hollow, were utterly routed by the sudden appearance of the seven Whippets, in line and each spitting furiously from four machine-guns. The tanks charged down into the hollow and up the other side, then turned and charged back, crushing unnumbered wounded and dead beneath their tracks, and shooting down the panic-stricken survivors in swathes. Over four hundred of the Germans died within those few minutes and the two battalions as such had virtually ceased to exist. In all, the episode provided such a convincing demonstration of the value of armour, mobility and inter-Service co-operation, that it is difficult to understand upon what grounds they were so long denied.

The gains won for the Germans by this last spasm of the Michael offensive did not remain in their hands for many hours. Shortly after 10 p.m. that night, a counterattack by one British and two

Australian brigades, made in fitful moonlight and with the aid of a few isolated light batteries, swept up to the outskirts of Villers-Bretonneux, and in two hours of street-fighting with bomb and bayonet, cleared the town.

In the morning, the front lines of both armies were virtually in the same positions as they had been twenty-four hours before. Only the wrecked tanks, the shattered, smoking buildings and the torn bodies weeping their blood into the impartial earth, told of the battle that had been fought.

Thus Michael died – to be followed within a few days by Georgette.

They had between them won a greater area of Allied territory for the Central Powers than all the attacks made by both sides on the Western Front during 1915, 1916 and 1917 added together. Yet they had failed to win victory. Only the graveyards, the hospitals and the prison camps benefited – if benefit can be said to accrue to such negations of life.

Since March 21st, 28,128 soldiers of the Allied Powers had been killed, and 56,639 of the Central Powers; while respectively 181,338 and 252,186 nursed their wounds in hospitals, and the prison camps and lists of missing accounted for 330,000 more, 290,000 of whom were British or French. These figures, like all the dreary numbers in statistical tables, have been added and divided, sub-divided and subtracted, affirmed and denied in a hundred different permutations in order to support or condemn one or other theory of war.

But taken as they stand, they tell the tale of human folly in terms of human suffering.

Neither was to receive an even temporary check.

6. Crisis:
The Battle of Chemin-des-Dames

WHEN in 1916 Hindenburg had assumed the position of Chief of the General Staff of the Field Armies, there had been some difficulty in deciding how the key figure in the partnership – Ludendorff – should be called. He had solved the problem himself by selecting the title of First Quartermaster-General – a traditional post in the Prussian Army which had, in fact, never been particularly concerned with logistical problems. Nevertheless, if Ludendorff's duties, and more especially his powers, ranged far wider than those of even the most exalted storekeeper, the title in its generally accepted sense was by no means inapt.

Ludendorff looked like a quartermaster. Moreover the class from which he came – solid and bourgeois middle-class – has produced the bulk of the quartermasters of this world, and it is possible that so far from breaking the tradition, Ludendorff was in reality nothing but the most brilliant offspring of his social milieu. All the qualities of the perfect quartermaster seem to have been his – integrity, industry, an immense capacity for detail, great powers of concentration and a fundamental ignorance of the world apart from his own. Above all, he possessed supreme competence – which is the most one can expect from a quartermaster, and a great deal more than one usually gets.

Human nature being as it is, we rarely accord to those who possess an efficiency beyond our own, very much in the way of sympathy or compassion when, despite their earnest and worthy efforts, their plans miscarry. Genius tormented by capricious Fate is tragedy: honest endeavour mocked by Fortune sends us uncaring on our way, slightly relieved that we have now an excellent excuse for not trying harder ourselves.

Ludendorff in 1918 was made much sport of by an extremely fickle Fortune. Twice his carefully laid and meticulously prepared

135

projects had received at their outset such gratuitous and unexpected opportunities as to tempt him onwards to greater hazards than he had originally intended, only to lead him to final frustration. History has not accorded him much sympathy – one notable authority has even dubbed him the Robot Napoleon, an epithet hardly calculated to inspire memorial devotions.

Perhaps he tried too hard to cover his bets.

On April 17th, two days before the lull in the Lys battle, he had issued orders for the group of armies under the Crown Prince to prepare for the possibility of yet another large-scale offensive, this time against the French, in the area adjacent to the southern edge of the now moribund St. Quentin attack. It was here that the original line of the Western Front had curved around from a roughly north–south orientation to west–east, before commencing its sixty-mile straight run to Verdun.

Here lay the Chemin-des-Dames.

Although the name referred originally only to a road, usage and time had combined to extend the area covered by the appellation until it embraced the whole of a fifteen-mile long, deeply ravined 'hog's back' ridge, lying between the River Aisne (to the south) and the Ailette (a tributary of the Oise), along the northern edge of which lay the German line. The French held the ridge, and had done since the previous October when an army under General Maistre had stormed it and hurled the occupants into the marshes fringing the Ailette below. For reasons which do not appear obvious the French now considered that the whole position need not be held in great strength, as its natural features rendered it completely impregnable. This was the quiet front to which the five British divisions who had been battered on the Somme and then even more cruelly mangled on the Lys, were to be sent in due course to rest and recover their strength and morale.

As reports upon the preparations made by the armies of the Crown Prince reached Ludendorff, coinciding with his growing realization of the opportunities still open to him for victory against the British in the Flanders plain now that the weather promised the essential firm ground for attack, his mind began to run on much the same lines as it had done a month previously. 'The most favourable operation in itself . . .', he writes, 'was to continue the attack on the English Army at Ypres and Bailleul. . . . Before we would

136

attack here again, the enemy must become weaker.' Having launched Georgette in order to sap the enemy's strength away from the Amiens front and so prolong his Michael offensive, he therefore now decided to launch yet another attack in the south in order to sap their strength away from the Lys: and not only from the Lys itself, but also from the Arras front – for Haig's staunch belief that Ludendorff wished to drive across Vimy Ridge to Béthune was by no means totally unjustified.

Ludendorff was acutely aware that time was on the side of the Allies, and that if victory eluded him for too long the arrival of the American armies would deny it to him completely. It was thus essential for him to retain the initiative, and once stagnation engulfed Georgette as it had done Michael, then the only way in which he could do this was to launch a third offensive somewhere.

In early May therefore, the preparations in the south received encouragement, and the possibilities of an attack there hardened into certainties: the battering train was transhipped yet again, reserve divisions were concentrated around Laon, and definite orders issued for an attack by the Seventh and First Armies under Generals von Böhn and von Below respectively, to take place at the end of the month against that sector of the front lying between a point north of Soissons, and Rheims. With an understandable lack of continued faith in the practice of naming his operations after saints, and scorning the classical and religious proclivities which had dubbed the originally conceived attacks in this area Archangel and Achilles, Ludendorff turned this time with fervent hope to his Prussian precursor, and christened what he had good reason to believe might be his last chance, 'Blücher'. Perhaps he hoped for an Iron Cross with Golden Rays himself.

Even as the preparation for the attack proceeded, however, it would seem that fortune began mischievously to speed it onwards, towards exactly the same stages of beckoning success and final disaster as had attended Michael and Georgette. The very qualities which had brought Ludendorff to his eminence and which he had developed and given in unqualified measure to his country's service, now served in part to bring his plans to ruin. For although he desired only a limited advance across the Chemin-des-Dames – and that solely in order to attract French reserves south and thus leave the Flanders plain vulnerable to his main design – he could not restrain the professional competence developed by both himself and his Staff, largely as a result of their efforts and experiences during the previous few weeks.

If the preparations for Michael had been imaginative in concept and efficient in execution, those for Blücher were brilliant in both. Bruchmüller (now nicknamed 'Durchbruchmüller'*) was given sole charge of the artillery, and produced schedules and directives for the barrages which were masterpieces of the gunner's art; assault and reserve divisions moved to their allotted areas with the smoothness and precision of the wards of a mortice deadlock, and perhaps most fatal of all for the essential limitations to Ludendorff's plans, the precautions for ensuring surprise were elaborated to an extent unprecedented since the episode of the Trojan Horse.

Military ingenuity and endeavour could hardly have reached greater heights had Blücher been intended as a final triumphant victory over enormous odds, and infinite trouble was taken to conceal the movement of all troops and supplies. No vehicle on road or rail bore a label or distinguishing mark, axles of all transport were well-greased and even fitted with leather coverings, iron-rimmed wheels were padded with tyres of wood-wool or rags, and every piece of loose metal on harness or equipment was wrapped in straw. No troops moved by day, and if at night they were spotted on the open road by enemy aircraft, their officers or NCOs had strict instructions to turn them about as though marching them to billets in the back areas instead of to the front. This might mean that they then had to march twenty miles to cover five – but they slept on arrival, and each night as the divisions moved closer to the front, the woods, the villages, the barns and isolated farms filled up with troops forbidden to leave cover during the day, or to light fires at any time.

And even Nature provided a gratuitous contribution, for the marshes and river bottom of the Ailette swarmed with frogs, which at night kept up such a deafening chorus that no one on the heights of the Chemin-des-Dames above heard any of the accidental or completely unavoidable sounds of preparation.

Any further elements required to ensure an initial sweeping success for the Blücher offensive were contributed by the Allies.

* Literally, 'Throughbreak' Müller.

Both Haig and Foch – supported in their view by British and French Intelligence – were convinced that Ludendorff's offensive schemes would be directed against the front north of the Somme, and in this they were of course basically correct: where they were mistaken was in believing that he would attack there next. Even Pétain's objections to strengthening the Arras sector at the expense of his own seems to have been motivated more by a disinclination to part with his divisions than to any genuine belief in the imminence of an attack upon his front – and as such they met with a certain amount of disregard. It was as a sop to his complaint, far more than as a genuine replacement of strength, that the exhausted British divisions were sent down to him after the Lys battle.

The only factor needed to confirm the senior partners of the Alliance in their view that no danger threatened south of the Somme was provided by the junior partner – America – who had been proclaiming with increasing vociferousness ever since April 23rd that the next German attack would be across the Chemin-des-Dames.

To be fair, the first suggestion by the Americans to this effect would appear to have been based far more upon a shrewd guess than upon reasoned premises. When put to it, however, they produced a logical argument in support of their opinion and in mid-May placed it before the French: it was the work of the chief of the 'Battle Order' sub-section of Intelligence, a certain Captain Hubbard, and was in itself a remarkable piece of inductive reasoning.

The offensives delivered so far by the Germans, Hubbard argued, had all been distinguished at their outset, firstly by striking use of the element of surprise, secondly by strong concentrations against weak fronts. No present sector of the Allied front offered Ludendorff the chances of further exploitation of these factors to such an extent as did the Chemin-des-Dames, as evidenced both by the certainty of British and French opinion that danger threatened elsewhere, and also by the presence of the exhausted divisions recuperating on the front.

Basically, of course, what Hubbard was trying to do was to persuade the French CQG that the next blow would fall on the Chemin-des-Dames, precisely because they thought that it wouldn't; and it is conceivable that the attempt was not made with the greatest degree of tact or diplomacy. Whether it was or not, the American view was rejected out of hand, in the first instance on grounds which cannot be said to have been either objective or even rational: pique, it would seem, played a major part in French reaction. That the Americans would not submit their improvised and amateur armies to French direction and control was bad enough. That their juvenile Intelligence organization should have the effrontery to disagree with one which had already experienced four years of actual warfare, preceded by forty years of preparation, and belonging to an army with a tradition firmly based upon the longest unbroken series of military blunders that history could show, was just not to be borne.

This was a pity, for Hubbard had supporting evidence for his theories. For instance, a large group of German 'Storm Divisions' had been identified around Hirson, just behind the Ailette, and a Guards Division which had not apparently been employed since March 26th, had also made its appearance in the neighbourhood. Moreover, American assessments of Ludendorff's available reserves showed that he had almost exactly the required strength to deliver an adequately mounted offensive on a front corresponding in length to that of the Chemin-des-Dames, that this strength was moving towards that area, and that all these individual divisions would be ready for offensive action at about the same time. By dawn on May 27th, proclaimed Hubbard and his colleagues, a German attack would be poised for a sweep southwards to at least as far as the Aisne.

But it was no use, for they were not only talking to offended dignity but were also up against a mood of deep disappointment, and indeed distrust, of American promises and intentions. Haig's diary entry of April 3rd seemed to have been justified.

The honeymoon consequent upon Pershing's generous offer of his troops to the Allies in their dire emergency lasted only as long as the mood in which he made it – which was not very long for he appears to have been prone to second thoughts. As a result of these, despite the publicity which his offer received and the grandiloquent terms in which it had been reported in the French press, Pershing still would not allow his troops to be used in less than divisional strength. It takes some time and organization to transport full divisions – especially the double-size American divisions – and it was thus three weeks before even one of them made its appearance in any part of the line which might have been described as active, and this was only at Cantigny on the southern flank of the Michael salient – eight days after the commencement of Georgette.

There were also many bitter arguments between the British and French civil and military chiefs on one side, and Pershing on the other, upon the subject of the employment of the American troops now being shipped by the British in increasing numbers and due very shortly to arrive in French ports. As soon as the glad tidings of Pershing's gesture of support had reached Lloyd George and President Wilson, they had very quickly reached an agreement whereby 120,000 American infantry and machine-gunners would be shipped each month for the four months of April, May, June and July, in battalions to be brigaded with British or French divisions. In order to provide the shipping for this, Britain would forgo large cargoes of food and raw materials, and in consequence be forced to lower the rations of her population to something not far above starvation level.

Having accepted this risk and put the necessary administrative machinery into motion, all parties concerned were provoked to considerable anger when on April 7th General Pershing repudiated the arrangements, insisted that only the first 60,000 Americans to arrive should be used to buttress the sagging Anglo-French front and that all the shipping made available should then be used only to bring across full American divisions to join the army under his command.

The British and French troops, he argued, were inferior in physique and morale to the Americans – and he did not wish his troops to be infected with European scepticism by too close a contact with their armies. 'Moreover,' he declared, 'the American people themselves would not have approved even though the President and his advisers should lean that way.'

Colonel MacArthur must have been following this exchange with close interest, and the fact that Pershing won all along the line cannot have escaped him.

All through the latter half of April the arguments wrangled back and forth. At a conference held at Abbeville on May 1st and 2nd, Pershing crisply agreed that he was quite prepared to stand by and watch the British Army pushed into the sea and the French Army driven back south of the Loire, confident that when the American Army was formed to his own specification, it could then take on the Central Powers and defeat them single-handed. To the combined pleas of the British, Italian and French Prime Ministers, he replied,

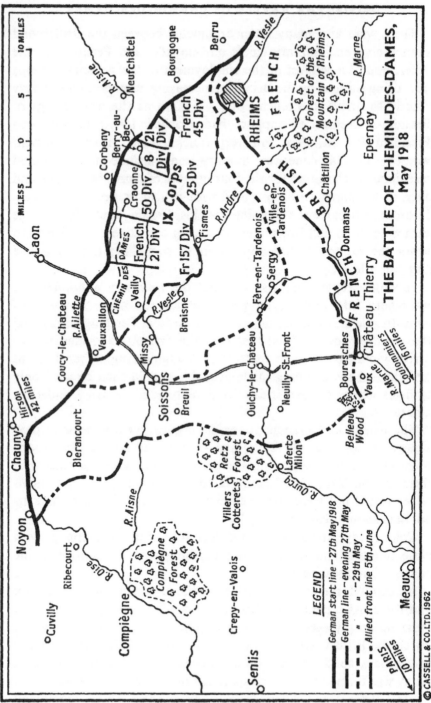

THE BATTLE OF CHEMIN-DES-DAMES, May 1918

LEGEND
——————— German start line – 27th May 1918
— — — — German line – evening 27th May
—·—·—·— "   "   – 29th May
——————— Allied front line 5th June

PARIS
10 miles

© CASSELL & CO. LTD. 1962

'Gentlemen, I have thought this programme over very deliberately and I will not be coerced' – banging the table with his fist as he spoke.

This being so, one cannot but feel sympathy for those who wished that Pershing had not taken the trouble to drive to Clermont on March 28th and raise everybody's hopes with his announcement of a programme of co-operation. The true value of that announcement, however, was to be felt in the future when the American armies began to swell at the astonishing rate of a quarter of a million men every month, as a result of the shipping programme initiated because of it.

But this could not be foreseen in early May, and the cavalier treatment accorded to Hubbard's appreciation of Ludendorff's intentions was a reflection of a not unnatural distrust of American thought: for even if the prognostications of his Intelligence service were accepted, Pershing made it quite clear that he would not contribute American divisions to reinforce those now standing in daily increasing danger of annihilation, along the heights of the Chemin-des-Dames.

Four French divisions held the greater part of the Chemin-des-Dames ridge, as far east almost as the village of Craonne where they met the flank of the first of the British divisions, the 50th Northumbrian, which had been cut to pieces in the battle for the village of Estaires in the opening days of the Georgette offensive and then forced to remain in action until the lull ten days later. The front from the 50th Division's right flank around to the outskirts of Rheims was held by the 8th and the 21st Divisions, which had fought at Villers-Bretonneux and Voormezeele respectively in the immediate past, and at Albert and below the Flesquières Salient just beforehand. In reserve was the 25th Division, recovering from its experiences at Ploegsteert and Bapaume. The 19th Division was still to arrive.

When the men of these divisions had first arrived in this delightful Champagne country, blossoming now in the warm spring sunshine, the contrast from the drab mists and mud of the Flanders plain had been to them a blissful revelation. The verdant countryside was broken by hills among which nestled charming villages untouched by war, and soft valleys lush with cornfield and vine. And if the trenches were shallow and insanitary to a degree, they were nevertheless so screened in foliage as to resemble more the brambled hideouts of childhood games, than the fortifications of more adult pursuits. Not that this mattered, for peace reigned here. This was a cushy front.

At first.

But after a week or more they began to wonder, for in addition to glorious weather, May brought an increasing feeling of tension along the entire front coupled with – or possibly caused by – an almost imperceptible daily increase in the amount of German artillery fire to which the front was subject. And if the troops felt uneasy, the battalion commanders, once their nerves and muscles had relaxed sufficiently for them to notice phenomena other than the euphoric quiet which now surrounded them, were horrified at the manner in which their men were arbitrarily disposed along a shallow defensive line. They reported their dismay to brigade and thence divisional commanders, who after due consideration forwarded their reports to the corps commander.

Unfortunately there was nothing he could do about the situation, for these British divisions were now in the command area of the French Sixth Army, and as such came under the control of a certain General Duchesne, whose choleric disposition was such that he fiercely resented any criticisms of, or divergence from, his own ideas – even when inspired by superior officers of his own nationality. Pétain himself had given orders that all defensive arrangements were to be based upon a system of depth and elasticity – but Duchesne had been Chief-of-Staff to Foch in the early days of the war when the military creed had been based upon the offensive, the massing of infantry in the front line and immediately behind it, and the rigid refusal to give up a yard of ground; and four years of warfare had not served to modify his ideas.

Having completely disregarded Pétain's orders, it was thus unlikely that he would be amenable to suggestions from subordinates; and when the subordinates were British – and those moreover who had disgracefully retired in the face of the last two German attacks – their suggestions were met with flat rejection worded in the most insulting terms. When they remonstrated further, he dismissed them with a basilisk stare and breathed a curt 'J'ai dit!'

All troops, then, British and French, were herded up towards the front line, in trenches not conspicuously suited to withstand heavy

The Ideal

Reality: Passchendaele, November 1917

Reality: near Essigny, February 1918

Reality: Le Barque, spring 1917

Haig, Joffre and Lloyd George

Field-Marshal Paul von Hindenburg, Kaiser Wilhelm II and General Erich Ludendorff

Field-Marshal Sir Douglas Haig

General Sir Hubert Gough

General Sir Henry Wilson

General Foch and General John J. Pershing

The Americans

Night scene in the German trenches

Minenwerfer crew in action

Bombing forward

Breakthrough

The second wave waiting to go in

Picquet waiting at a road block. The Lys, April 1918

Moving up

German tanks in action, June 1918

The tide turning: German Storm Troops under
attack during the fighting in the Marne Bulge

General Pétain   General Foch

British attack through wooded country near Tardenois: July 22nd, 1918

Mark V tanks of the 4th Battalion, Tank
Corps, at Meaulte, August 22nd, 1918

British armoured cars at Biefvillers, August 25th, 1918

Wire belts in the Siegfried Line, stormed by the Australians

German machine-gunners

British Mark IV Female tank attacked by flamethrowers

From the German angle

Near Dury, after the battle of the Drocourt-Quéant
Switch, September 2nd, 1918

The cost of the assault

Scene on the battlefield

Canadians in the Wotan Line, September 2nd, 1918

German machine-gun post

Americans in the Argonne

German trench, summer 1918

Concrete defences in the Siegfried Line, under attack

British artillery crossing the Canal du Nord

Canadian patrol in Cambrai, October 9th, 1918

Prince Max of Baden

General von Seckt

Grand Hotel Britannique, Spa

The Kaiser (fourth from left)
and his suite on Eysden railway
station, November 10th, 1918

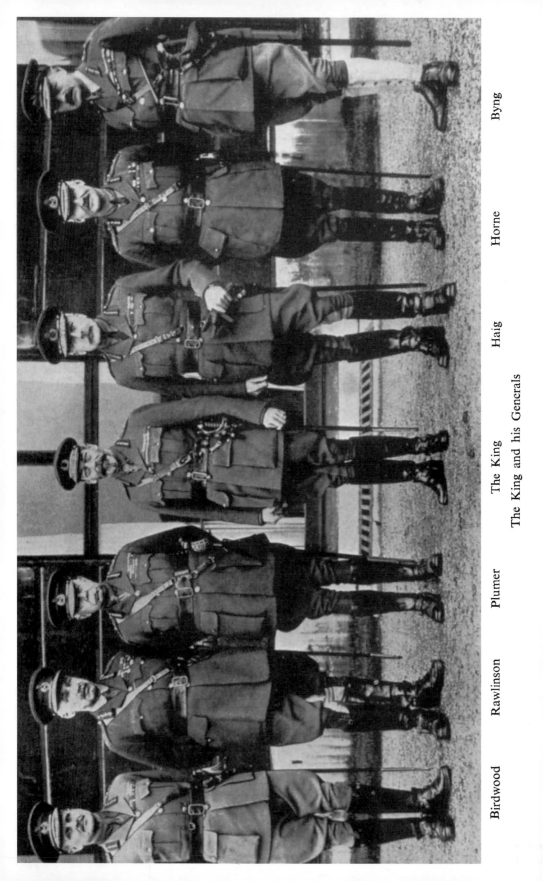

Birdwood   Rawlinson   Plumer   The King   Haig   Horne   Byng

The King and his Generals

bombardment, and given orders which were in flat contradiction to the lessons learned during the last few weeks. The French front-line divisions and the British 50th and 8th Divisions were ordered to sandwich their infantry, and even their guns, between the Ailette and the Aisne, giving them a maximum depth of five miles, and on the 8th Division's front an average depth of only three miles.

Thus did French autocratic intransigence combine with German efficiency and Nature's collaboration, until there was really nothing lacking to ensure Blücher's sweeping success. Knowing the strict limitations which Ludendorff not only desired but upon which he was also basing his future plans, it is almost possible to feel sorry for him were one's sympathies not otherwise fully engaged.

During the last week before the attack two events occurred which might have eased the fate of the defenders of the Chemin-des-Dames. The first was the conversion of Colonel de Cointet, Chief of the French Intelligence, to the American view of the imminence of the attack, but this was negated both by the French Operations Section which refused to believe their own Intelligence, and by Duchesne's attitude, which was nothing short of contemptuous.

The second event was the escape of three French prisoners-of-war from their camp not far behind the German lines, as a result of the massive reorganization of life there consequent upon the preparations for the attack. They reached the British lines just before dawn on May 25th, where they were admitted, fed, and closely questioned upon the conditions existing on the far side of the Ailette. Any doubts still existing in the minds of those conducting the interrogation as to the precariousness of their position were quickly dispelled, and a strongly worded report was forwarded to Sixth Army Headquarters.

But Duchesne's reply read coldly: 'In our opinion there are no indications that the enemy has made preparations which would enable him to attack tomorrow' – and in any case, when light did at last dawn upon his shadowed mind, his reaction to the army's danger was merely to compress it even tighter into its sepulchre.

This occurred on the afternoon of May 26th, as a result of the capture early that morning of two German soldiers on the front of one of the French divisions. One of these soldiers was a candidate officer, and he declared effusively to his interrogators at Duchesne's headquarters, that so far as he knew there were no intentions of any

German attack in that area in the immediate future. The second soldier, however, a private in a Jäger battalion, revealed that assault and Guards battalions had already moved up into attack positions, that grenades and ammunition had already been distributed and that so far as he could judge the offensive would be launched in a matter of days if not hours.

When the candidate officer was recalled for questioning he was informed (correctly) that the laws of war had in no way forced him to give the information which he had volunteered, but that should his information prove to be false he could be shot as a spy; and if this information came as a surprise to any present who had studied the Hague Convention in detail, it came as a severe shock to the candidate officer, who presumably hadn't. After a few moments' reflection he admitted that his previous statements were incorrect, and the floodgates of his mind then opened to let out a remarkably comprehensive description of the military forces about to descend upon the luckless Sixth Army.

It was by now 3 p.m. on May 26th: the attack would commence at 1 a.m. on the morning of May 27th.

The signals went out, those troops not already occupying their battle positions moved into them, and the atmosphere at Sixth Army Headquarters, which had until then – according to the French writer Pierrefeu – been dominated by 'Une humeur de dogue, un grondement perpetuel', calmed under the impact of the sudden realization of impending catastrophe.

This must have been a great improvement for everyone there, causing – even amid sorrow – much more contented conditions for the Staff. Another factor which might have contributed to their well-being was the considerable distance which separated them from the front.

Until midnight, the troops lining the ridge and holding the curving right flank counted the hours: after midnight, they counted the minutes. Four French and three British front-line divisions – the latter composed solely of tired or raw troops – faced eighteen fresh German divisions with seven more in close support. A relatively small proportion of the defenders, however, would ever see many of their assailants, for even more fatal to them than the preponderance of enemy troops was the weight of Bruchmüller's artillery barrages, due to fall soon upon trenches crammed tight with troops as a result of Duchesne's blind stupidity.

But first of all, before the steel and the high explosive trod them into the ground, all Allied positions between the Ailette and the Aisne were thoroughly drenched with gas. Between 12.45 a.m. and 1 a.m., thousands of gas-shells phut-phutted into the soft ground and spread their choking poison across the face, the crest and the rear slopes of the Chemin-des-Dames, and the saucer at its eastern end which held the British. There was little point in the gas casualties trying to make their way back to the aid posts or to the casualty clearing stations, for they were under no illusions as to the time still available for the journey.

Promptly at 1 a.m., the 3,719 guns of Bruchmüller's 1,158 batteries opened fire in a bombardment which in the opinion of the few remaining survivors of previous offensives had had no equal in the history of the Western Front. The whole length of the Chemin-des-Dames crest disappeared under a line of erupting fire, while the front face of the ridge was closely pocked with the flame of bursting shells and mortar bombs. Never before had drum-fire been so consistent, so concentrated or so prolonged, and within minutes it seemed as though the whole fifteen-mile-long hill was quivering under the shock of hammer blows and shaking the surface of the valleys around.

Penned inside dugouts which threatened to collapse and bury them, stifling under the pressure of fear and the moist strangulation of sweat-filled gas-masks, the luckless thousands of Duchesne's army waited for death or action to end their sufferings. For some the ordeal became unbearable, and by the end of the two and a half hours of the barrage, many men had gone mad and either torn off their gas-masks and choked to death, or rushed out into the tumultuous night to be blown to pieces, or ended their torment by their own hand and their own ammunition.

At 3.40 a.m. the German Storm Troops began to move forwards behind the wall of their own bursting shells, through scenes of carnage and destruction beyond even the imagination of a Dante or a Hieronymus Bosch.

The first reports of the assault received by Duchesne and his Staff were to the effect that enemy balloons were rising from the front trenches of the Allied positions, and by midday the Germans were five miles ahead and across the Aisne – aided by the fact that Duchesne had delayed until too late the order to destroy the bridges. The Storm Troops had reached the river across a carpet of annihilated British and French infantry battalions, and through the desperate but feeble resistance of the survivors of those few battalions who constituted what Duchesne had insisted upon regarding, right until the end, as his rear support units.

On each flank, the survivors of the disaster hurriedly rewove a system of defence in order to try to confine the width of the breakthrough, and in this they met with some success – due, however, more to the ever-forward flow of the German assault than to their own efforts.

By the evening the central German spearhead had reached the next river to the south – the Vesle – on both sides of the town of Fismes, and the following morning they crossed the river and surged onwards towards the Marne, at the same time broadening their advance in order to threaten the important rail centre of Soissons on the west flank of their attack front.

In one day therefore, the German assault troops had advanced twelve miles – a feat which had long been considered impossible upon the Western Front by Allied commanders, who were thus thrown into confusion and dismay.

Ludendorff was rather surprised, too.

'I had believed', he was later to write – after sufficient time had elapsed for his memory to make those adjustments which flatter the self-esteem of all of us as we grow older – 'that we would succeed merely in reaching the region of Soissons and Fismes.'

This was undoubtedly the truth, but not quite all of it, for if his original intention for the Blücher attack was merely to attract French troops away from Flanders, it was essential not so much that his own troops should reach the region of Soissons and Fismes, but that they should not reach much farther.

But nothing succeeds like success, and it would have taken a greater man than Ludendorff – and one much more clear-headed than his recent experiences had left him – to rebut the congratulations which poured into his headquarters, and to assert that what everybody was assuming to be a great victory bade fair to develop into utter catastrophe.

There was in any case so little that he could do to arrest the forward surge of his troops – even if the glowing terms of the first reports of the advance did not drive such intentions out of his head. Launching a successful attack is not unlike throwing down a bucket of water: unless one acts with extraordinary rapidity and decision during those vital first few seconds, no attempts to dam or channel the flood are of any avail, and there is nothing to do but wait until the waters lose their impetus and reach the limit of their dispersion.

And though the Allies made attempts to dam the flood – at first futile but as time went on gradually more successful – Ludendorff did nothing. Instead, despite the lessons of the last few weeks, he reinforced his forward divisions during the second day of the attack (by which time they had crossed the Vesle and secured the heights to the south of the river) to such an extent that on the third day, May 29th, they not only captured Soissons, but also made an imm-ense bound forwards to beyond Fère-en-Tardenois, twenty miles from their original start line.

Yet already the form of the trap into which he was being enticed was there for eyes that wished to see: the progress was all in the centre, where an apex was forming to a rough triangle whose height rapidly increased but whose base was only fractionally widening. To the east, the two British divisions originally in the centre, the 50th and the 8th, had been virtually annihilated (the 2nd Battalion of the Devons, for instance, had fought on the north bank of the Aisne until every man was either dead or too badly wounded to stand) but the 21st Division and the 25th in reserve, although badly mauled, had hinged back from the outskirts of Rheims and were holding fast on the flank. They were ably supported by the Algerians of the French 45th Division in the north, and only slightly incon-venienced by the French stragglers and civilians who assailed them with curses and 'hostile demonstration'. Despite their weakness in numbers and the growing exhaustion of the survivors, the British divisions even managed to extend their front in order to continue to hold the flank of the German advance, until at last help came in the shape of the 19th Division, which had just arrived from the north for its spell of rest – and was somewhat vexed by its reception at the hands of the local inhabitants, some of whom spat at them.

But this happened on May 30th – during which Storm Troops of General von Böhn's Seventh Army had reached the Marne: and before

149

Ludendorff's pale blue and slightly protuberant eyes appeared a vision of Paris, less than fifty miles away and straight up the corridor between the Marne and the Ourcq.

It was enough to blind any soldier in Ludendorff's position, unless he happened to be a military genius of the calibre of Marlborough, who would have seen beyond the glitter, or Wellington, whose cold common sense would have precluded his interest in any other object than that of a convincingly beaten enemy army.

Carried by the flood of his own success, insensitive to the thrusts which Pétain had all the time been directing at his western flank, Ludendorff rushed every reserve division he could bring to the area through the gap between Soissons and Fismes, wheeled them westwards, and bulged out the side of his triangle towards Paris.

Now indeed it seemed to the watching and unthinking world that the end was near and the chance which had been fumbled by von Moltke in 1914 would be redeemed from virtually the same area by Ludendorff in 1918. There appeared to be nothing between the German armies and the French capital but the few hastily committed reserve divisions which Pétain was flinging before the onslaught, only for them to be swept away like sand-castles before the seventh wave. Victory was surely inevitable.

That essential lightweight, the Kaiser, certainly thought so – as did the Crown Prince whose armies seemed likely to bring it about, thus adding immeasurably to an already pluming self-approbation; and from his actions it can well be assumed that Ludendorff himself was not unhopeful.

Yet the recurring pattern was forming clearly enough: for the attacker – the ever-lengthening supply lines to feed an ever-widening front; for the defender – the falling-back upon his own reserves. After a peak of progress on the 29th, every hour brought the German armies a slackening of impetus – of which there were many signs Ludendorff should have recognized. Perhaps the chief of these was the bout of violent and widespread drunkenness throughout his armies, a reflection of a psychological condition for which Ludendorff had made no allowances, and indeed of which with his limited field of knowledge he may have been completely unaware.

For far too long these German troops had been deprived of everything but the bare minimum necessary for fighting efficiency, and they were all only too well aware that their families at home did not receive even this. The capture of Albert had given them the first taste of luxuries for which they had long yearned and with which they now found themselves surrounded. The same diarist who described the scenes at Albert, Rudolph Binding, later wrote:

Had I not seen yesterday an officer younger than myself sitting beside me in the car suddenly call out to the driver to stop at once, without so much as asking my leave? When I asked him in astonishment what he meant by stopping the car when we were on an urgent mission, he answered, 'I must pick up that English waterproof lying beside the road'. The car stopped. He jumped out, seized the waterproof, and then jumped joyfully back again, as if refreshed and waked to a new life.

If this lack of restraint can seize an officer, imagine what effect it must have on the private soldier, to have craved and hungered and thirsted for months on end ... with the private soldiers, according to taste, it was the coloured picture postcard, the silk curtain, the bottle of wine, the chicken, the cow, but in most cases the wine.

And now they were in the Champagne country, and the cellars of Soissons and Fismes and the surrounding villages, had been full. Soissons, on the evening of May 29th, was thronged with reeling, totally unmanageable troops, while at Fismes on the morning following its capture the roads had to be cleared of the insensible bodies of the weaker-headed of the celebrators in order to let the transport through – transport driven by men only too eager to join and reanimate the tiring revels whose strains came to them from the houses on each side: and this at a time when every moment counted if victory was to be gained.

Not only did the actual time spent in drinking and drunkenness form a loss of thousands of man-hours, but in the sullen inertia of the hangover period it was extremely difficult to get the men moving forward again, and those in action soon afterwards were still suffering a loss of efficiency which must have cost many of them their lives.

While the German troops drank, and slept, and looted until herded back into the line by Feldpolizei suffering the same pangs as themselves, French troops had been working hard under the cold and logical direction of Pétain. The divisions he had flung down before the onslaught had not been sacrificed in vain for they had won him time – the time necessary for the larger part of his reserves to dig a long, curving defensive position between the two rivers, against which the German advance eventually beat with anger and no little force – but with no more effect than tidewaters against the containing harbour wall.

Now followed an event which Sir Winston Churchill has described:

Suddenly the roads between Provins and the front towards Meaux and towards Coulommiers began to be filled with endless streams of Americans. The impression made upon the hard-pressed French by this seemingly inexhaustible flood of gleaming youth in its first maturity of health and vigour was prodigious. None were under twenty, and few were over thirty. As crammed in their lorries they clattered along the roads, singing the songs of the new world at the tops of their voices, burning to reach the bloody field, the French Headquarters were thrilled with the impulse of new life. 'All felt,' says Pierrefeu, 'that they were present at the magical operation of the transfusion of blood. Life arrived in floods to reanimate the mangled body of a France bled white by the innumerable wounds of four years.' Indeed the reflection conformed with singular exactness to the fact. Half trained, half organized, with only their courage, their numbers and their magnificent youth behind their weapons, they were to buy their experience at a bitter price. But this they were quite ready to do.

They were, indeed, and one can only regret that national pride demanded they should pay this price, rather than profit by the hard-won experience of others.

The first Americans in action as a unit against a still flowing German advance – apart from the isolated engineers who had helped stem the flood at Amiens – were the men of the 7th Machine-gun Battalion, who reached the south bank of the Marne shortly before the Germans reached the north bank, near Château Thierry. These Americans were extremely fortunate. Not only did they have just the right amount of time in which to dig themselves in and site their forty-eight guns to excellent advantage, but they were also in the middle of a section held by a French colonial division of hardened veterans, who were delighted to see them and glad to help.

The result – when the Germans arrived and attempted to cross the river – was a brisk, hard-fought action in which the battalion acquitted itself extremely well, beat off two determined attempts to cross the Marne bridges by the enemy, suffered no casualties, and saw a satisfactory end to the fight when French engineers eventually blew up the bridges. As this had been the first time they had been in action – they were from the 3rd Division which had not occupied even a quiet section of the line before this – they had every reason to feel thoroughly pleased with themselves. They had carried out the task which had been set them, their organization had worked well before the action had commenced, and no one's nerve had failed after it had been joined.

Neither had neighbouring troops retired without warning and left their flanks exposed, nor had the weather blindfolded them with fog, nor clogged their weapons with snow or mud.

The main American contribution to the halting of the German attack, however, was provided by the 2nd Division (of marines and regular infantry) who during June 1st were deployed on each side of the Paris–Château Thierry road, on the right flank of the main French defensive position. All through the following day, the Germans attacked along the whole length of the front held by the Americans, only to be beaten back time after time by withering and accurate rifle and machine-gun fire from the American rifle-pits. Keen eyes, cool nerves and exceptional markmanship distinguished the defence, and the enthusiasm and confidence which the Americans felt in themselves as a result of this first success infected the French alongside, until the whole defensive line from Villers-Cotterets in the north down to the Marne itself was fighting with renewed hope and vigour.

Inevitably, the tiring German troops became aware of the new spirit abroad in the Allied lines, and their own despondency communicated itself upwards through the hierarchy. When the belated arrival of their field artillery, and its use against the Americans, failed to breach the line or even to push it back, the Crown Prince, acting on the advice of von der Schulenberg, called off the attacks and instructed his troops to dig in and await events. So far as could be seen, the war of attrition was due to start again, the road to Paris was blocked.

Thus for the third time, Ludendorff had fallen into a trap which he had dug himself. Bitterly, he confirmed the Crown Prince's orders and made what dispositions he could to repel counterattacks and to hold a line now stretched even further, with reserves once more diminished.

Fortune, he may well have felt, had played him false again.

One can sympathize. But it might be more realistic to say that competence alone can only act within clearly foreseen limits, and that it needs a higher – or at any rate, rarer – quality to recognize true opportunity and to divine the best method for its exploitation. This quality, Ludendorff did not possess.

7. Point of Balance

THE German troops opposite the Americans had not long to wait for the expected counterattacks. On June 6th, the marines of the U.S. 2nd Division received orders to straighten a portion of their front, thus giving the defenders only five days in which to prepare themselves. Unfortunately for the Americans, this proved quite long enough for the experienced troops of General von Böhn's Seventh Army.

On the American's left flank, the 4th Marine Brigade held a line which curled around the southern and western edges of a wood – Belleau Wood. It lay some eight miles west-north-west of Château Thierry on a hill which dominated the surrounding countryside, and if its trees were slender in form, they were so close together as to reduce visibility to less than ten yards. The six hundred acres of ground it covered were jumbled, boulder-strewn, cut by ravines which fell so sharply that the branches of the trees in the bottoms brushed the boles of those on the banks, and within this natural fortress the German troops – veterans, some of them, of fighting upon both Russian and Italian fronts – had constructed during their five days' occupation a system of well-concealed machine-gun posts with interlocking fields of fire.

Immediately west of the wood lay the small village of Bouresches, whose stone-built cottages were in the same period transformed into rifle and machine-gun posts with interlocked fields of fire. From its nearest edge to the American lines lay fields thigh-deep in winter wheat, green, rustling, beaded with scarlet poppies – and two hundred yards across, while to the west and then north around the flank of Belleau Wood the ground was similar, but increasing in width to over four hundred yards on the extreme flank of the brigade front. Across this the marines must advance, before they could even begin the task of locating, and then destroying, the enemy posts.

During the afternoon of June 6th – twenty-six years exactly before the Normandy landings – the men of the attacking battalions waited in their lines, smoking, talking quietly among themselves, looking out curiously over the open ground at the innocent pastoral scene of leafy wood and soft-toned village. The weather was perfect June – heat haze, dancing midges, gentle breezes; and the utter lack of movement might well have been explained by the admirable local peacetime habit of an after-lunch siesta.

This peace was rudely broken at four-thirty by a bombardment of the wood and village by Franco–American artillery, whose commander had decided to adopt the new German practice of firing barrages without any form of preliminary registration, but also – unfortunately – without bothering to adopt the other new German practice of deducing correct ranges and bearings by mathematical calculation. The first twenty minutes of the barrage therefore, was completely wasted from the infantry's point of view, for the vast majority of the shells soared away high over the woods and the village, to crash to earth far in the rear – only a tiny proportion having the faintest military use, and that only by accident.

When at five o'clock the marines climbed out of their trenches, the gunners were just beginning to find their target areas – but in accordance with orders, they now ceased fire.

Five yards apart, in four ranks, twenty yards between each rank, the marines advanced. Nothing had been seen like it, in mass innocence, in hope and at the end in unavailing heroism and self-sacrifice, since the British attack on the Somme in 1916 – and it is quite possible that the lack of immediate reaction from the enemy was due to disbelief that in 1918 such naïveté could still exist. For nearly a hundred yards the marines walked forwards in silence, broken only by the threshing of the young corn as they waded through it, by their officers' whistles or shouted commands, and by the sounds of their own breath in throats dry with fearful excitement.

Then with the sharp crack of a thousand snapping sticks, the hidden machine-guns opened fire and the air above the wheatfields filled with red-hot nails, each humming like an angry hornet. There were cries of pain and anger as the men went down, shouted orders and warnings as others swayed momentarily out of line to go to their aid; gaps appeared everywhere through the marching phalanx, and inexorably the front line melted into the ground. But all along the front of the advance, the spacing was held, the pace maintained – for as yet the marines still believed in the wisdom of their training:

it took another hundred yards and the deaths of half of those who had started out to force the survivors to begin thinking for themselves.

As their bodies were fit and their nerves sound, they thought to some purpose. Those on the left flank with still two hundred yards to go to the edge of the wood and no chance whatsoever of arriving there, went to ground; but those in the centre and on the right who were already close to their objectives when they came to their senses, covered the last few yards in a storming rush. Unfortunately, they then found that their troubles were just beginning, and that they had neither the weapons nor the technical ability to deal with them. Some form of high explosive or liquid fire is needed to blow or burn out the occupants of blockhouses, be they of stone or concrete – and Pershing, having spent his formative military years fighting Indians, had been content merely to equip his men with rifles, with which, to be sure, they were extremely expert.

In Bouresches, the marines were faced with three alternatives. They could use their markmanship and endeavour to shoot it out with the enemy through the narrow windows of the cottages, they could try to reach the doorways and attack inside the crowded rooms with the bayonet, or they could mass and flood through the village using a combination of both methods, and rely upon German morale to crack when the machine-gun posts found themselves surrounded.

In the face of the interlocking fields of fire, the first method was soon abandoned, but during the early part of the evening there were many attempts by single men or men working in pairs or trios, to put into effect the second method. Periods of comparative silence would suddenly end with screams and curses, the crunch of rifle-butts on flesh and bone, the bark of revolvers: but rarely did the machine-gun remain silent when next Americans moved in front of it.

Then the only surviving officer – Lieutenant Robertson – collected all the men he could find, and organized an attempt at the third method. Fortunately for American arms, it was dark before he could put it into effect. They crept forwards silently at first until the leading group were already past the outlying houses, and then were seen and fired on. The group immediately rose to their feet and charged forwards, followed by the remainder of the battalion's survivors, and the night was full of fire and fury, the whine of ricocheting bullets, the clash of bayonets.

The Gods who protect the young and inexperienced by blinding them with courage and hope now aided the Americans, and by 2 a.m. the village was in their hands; but of the battalion which set out to capture it, only twenty men were still on their feet, and they had very little ammunition left. Fortunately, they were reinforced and re-supplied in time to beat off the inevitable German counterattacks, and the village thus remained in American hands.

But in Belleau Wood, the position was bad.

The western side of the wood had not been reached at all, as those who had intelligently gone to ground in daylight when the task was patently impossible, had been withdrawn to their own lines as soon as darkness had fallen sufficiently to give them some chance of success. This left unsupported those survivors of the 6th Marines who had reached the southern edge of the wood, and although they had been able while daylight lasted to put their skill with the rifle to good effect, and gain some penetration, when darkness fell the flashes gave away their positions with the result that they were bombed back to the edge again.

There they lay all night, and early in the morning another company came up in support – but once more as they tried to force their way through the wood, they were caught in the interlocking machine-gun fire. Their skill, their pride, their fierce determination, took them that June day almost three hundred yards through the chaos of tumbled rock and thick, concealing foliage – but at night, once again, they were bombed back to the line from which they started; and of the two hundred men who had joined them in the morning, only eleven came out with them at night.

The whole process was repeated the following day, but on June 9th the marines were withdrawn completely from the wood, which was then subjected to a bombardment from two hundred guns. If the artillery eliminated any of the machine-gun posts, it also felled many of the trees – which thus served both to obstruct the next advance through the wood and camouflage and protect the defenders to an even greater degree. 'The trees looked like someone had cut them down with a scythe,' wrote one of the marines in a letter home, but the scythe had not cut low enough, and when they went in again after the bombardment, the marines found that the debris had choked the wood completely.

However, they crawled forwards through it – and if they had not yet been reduced to the mole-like existence of the other armies on the Western Front, they were at least beginning to appreciate the reasons for it. They also took with them a supply of grenades, and they borrowed or cut themselves cudgels. With this help, they remained in the wood that night.

On June 12th they were withdrawn again, an even larger concentration of guns bombarded Belleau Wood and a fresh battalion was sent into the attack. Fortunately, the marines were prepared to learn from each other, even if they had not been given much chance of learning from their allies, and this time the wood was cleared along its eastern and southern edges, and nearly half-way up the western edge. But beyond that they could not go, despite their reinforcement by infantry from the U.S. 3rd Division, despite also their increasing use of such trench weapons as light machine-guns (the French Chauchat), light mortars, grenades, clubs, and even sawn-off shot-guns – upon which the American High Command had looked with a disfavour amounting almost to contempt when they had seen them in use in the British and French trenches.

Finally, on June 25th, nineteen days after it had first been attacked, Belleau Wood fell completely into American hands as the result of a fourteen-hour bombardment followed by a creeping barrage, behind which the marines advanced in a manner strikingly similar to that of the British attack on Loos in 1915.

The Americans were thus making technical progress at a somewhat quicker rate than their allies had done, but they had nevertheless started with exactly the same preconceived ideas. Their progress, moreover, could well have owed at least some of its speed to the fact that they had allies who had already trodden the same path, and who were willing to guide them, even if their proffered short cuts had been spurned.

In all, the 4th Marine Brigade suffered 5,711 casualties, and lost almost half of its officers. The Commanding Officer had also been badly wounded, and when interviewed in hospital remarked: 'Don't feel so bad about me. It's my own fault. I shouldn't have been so close to the front in a first-class war.'

Given another year of war, perhaps even the Americans would

have found their Corps Headquarters established some forty miles behind the line.

In the meantime, another battle had been fought out between the French and the Germans, some forty miles north of the scene of the American ordeal. Although small in scale compared with the three gigantic conflicts which had preceded it – one on either side at St. Quentin and the Chemin-des-Dames, and the Lys battle far away to the north – it was significant in revealing the lessons being learned by the respective army commands.

The first lesson concerned the value of time in military affairs. Twelve days had been allowed to elapse between the close of the main German advance towards Amiens and the opening of the Lys offensive, while twenty-six days had gone by from the end of Georgette to the launching of Blücher across the Chemin-des-Dames. It was beginning to dawn upon a number of interested observers on both sides of the line that such a lapse of time between two attacks lost for the second opportunities which may have been created for it by the first.

Whether Ludendorff's Chief of Operations, Lieutenant-Colonel Wetzell, was the first to realize this fact or not, is immaterial: he was certainly the first to try to do something about it. During the planning stage of the Blücher attack he had suggested that as soon as the Chemin-des-Dames had fallen and the main purpose of Bruchmüller's battering train had been accomplished, it should be immediately transferred a few miles westwards, to the stretch of line immediately adjoining the Blücher front. This front – between Noyon to the east and Montdidier to the west – was still held by von Hutier's Eighteenth Army, on the flank of its original sweep forwards from la Fère.

Wetzell's suggestions had not been accepted at the time, as Ludendorff's aspirations had been fixed upon developments which he hoped would allow him to tranship his heavy artillery back to Flanders, in order to smash the British. But once the Quartermaster-General temporarily relinquished these hopes for the more alluring prospects of an advance on Paris, then the benefits to be conferred upon the main advance westwards by a second attack converging with it from the north were immediately apparent. One of the reasons for the belated arrival of field artillery opposite the Americans was that most of the available transport facilities were already engaged moving heavy guns and trench-mortars into position west of Noyon.

This task was a formidable one in the most favourable circumstances: when it had to be accomplished across a countryside full of reserves being rushed across the line of movement in an attempt to prolong the battle raging to the south, delays were inevitable. Men, horses and machines were already feeling the strain of the previous battles and of the continual movements between them, and it was thus six days after the Crown Prince had called off the attacks between Château Thierry and Villers–Cotterets, before von Hutier could announce that he was ready to launch another offensive. But as even this represented a considerable improvement upon previous performance, Wetzell and his colleagues were not unhopeful.

Their hopes were unjustified; Pétain had not been so fully engaged upon damming the flood to the south that he had been totally unaware of danger threatening elsewhere.

For one thing, Pétain – and others on the Allied side – was acutely conscious of the fact that after the battles of St. Quentin and the Chemin-des-Dames, the Germans occupied two vast salients jutting into France, in general outline not unlike that of a rather untidily filled brassière. The shortening of the German line consequent upon the elimination of the Λ between the salients would yield to Ludendorff an extra reserve of strength which all thought he could not eschew, and it would, moreover, bring the Germans to within forty miles of Paris along a wide front. Allied Intelligence therefore kept a very close watch upon the Noyon–Montdidier area, and as Wetzell had been inclined to sacrifice secrecy to speed in his movement of the battering train, both Foch and Pétain were well aware of the impending danger.

They had, however, differing views upon how it should best be combated. This was unfortunate, for one of them was completely right in his proposals and the other completely wrong – and the compromise in defensive tactics which resulted was therefore not as satisfactory as it could have been.

Pétain was right.

He had been right in his suggestions for the defence of the Chemin-des-Dames, but had there been foiled by the blatant disobedience of General Duchesne; on the front between Noyon and Montdidier he was to be partially foiled by the reluctance of Generals Humbert and Debeney – who shared Duchesne's opinions but not his arrogance – to fall in completely with his schemes, and their intransigence had been stiffened by Foch, who issued a directive ordering 'a foot-by-foot defence of the ground'.

Nevertheless, Pétain was able to insist that his plan for an elastic system of defence was used to some extent. Mr. Churchill, who was staying in Paris at the time, visited this portion of the front on the evening of June 8th, and later described the situation:

A strong picquet line of detached machine-gun nests, carefully concealed, was alone in contact with the enemy. Behind these devoted troops, for whom an assault could only mean destruction, was a zone three or four thousand yards deep, in which only strong points were held by comparatively small forces. It was not until at least 7,000 yards separated them from the hostile batteries that the real resistance of the French Infantry and Artillery was prepared. When one saw all the fortifications and devices, the masses of batteries and machine-guns, with which the main line of defence bristled, and knew that this could not be subjected to heavy bombardment until the stubborn picquets far in front had been exterminated, it seemed difficult to believe that any troops in the world could carry the whole position from front to rear in a single day. . . . The presage of battle was in the air. All the warnings had been given, and everyone was at his post. The day had been quiet, and the sweetness of the summer evening was undisturbed even by a cannon shot. Very calm and gallant, and even gay, were the French soldiers who awaited the new stroke of fate.

Perhaps here lay the seeds of trouble. Gaiety may well be a good mood in which to launch an attack, but for the conduct of a resolute defence, grim determination would appear to be the desideratum.

Early the following morning, Bruchmüller's artillery began once more its thunderous overture. The bombardment blotted out the picquets and the strong-points of the intermediate zone, and at its farthest limits rained down upon those positions inspected by Mr. Churchill a few hours before, to such effect that the seven French divisions holding them proved utterly inadequate to beat off the attack which followed. This was delivered by thirteen of von Hutier's divisions (nine in the first wave), rested after their labours south of the Somme but still cock-a-hoop with success, who swept across the obliterated forward defences and fell upon the French with such ferocity that Storm Troops had broken through the first position and occupied seven miles of the second before 11 a.m. By the end of the day, von Hutier's divisions on the left flank of the offensive had reached the north bank of the river Matz – over seven miles in front of their start line – and on June 10th the river was crossed in the centre of the attack front, which thus bulged slightly (but only slightly) towards Compiègne.

There the offensive was finally halted by the reserves which Pétain had held in the area, aided on their left by violent counter-attacks launched on Foch's orders and under the direction of the fieriest of the French generals, a short, dark, flamboyant Gascon named Mangin, who shared with the British General Deverell the dubious distinction of being nicknamed 'Butcher' by his troops. These counterattacks did not regain much ground, but they served to distract the attention of the German command from more vulnerable parts of the French defensive line, and affected an already despondent Ludendorff so much that on June 11th he called off the offensive, together with a secondary one which had been launched in its support by the German Seventh Army, westwards from a point just below Soissons.

'The action of the Eighteenth Army', he wrote, 'had not altered the strategical situation . . . nor had it provided any fresh technical data.'

Possibly not: but the action in itself did provide one fact of arresting strategical importance. For the first time since the opening of the German 1918 Spring Offensive eleven weeks before, a German advance had been halted by factors other than its own exhaustion, and in one place the advance had been beaten back.

Of recent years there has been a great increase in the practice of entrusting the management of large business organizations to accountants, irrespective of their knowledge of the technicalities of the business itself. There is much evidence to support a contention that after 1915, the war on the Western Front resembled nothing so much as the activities of two vast and competing firms of civil engineers, whose staffs were generals, whose capital assets were guns and ammunition, and whose liquid assets were the unfortunate troops. In order to assess the true strategical situation at the close of the battle of Noyon, it is instructive to endeavour to see it through the cold eyes of a member of the book-keeping profession – perhaps, for the sake of argument, those of one who had recently been offered seats on the boards of both firms and who was trying to make up his mind which would prove the most advantageous to accept.

If the possession of real estate in France and Belgium be taken as the criterion of success, then undoubtedly Germany had made great progress during the past few weeks, to the direct loss of her competitor. The cost, however, can be seen to have been excessive.

At the start of the St. Quentin offensive, Ludendorff had deployed 192 divisions along the Western Front and by the middle of May he had apparently increased the number to 207, while the Allies showed on paper that they had increased the number of their divisions from 178 to 188 over the same period. In view of the events which had taken place during that time, these figures are at first sight surprising, but the extra German divisions were all late arrivals from the eastern Front, while the increase in the number of Allied divisions had been brought about by the transfer to France of British divisions which had been serving in Italy, Salonika and Palestine, together with the arrival of more Americans.

The vital question, of course, related to the maintenance of divisional strengths, and in this regard it was significant that by the end of the battle of Noyon the average strength of German field battalions had been reduced from 807 men to 692, and this despite the arrival at the front of 23,000 recruits of the 1899 class as well as 60,000 men withdrawn from such services as the Field Railways, the Motor Transport and even the Air Force. The bottom of the barrel would seem to have been in sight, if not actually being scraped.

It had also become disturbingly visible to the British and the French – but there were important differences of degree. There had been 88,000 men on leave from the British Army – incredible though this may sound – on the evening of March 21st, and another 30,000 attending courses or at depots in France, and these factors had been partly responsible for the low rifle strength of many of the Fifth Army's battalions. When the battalions were decimated, these men were immediately available as replacements. There had also been 100,000 men retained in England for a variety of reasons – the official one being as a guard against possible invasion – and the Government's decision to lower the age limit of troops made available for sending overseas from nineteen years to eighteen and a half, made up a total of 170,000 men ready to take the place of those who were lost in the battles.

Thus, while after the attack on Mont Kemmel in March Haig had been forced to reduce ten of his divisions to cadres, by July they had all been reconstituted.

But above all, so far as the Allied 'liquid assets' were concerned, the immense reserve of American man-power was being made available just as fast as Britain could ship it across the Atlantic – and by the end of May, three-quarters of a million men in the prime of life had arrived in France, and there were many more to come.

If numbers of men formed the criteria, therefore, the advantages would not appear to lie with the Central Powers: and by the end of May, there was no longer any reason for them to believe that their inferiority in quantity could be offset by any marked superiority in quality.

The formation of élite military units in any large quantities seems to offer to an army commander about to launch an attack a solution to many of his problems – and if the attack is successful and victory is gained then the practice is justified. But if victory proves elusive, the tasks of pursuing it are invariably entrusted to these élite units, who have already borne the brunt of the attack, and they are thus slowly but surely crumbled into disintegration.

This fate had overcome many of Ludendorff's Storm Troop divisions and as a result he was soon to be left with an army from which he had himself drained the finest elements. In this residual army were many weak and indeed undesirable factions, who as early as April had been responsible for some ugly incidents. Desertion had increased, troops had failed to return from leave, and many of those who did return as far as the railheads behind the lines then joined up with others as sullen and mutinous as themselves to roam the back areas, defying the Feldpolizei, raiding stores dumps, and generally spreading confusion and dismay.

And there was nothing to restore their morale.

The British and French Commands were faced with troubles of a similar nature – especially immediately after the main retreats – but once American troops arrived in the neighbourhood in more than token strength, then there began a steady, if sheepish, return to their units by the absentees. With an obvious accession of strength to the Allied cause came a return of hope to those previously sceptical of Allied fortune, and with it a return to duty. Thus Allied morale, despite a succession of apparently disastrous defeats, was higher than that of the supposedly victorious Germans.

The physical health of the Allied troops was better, too. During April, the Western Front received its first visitation of what later came to be known as 'Spanish influenza', and although it put nearly fifteen per cent. of the British Army into hospital, the men were soon on their feet again and the only fatalities were among those who had caught the fever in addition to other weaknesses, caused either by illness or wounds.

But among Prince Rupprecht's Army – in which the sickness was known as the 'Flanders fever' – the percentage of those affected was higher, and owing to inadequate medical facilities and to general weakness caused by months of undernourishment, many of the sick did not recover. This was yet another factor resulting from the naval blockade of Germany, another consideration for the mythical accountant to bear in mind; and as the epidemic was to roll in waves across Europe, each wave larger than the preceding one until the peak was reached in the following November, it was to become a factor of increasing significance.

So far as the capital assets of the two enterprises – the material of war – were concerned, a very similar position existed. Guns and ammunition captured by the Germans during their advances had never exceeded the quantity used up or wrecked as a result of the fighting, and although the factories in the Fatherland were still in existence, there was a woeful shortage of raw materials from which to manufacture more.

But with command of the seas and American sources at her disposal, Britain suffered no such disadvantages, and as in the Napoleonic Wars, she was the granary of Europe: none but her friends would eat, and her foes would starve. Few appreciated this so well as Mr. Churchill, whose buoyant optimism was such that despite the disasters of the Chemin-des-Dames and the annihilation of the gallant French whom he had visited on the evening before the battle of Noyon, he could still relax and enjoy himself in Paris.

'Paris was calm and even pleasant in these days of uncertainty,' he wrote. 'The long-range German cannon, which threw its shells about every half hour, had effectually cleared away nearly all those who were not too busy nor too poor. The city was empty and agreeable by day, while by night there was nearly always the diversion of an air raid.'

Whether he enjoyed himself more then than in 1940 must be difficult for him to decide.

Thus, so far as accountancy was concerned, there could be little doubt as to which side – despite the lines on the maps – was in the most favourable position, and it is significant in many aspects of the situation that after the battle of Noyon, Pétain so far abjured his habitual pessimism as to announce that 'If we can hold on until the end of June our situation will be excellent. In July we can resume the offensive; after that victory will be ours.'

For he, of all the army commanders of the Great War, had best appreciated its basic economics.

It is a great pity that Pétain's lucidity of mind was not combined with a wider outlook upon life, and that the whole tone of his personality inclined him to regard all possibilities in the bleakest light. He rarely kept his opinions to himself, with the result that practically everyone who came into contact with him left his presence somewhat depressed, or at the least irritated. In 1914 he had been a favoured officer of General Lanrezac, whose Anglophobia had been so great that at his first meeting with Sir John French – the original Commander-in-Chief of the British Expeditionary Force – he had treated that officer with such unpardonable rudeness that inter-Allied co-operation could not really be said to have existed for the first few weeks of the war. Though Pétain had been retained when Lanrezac had been discharged (for failure of nerve during the 1914 retreat to the Marne), there is no doubt that Pétain shared Lanrezac's feelings towards their country's ally, and retained them for the rest of his life. In the First World War, they barred him from the Supreme Command, and in the Second, they ruined him.

Within twenty-four hours of the breakthrough across the Chemin-des-Dames, Pétain had moved sixteen divisions into position to bar the road to Paris – and of these sixteen, four had been taken from behind Amiens, where they had been placed especially to guard the joint between the French and the British armies. This he had done without requesting the permission of his official superior, General Foch, and on the following day he had stripped away all reserves

167

behind Montdidier, asked Foch for the French Tenth Army waiting in reserve behind the British front at Arras, and also for the whole of the French force still holding the front west and south of Mont Kemmel.

Two days later, he 'urgently requested' that the five American divisions training in the British section of the line should be placed at his disposal.

All these requests were granted by Foch, who then asked Sir Douglas Haig – who had not been consulted at any stage, and was thus somewhat nettled by the abrupt removal of so much of the force under his command – for three British divisions to move south in order to guard the now naked joint. Commendably, Sir Douglas Haig agreed – restraining himself to a pointed comment upon the rapidity with which reserves could now be rushed south, compared with the pace at which it had been possible previously to ship them north – and the British divisions moved into the area on June 8th.

The next day, Pétain asked for them to be placed under Humbert, in order to hold the west flank of von Hutier's attack, and was aggrieved when Foch refused him. He was even more aggrieved a few days later when he received instructions to the effect that as the battle of Noyon was now concluded, and it appeared to Foch that Ludendorff's next move would be the long-awaited onslaught on the British at Arras, he was to send artillery units north immediately and prepare to release infantry divisions to support the British, with the same promptitude which they had displayed in supporting him.

This was so far from the position as Pétain saw it that he invoked the clause in the Beauvais Agreement which allowed him right of appeal to his own Government, and sent a strongly-worded protest against the orders to Clemenceau. It was, however, to no avail, for Clemenceau had become increasingly wearied by Pétain's pessimism, and now favoured Foch to such an extent that he not only confirmed Foch's instructions, but also rescinded Pétain's right of appeal, placing him specifically under Foch's direction.

This was unfortunate, for Ludendorff after Noyon still considered 'that the enemy in Flanders was so strong that the Second Army could not attack yet', and as his entire front in the Marne bulge had to be supplied through the single railway junction of Soissons on the extreme west, he was under pressure from his Staff to mount yet another attack in the area in order to capture Rheims and give himself another supply line on the east. The German position in the Marne bulge was in fact rapidly approaching a supply crisis, and Ludendorff knew that he must either get on, or get out.

This was Pétain's reading of the situation, and he was, as usual, right.

Before the development of the German threat to Rheims, there were a number of smaller actions of some importance taking place along the front, and one of these was indicative of the contribution which American arms were capable of making, when their soldiers were not fettered by out-of-date concepts of warfare, but were allowed to exploit their individual skills within the framework of their national propensity for large-scale and detailed organization.

On the right of the section held by the Marine Brigade was one held by two brigades of American regular infantry, also of the 2nd Division. There was an indentation in their line around the southern outskirts of the small town of Vaux, and while their companions of the Marine Brigade had been undergoing their searing ordeal in Belleau Wood and Bouresches, these infantrymen had been quietly but very effectively preparing an attack upon the place. It was such a model of careful planning and preparation that it is difficult to understand why the marines of the same division could have been allowed to pour out their youth and gallantry in such wasteful profusion.

Vaux, like Bouresches, was built of stone – in which every house could be turned into a small fort. From picture postcards, from aerial photographs, and – most useful of all – from the memories of the town stone-mason who had worked in practically every house in the town and who now lived just behind the American lines, an accurate picture of every street and alleyway in Vaux was built up, and to every house was allotted a group of men whose task would be to find it, and then to clear it of enemy occupants.

The barrage began at 6 a.m. on the morning of July 1st, and it was carried out by the gun-crews who had recently gained experience on Bouresches and Belleau Wood. For twelve hours the shells crashed down upon the little town, then at 6 p.m. the range abruptly shortened into a creeping barrage in front of the infantry, as they climbed out of their trenches and walked forward. It was all well-conceived and well-executed – and if there was little attempt at surprise, it would seem, nevertheless, that the bombardment had been sufficiently accurate to dislocate the morale of the enemy in Vaux.

It took twenty-five minutes for the infantry to reach the nearer outskirts, at which point the barrage lifted to the farther side of the town to deter any German reinforcements who might be thinking of an immediate counterattack.

As it lifted, the infantrymen raced forward, each upon his own set and separate mission . . .'and their bobbing tin hats', as the *New York Times* reported it, 'were gone into the roaring evening.'

The surprise which had been missing before now entered into the American attack, in the form of a slick efficiency which had not been seen on the Western Front during the previous four years – it is, indeed, fair to say that it had quite possibly never even been imagined. The careful siting of the German machine-guns, each to cover the approaches to at least two more, was rendered useless by the death or capture of practically all the crews at virtually the same moment. The first Americans to enter the town had the furthest to go, but Vaux is a small town and they were breaking into the houses which formed their own particular targets within minutes of the lifting of the barrage and while many of the Germans were still sheltering in cellars, deciding whether or not the time had arrived to man their posts.

As there were considerably fewer of these posts than the Americans had allowed for, those few Germans who managed to bring their guns into action soon found themselves being shot down from neighbouring buildings which they had believed empty, and so within twenty minutes of entering Vaux, the Americans were in control, and at a loss of only forty-six fatal casualties. And when eventually the American bombardment of the far approaches to the town ceased, it was only after the infantrymen had been given sufficient time to site their own machine-guns in nests with interlocking fields of fire – on the northern side of the town.

Very careful planning, imagination, and an admirably business-like efficiency marked the entire enterprise – and if Vaux was not so heavily fortified or garrisoned as had been expected, this does not detract from the dash and valour of the troops, who were not to know this. When the German counterattacks came, they were beaten off with the cool resolution only achieved by troops who have gained just enough experience to give them confidence, but not so much as to warp their nervous systems out of true.

Four days after the American attack on Vaux, a second action was fought, many miles away to the north-west, which was just as full of significance as a pointer to the battles of the future.

Some four miles north-east of Villers-Bretonneux lay a ridge surmounted by the ruined village of Hamel, with a small wooded area – Vaire Wood – just to the south. The ridge gave excellent observation to the Germans of the positions held by the Australian Corps, and their commander, Sir John Monash, was eager to capture it.

Monash was a Jew – and it is indicative of his ability that despite the prejudice which existed both in military circles and in the Dominion against members of his race, he had risen to the rank he then held. As he was an engineer by profession and not a regular soldier, this feat was even more remarkable, but examination of his subsequent career provides the clue to his military success on the Western Front. After the war, he created the Victoria State electricity scheme, one of the greatest works of engineering in the world, vast in scale and a masterpiece of organization: he possessed, in fact, the 'Big Business' type of brain which the vast complex of the modern army had made necessary for successful command.

For the operation, Monash was given the use of five companies of the Tank Corps, comprising sixty fighting and twelve supply tanks. There was some opposition to this in Australian circles, for their previous experience of co-operating with tanks had been limited to an unfortunate episode at Bullecourt during the previous year, when the machines had broken down, and through a tragedy of muddle and mismanagement the action had ended by the tanks firing on their own infantry.

These tanks now being offered, however, were the new Mark Vs, and when once Monash had been convinced of their efficiency, he organized and rehearsed the whole operation in such detail that no misunderstandings could wreck the enterprise. Ten battalions of Australian infantry were to make the attack along a front of three and a half miles, against objectives which would require a penetration a mile and half deep, and as the American 33rd Division of National

171

Guardsmen was training in the area, the offer was made and accepted for four of their companies to go forward with the Australians. 'You're going into action with some mighty celebrated troops ...', the American colonel announced to his men, 'and you've got to get up to their level and stay there with them. There'll be a whole heap of people looking on at you ... and you've got to make good!'

In the Americans' honour, the chosen date of the attack was July 4th – a gesture which was nearly rendered vain by an order received from Pershing on the previous day that they were not to take part. They showed such disappointment, however, that the army commander, Sir Henry Wilson's friend Rawlinson, declared that it was too late for dispositions to be altered: and according to one authority, in order to ensure that any late action taken by Pershing to enforce his will was ineffective, many of the American troops disguised themselves in Australian uniforms.

At 3.10 a.m., by which time there was just sufficient light to distinguish friend from foe, the first wave of infantry began to move forward with the leading tanks just behind them. Gradually the tanks overtook the infantry and began to forge ahead, but the enormous noise of their engines was effectively disguised by aeroplanes flying low up and down the line of the advance, while artillery plastered Vaire Wood and Hamel with smoke and a certain amount of high explosive. As these positions had been subjected to a gas and high explosive bombardment of similar magnitude at exactly the same time each morning for the past week, the Germans were unaware of the vital difference on this particular morning until it was too late.

In the cool, soft air of early morning, the smoke clouds billowed into fantastic shapes, occasionally lit by soaring rocket or bursting shell, but the tanks and infantry were well on the way towards their first objectives before the doomed occupants of the village and the woods realized their danger. The previous slow succession of gunfire along the German front – almost casual, irregular, countable – suddenly quickened with urgency, and the Australian lines and the areas behind were pocked with shell-fire.

But by this time the British artillery had shortened their fire into a creeping barrage, the tanks were crunching through the German defences and the infantry were swarming through after them.

In Vaire Wood, many of the enemy were surprised still wearing

172

their gas-masks, and were hampered by them to such effect that they put up little defence. In Hamel, whenever the attacking infantry were held up by machine-gun nests, they waited until tanks either shot the posts to pieces or crushed them beneath their ponderous weight. Within two hours, a tricolour – placed there by an Australian officer – was flying from a roof in the farthest outskirts of the village, and when day broke completely, a growing crowd of prisoners was seen by observers in the original Australian lines, gathering on the ridge. All objectives had been gained, the first Congressional Medal of Honour to be awarded to a member of a National Guard division had been won by Corporal Thomas Pope for his action in disposing of the crew of a German machine-gun solely with his rifle and bayonet, and 1,500 prisoners had been captured, together with two field-guns and 171 machine-guns.

Australian casualties had been 775, American 134, and the Tank Corps had lost no tanks, although five of them had been damaged and thirteen members of their crews had been wounded. And in order to ensure that these losses were not increased by a sudden successful German counterattack, pickets and wire were carried forward by the supply tanks, and a hundred thousand rounds of ammunition were dropped into Hamel and Vaire Wood by parachute – the first time such an operation had ever been attempted, possibly because no one of sufficiently high rank on any of the army Staffs engaged in the war so far had possessed the imagination to think of it.

When asked how the Americans had conducted themselves, an Australian is reputed to have replied: 'They play a bit rough; but they'll learn the rules in time.'

They had made firm friends among the Dominion's troops – and so had the Tank Corps.

8. The Tilting Scale:
Second Battle of the Marne

BESIDES the instruction to hold divisions ready to send north to aid the British, Foch's orders to Pétain (which had caused the latter's use of his Right of Appeal to Clemenceau) had contained a tactical direction to the effect that first and second defensive positions on any part of the front should be occupied in strength as soon as an attack in that particular area was foreseen. Furthermore, in order to counteract Pétain's pessimism and 'defensive outlook', Foch ordered the replacement of Pétain's Chief-of-Staff, General Anthoine, by the younger and more ardent General Buat – an action of gratuitous disparagement in that Foch did not even pay Pétain the courtesy of a pretence at consultation about the move. There followed an exchange of letters which can have done little to smooth relations between the two men holding the highest positions in France's army, at a time of one of her greatest crises.

Foch's attitude to his subordinate was doubly unfortunate in that it severely restricted the power of the man whose view of the developing situation was more nearly correct than that of any other military leader on the Allied side, and that Pétain was obviously in some disfavour offset in the eyes of the French Army, the fact that twice in the immediate past events had proved him right.

It is one of life's major pitfalls that the experience which age brings is almost invariably accompanied by hardening of the arteries: and the arteries are as often mental as physical. Foch had been an apostle of the 'Spirit of the Offensive' for such a large proportion of his life that it was impossible for him to appreciate (or perhaps to admit) that in some circumstances a manœuvre entailing a planned retreat could pay high military dividends. Conditioned by this life-long attitude of mind, he was not happy with subordinates who thought otherwise, and although his position was not yet strong enough for him to dispense with Pétain as French Commander-in-Chief, he could, nevertheless, ensure that army commanders at lower

174

levels were more in sympathy with his own viewpoint. His recall of Mangin from virtual disgrace (brought about by the disastrous Nivelle Offensive of 1917) was an example of his intentions in this respect, as was the appointment of Buat: and he could not have been unhappy that the French Fourth Army, holding the line east-wards from Rheims, was commanded by General Gouraud.

Gouraud was a man very much after Foch's heart. He had indeed become something of a legend in the French Army as a result of his personal bravery – one arm had been shattered at Gallipoli, and both his legs had been broken – and he was naturally anxious that the legend should not be besmirched. Thus when Pétain approached him during the first week of July with plans for an elastic scheme of defence upon his front, Gouraud was sufficiently outraged as to refuse outright at first to comply with them, and when Pétain persisted, to hint at an appeal to Foch over Pétain's head.

Pétain, however, could turn a soft answer when occasion de-manded, and Gouraud had none of the egregious arrogance of a Duchesne: gradually, over the next week, Pétain brought Gouraud to see that his troops could be just as heroic beyond the range of the German artillery, and thus alive, as within the range, and dead. As, in common with most of his confrères, Gouraud had not clearly appreciated this point before, it must be said that for a man of his age, this acceptance of military reality was an intellectual advance of no mean order. And having made it, Gouraud quickly solved the purely tactical and local problems of turning his command area into a death-trap for any German troops unfortunate enough to be ordered to attack it.

But south-west of Rheims, Pétain was not so successful in per-suading either General Berthelot, commanding the French Fifth Army, or Degoutte commanding the Sixth, of the wisdom of his system of defence. This is not really surprising in the case of General Degoutte, for he commanded the forces holding the south bank of the Marne, a geographical location which had gained an almost mystical significance in the eyes of the French nation in 1914. He had only just received his command (in the place of Duchesne) and against suggestions that he begin his first battle with a voluntary withdrawal, he could, with apparent justification, point to the extreme difficulties facing any attempt by German forces to breach his forward positions, for they were guarded immediately in front by the river – eighty yards across at that point, and flowing fast. There were no bridges across it now, and marshes on the northern bank would surely slow the attacking troops, and thus allow his own front-line machine-gunners and massed riflemen to shoot them down. Faced with such arguments, and such confidence, and aware of the distinct lack of support from his immediate superior, Pétain had to be content with issuing his instructions, and turning a blind eye to their disobedience.

So far as Berthelot, commanding the Fifth Army below Rheims, was concerned, there was little real chance of ever persuading him to adopt any plan containing the elements of success, for although not lacking himself in subtlety, he seems to have been invincibly wrong-headed. Berthelot was a large, corpulent man, much given in summer to spending his entire working day still clad only in his nightshirt, and he shares History's booby prize with Sir Henry Wilson in that they were both almost invariably wrong in their military judgements, with a consistency which would be appealing had it not been so dangerous. Wilson's position had been such that he could be wrong more often, but Berthelot's errors were always greater in degree, as was typified in a discussion between the two men on September 12th, 1914. They were considering – five weeks after the outbreak of the war – how soon the Allied armies would fling those of the Central Powers back across the German frontier. Wilson's conjecture was four weeks, whereupon Berthelot rated him for undue pessimism and announced firmly that French troops would cross the Rhine by the end of the month.

In the face of such ingenuousness, Pétain's plans for a yielding and elastic defence on the eastern flank of the Marne bulge – along the line running south-west from Rheims to Château Thierry – met with little response, and so the French and Italian divisions under Berthelot, and the French and American divisions under Degoutte, were to be packed into position to act as compressed cannon-fodder for the German artillery barrages, with tragic results for themselves and considerable danger to the Allied cause.

It was fortunate that on the western flank of the Marne bulge, between the front opposite Soissons and Château Thierry, there was no need for Pétain to suggest a voluntary yielding of territory, as here waited the French Tenth Army, under the ferocious Mangin, with to his south the left-hand divisions of the Sixth Army under

Degoutte. Mangin was no more likely in the circumstances to fall in with plans entailing retreat on the west than Berthelot or Degoutte were on the east, but by now it had become quite obvious that only the eastern sector of the front was under immediate threat, so the offensive characters of Mangin and Degoutte could be put to good use between Soissons and Château Thierry.

Pétain's plan to block Ludendorff's intentions was divided into three phases. Firstly, the absorption of the German attack east and south of Rheims by elastic defence; secondly the attack by reserves, held in readiness, on the four sides of the two pockets formed as a result of this elasticity; and thirdly, when sufficient German reserves had been drawn into the pockets, by the launching of an attack on the west flank of the Marne bulge by Mangin's army which, at the very least, should cut Ludendorff's only supply route.

Given complete success, Mangin's force might drive through Soissons and straight across the base of the Marne salient, to fall upon the rear of the German armies, trapped in the pockets made by their own offensives.

If this plan demanded coolness of nerve to put into execution, it also needed larger forces than were immediately available under Pétain's command. As had happened before, he looked to Foch to provide them – from the British front.

Although Foch was unreceptive to realities which challenged his basic military outlook, he was always prepared to change his mind with regard to the day-to-day prosecution of the war.

On June 16th, believing that Flanders would be the area of the next German offensive, he had ordered the return to Haig's command of all British divisions south of the Somme, including those guarding the Franco–British joint behind Amiens and also the battered remnants of the five divisions whose period of convalescence on the Chemin-des-Dames had been so brusquely curtailed. By the end of June, however, he was ready to issue a directive pointing out that Paris was still in great danger and that a concentration of force should be held ready to defend the capital from both north and east, while five days later, after an interview with Pétain, he was so far persuaded towards the truth that he instructed Pétain to reinforce the Champagne area, south-east of Rheims.

At this point, he was obviously receptive to Pétain's pleas for greater strength, and so on July 11th, Pétain was authorized to draw reserves from the Amiens area, while Foch appealed again to the British for four divisions with which to cover once more the Franco–British joint. Two days later, he sent again to Haig's headquarters with a further request that the four divisions already on their way should now be placed immediately under Pétain's orders for use in the battle to come, while yet another four divisions came south to take their place astride the Somme, and at Amiens.

It is greatly to Haig's credit that he immediately approved the movement of six of the eight divisions which had been requested, and merely asked that the movement of the remaining two should await the outcome of a meeting between himself and Foch on July 15th. For it had become increasingly obvious of late that if Ludendorff's first thrust would endeavour to strike down through the Champagne front, it would be quickly followed by a hammer blow by Prince Rupprecht's Group of armies, aimed at smashing the Flanders front to pieces against the Channel coast. Haig's action in stripping his front of reserves at this particular moment was thus a striking testimony to his loyalty to the spirit of the Doullens and Beauvais Agreements, despite the fact that he had himself not benefited from them to the extent to which he had hoped.

Many months after the war had ended, a distinguished ex-member of the German General Staff wrote that after the attack across the Chemin-des-Dames, 'the Supreme Command renounced further plans for a decisive battle, and made other diversive offensives in the hope of something turning up.'

If this judgement is unduly harsh upon Ludendorff, it is nevertheless probable that it contains some elements of truth; for in the planning, mounting and delivery of the last German offensive, Ludendorff's grip upon events was uncertain.

He made several fatal errors.

Possibly his greatest was with regard to morale, for he allowed the attack to be christened 'Friedensturm' – 'Peace Offensive' – and encouraged the belief that this was the final stroke which would win the war for Germany, and thus release the soldiers from their bondage of slaughter and destruction and their families at home from the grip of hunger. If this gave added impetus to the first attack, it was to reap a sorry harvest in the grim days which followed.

But in the actual mounting of his offensives, Ludendorff disregarded two tactical factors essential for success. The first was consideration of the time element, for the battle of Noyon had ended on June 11th, while the first act of the 'Friedensturm' was not launched until July 15th. Granted that it was vast in concept – for the hammer-blow against the British in Flanders was to be delivered five days after the Rheims onslaught, and as such had been considered as an integral part of the plan – but time aids the defender more than the attacker, especially when the defender can watch the attacker's every move, and prepare himself accordingly.

For the second tactical factor which Ludendorff ignored was the provision of a cloak of secrecy over his concentration of forces. This lapse is the more difficult to understand in view of the exceptional pains he had taken in his first three offensives, to mask his strength and as far as possible his intention; and from this failure of concealment it may well be concluded that his mental and physical faculties were weakening under the enormous strain they had recently borne, and that he was no longer capable of retaining the initiative.

By the evening before the attack in the south, all his plans were known to the Allies. Forty-nine German divisions, in three armies, were to attack on either side of Rheims, while in the north thirty-one divisions of Crown Prince Rupprecht's Group of Armies waited to renew the battle of the Lys.

Even the time of the first attack was known, for on the Gouraud front, a raid captured a German prisoner who seemed unduly concerned to retain his gas-mask, and when it was taken from him he revealed that the inevitable gas and high explosive bombardment would begin at 1.10 a.m. Immediately instructions were issued and circulated, with the result that at 1 a.m., as the German infantry and Storm Troops made ready to clamber from their trenches and charge forward once more, they were suddenly trapped and their ranks decimated by a crushing barrage from the French artillery.

Ten minutes later, Bruchmüller's artillery opened fire, and the survivors of the assault divisions began their advance. They were accompanied east of Rheims by twenty tanks, of which fourteen were German, and six captured British.

Along a twenty-mile front the infantry raced forward easily at first, their only casualties caused by the widely spaced and isolated

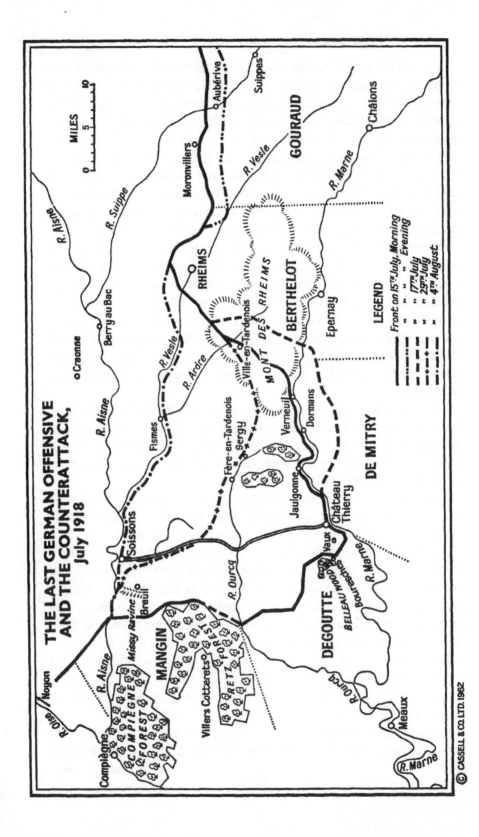

THE LAST GERMAN OFFENSIVE
AND THE COUNTERATTACK,
July 1918

MILES
0   5   10

R. Oise / Noyon
R. Aisne
Missy Ravine
Breuil
COMPIÈGNE FOREST
MANGIN
Villers Cotterets
RETZ FOREST
FORÊT

R. Aisne
R. Ourcq
R. Ourcq
R. Marne
Meaux

Soissons

DEGOUTTE
BELLEAU WOOD
Bouresches
Vaux
Château Thierry
R. Marne

DE MITRY

Jaulgonne
Dormans
Verneuil
Sergy
Fère-en-Tardenois
Ville-en-Tardenois

MONT DES RHEIMS
BERTHELOT
Epernay

R. Ardre
R. Vesle
Fismes
R. Aisne
R. Suippe
R. Aisne
Craonne
Berry au Bac

RHEIMS
Moronvillers
R. Vesle
R. Marne
Chalons
Suippes
Aubérive

GOURAUD

LEGEND

Front on 15th July. Morning
  "   " "   "   Evening
  "   " 17th July
  "   " 29th July
  "   " 4th August

© CASSELL & CO LTD. 1962

French machine-gunners, who nevertheless heroically manned their suicidal positions. But as the Storm Troops penetrated deeper and deeper into the French positions, machine-gun posts were encountered more often, and their withering fire cut wide swathes in the advancing ranks.

However, there was a great number of German troops – and this was the Peace Offensive which would bring them victory and release them for an honourable and glorious return to their families – so they pressed onwards; onwards through the flaming and thunderous night, onwards past the curiously empty and deserted French lines, onwards through increasing (and to the more experienced, puzzling) hostile shell-fire which soon accounted for nearly half their tank force, until at last they reached the area of smoking and cratered ground which marked the limit of their own artillery barrage.

And there, just beyond it, they saw the solid line of French defences, unshelled, unbombed, ungassed, the riflemen and machine-gunners waiting in safety and even some degreee of comfort, to shoot them down in the light of the star-shells and Very lights already bursting above, flooding the scene with garish clarity.

On Gouraud's front, few of the attackers ever reached his army's main defences, for they were killed in the open by bullet or shell-fire long before they could attack with the bayonet or even with grenades. Though the Storm Troops mounted attack after attack with enormous gallantry, launching them from shell-holes in which they had been driven for shelter, they had no hope of success in the face of emplaced defenders, undisturbed by high explosive or gas, unshaken by surprise.

And when daylight came, their position was hopeless: the remaining tanks were soon blown to pieces by French artillery, for there had been far too few to affect the battle. Binding on this day was acting as liaison officer between two of the assault divisions, and his account is as arid and cheerless as the country across which the attack was delivered.

I have lived through the most disheartening day of the whole War, though it was by no means the most dangerous. This wilderness of chalk is not very big, but it seems endless when one gets held up in it, and we are held up. Under a merciless sun, which set the air quivering in a dance of heat, and sent wave after wave up from the grilling soil, the treeless, waterless chalk downs lay devoid of all colour, like stones at white-heat. No shade, no paths, not even roads; just crumbling white streaks on a flat plate. Across this wind rusty snakes of barbed wire. Into this the French deliberately lured us. They put up no resistance in front; they had neither infantry nor artillery in this forward battle-zone. . . . Our guns bombarded empty trenches; our gas-shells gassed empty artillery positions; only in little hidden folds of the ground, sparsely distributed, lay machine-gun posts, like lice in the seams and folds of a garment, to give the attacking force a warm reception. . . .

After uninterrupted fighting from five o'clock in the morning until the night, smothered all the time with carefully directed fire, we only succeeded in advancing about three kilometres in the direction of the high-lying Roman road, which traverses the whole fighting front like a cross-beam. . . .

We did not see a single dead Frenchman, let alone a captured gun or machine-gun, and we had suffered heavy losses. On one of the chalk-hills I saw an artillery ammunition-column which had all its horses killed. What it was doing up there no one knows, for not even the guns had got so far.

Late in the evening, friend and foe were alike so exhausted that they left one another alone. . . . My face was burning as though it had been sprinkled with pepper. . . .

And later he was to write: 'Since our experiences on July 16th, I know that we are finished.'

Slowly, but inexorably, this feeling was to permeate the German Army.

But not immediately, for to the west of Rheims the German attack had met with considerable success – so much so, that although it could not hope to link up as had been intended with the attack to the east, it nevertheless progressed far enough seriously to under-cut the vital position of Rheims itself.

On the river line, from Château Thierry as far east as Dormans, two French divisions and the American 3rd Division (who had been there ever since their machine-gunners had repulsed the German attempts to cross the river at Château Thierry) suffered considerably as a direct result of Degoutte's conviction that the physical difficul-ties in the way of an attacker in that area were too great to be overborne.

Although the French counter-batteries opened fire – as on the Gouraud front – ten minutes before the German guns, this did not spare the Allied troops in the forward positions their ordeal of gas and high explosive; and much of the ingenuity which had been used in Ludendorff's previous offensives to provide his forces with camouflage, was now employed to throw them across the river. Pontoons, rafts, rowing-boat and even punts were used to ferry the German assault infantry through the shell- and bullet-churned waters, and by a magnificent feat of military engineering, skeleton bridges were rapidly built, across which the Storm Troops charged to fall upon the gassed and shell-shocked defenders.

Once the infantry were across the river, the assault tactics which had been used at St. Quentin sixteen weeks before paid excellent dividends – though not so high as previously, for when daylight broke, it brought no fog. Nevertheless, many Allied units were surrounded, many companies obliterated, and one position held by a battalion and a half of the American 38th Infantry was subjected to such continuous and violent attack during the whole of July 15th that by nightfall only four hundred of the fifteen hundred men engaged were still on their feet, and these were limp with exhaustion and minor wounds.

To the north-east, on Berthelot's front, the German penetration had been greater as the assault divisions had had no river to cross – and by nightfall they had pressed forward for five miles along the valley of the Ardre, to reach the slopes of the Mont des Rheims. Here, however, they were held, for Pétain had concentrated – and concealed – his reserves in the woods which clothed the hillside, and they were thus available to buttress the sagging line.

Gradually the impetus of the attack was absorbed and as night fell the advance was halted along the whole front – east of Rheims by what was to become known as the 'Gouraud Manœuvre', immediately south-west of Rheims by Pétain's reserves, and further south by the exhaustion of the Storm Troops, coupled with the containment of their left flank as more of Pétain's reserves came into action. Here the attack suffered also restraint from Supreme Headquarters, for Ludendorff sensed danger in allowing his troops to press too far south of the river: he had no wish to be again presented with a situation similar to that after March 22nd, with one flank of his offensive vastly out-distancing the centre.

With the halting of the advance, the defensive crust hardened – and by midday on July 16th, faced with complete failure on one front and stalemate on the other, Ludendorff decided that the attack must cease. Furthermore, 'Once the difficult decision to suspend the offensive of these armies had been taken, it was useless to attempt to advance further across the Marne or to leave our troops on the southern bank.'

After which decision, he immediately left for Tournai in order to supervise the long-awaited attack upon the British. Bruchmüller's battering-train was already *en route* – a fact which had not escaped Allied Intelligence.

The enforced employment of the French reserves to stop the collapse of Berthelot's front had left Pétain short of troops for the second phase of his plan – the pressure on the sides of the new pockets which was to draw in more and more German strength and open the way for Mangin's advance across the base of the Marne Salient. This advance was due to begin on July 18th, but during the morning of July 15th – by which time it had become obvious that he would need more strength and more time therefore in which to amass it – Pétain had ordered a postponement. He had also instructed both Mangin and Degoutte to release some of their reserves to move eastwards in order to undertake the application of the essential second-phase pressure.

This modification of plan might well have been justified in the eyes of all concerned, had it not at this point appeared that danger now loomed most threateningly in the north. From the British point of view, not only did Haig feel in urgent need of the immediate return to him of his own reserves, but also of reinforcement by every division which could be rushed up to the support of the Lys front.

Foch and Haig were due to meet at Mouchy on the 15th, and on his way to the rendezvous Foch called at Mangin's headquarters to learn with extreme annoyance of Pétain's latest instruction. As Foch had specifically promised the British that Mangin would attack and as he himself was unsympathetic to any other form of warfare, he immediately cancelled Pétain's orders, instructed Mangin to press forward with his arrangements with all possible speed, and telephoned Pétain to the effect that 'There can be no question of slowing down, still less of stopping Mangin's preparations. In case of urgent, extreme need you may take troops absolutely indispensable, informing me at once.'

Foch then proceeded to his meeting with Haig, where he persuaded Sir Douglas that the most efficacious method of relieving danger in Flanders would be to allow the British divisions in the south to remain there, and to reinforce Mangin's thrust yet further with the two divisions still withheld in the British area.

As Haig was still prepared to accept Foch as his Supreme Commander despite his doubts of the value of French promises of offensive action, he therefore took the risk of agreeing, and accepted the responsibility with the feeling that he was acting in the main interest of the Allied Cause. So far as his own position was concerned, as he remarked caustically during the evening, 'If the dispositions proved to be wrong, the blame will rest on me. On the other hand, if they prove right, the credit will lie with Foch. With this, the Government should be well satisfied!'

At 4.35 a.m. on the morning of July 18th, after a violent cloudburst had drenched the whole area, Mangin's offensive was launched to the south of Soissons, aimed primarily at cutting the Soissons–Château Thierry road in order to starve the main mass of the German troops in the salient of all supplies: and if Pétain hoped that the advance would be so successful as to close the neck of the salient completely, it would seem that Foch was content merely that, at last, an Allied advance had begun.

The secrecy which Ludendorff had failed to maintain on the east of the salient three days before was achieved by his enemies on the west – and by methods markedly different from those previously employed by the Germans. Not for the French or the Americans the tedious details of camouflage and wrapped accoutrements: instead, the attacking divisions arrived at their start line from many miles away, and hardly paused before plunging into battle.

True, the Compiègne Forest and the Retz Forest near Villers-Cotterets extended many miles back from the front line, and in the shelter provided by great oaks in full leaf, the American 1st and 2nd Divisions and the Moroccan Division, who were to be the spearhead of the attack, spent the forty-eight hours immediately preceding zero hour. But not close to the front, and the marines of the American 2nd Division did not begin their approach march until after dusk. They covered over five miles – through drenching woods, along winding forest paths, and in complete darkness –

before they arrived at the foot of a steep rise which seemed to tower above them, stretching up limitlessly into the sodden, inky night.

Sweating, stumbling, their backs and legs aching with the effort, they hauled themselves and their weapons up through thinning trees until at last they broke clear of them, then further up and on to the wide crest of a long, grass-covered ridge. Here the men lay – so thickly that the last arrivals could hardly find a place to rest – gasping for breath and with that complete muscular relaxation which only the young and the fit ever achieve, for only they are capable of the effort which makes it necessary.

As the leading files recovered and began to lift their heads and turn to look about them, a red Very light curved up from the dark plain below, and as though it were a signal, French 75s behind and immediately in front opened fire from positions into which they had been manhandled only a matter of hours beforehand.

As the marines dragged themselves to their feet and moved forward – together, though they could not see them, with infantry of seventeen other divisions spread out in a line twelve miles wide – three hundred and forty-six Renault tanks also debouched from the woods and ground their way across the ridge and on towards the enemy lines.

For the first hour, as daylight grew, it seemed that nothing would ever stop the advance: the German wire was thin, their trenches incomprehensibly shallow and unsystematic, their machine-gun posts – although gallantly manned – unavailing against the armour of the tanks. There was plenty of cover, too, for the men on foot, and the ground was humpy so that they could dive into hollows for protection when machine-gun bullets scythed too dangerously close, or stalk the machine-gun crews through the close-growing wheat.

Within an hour they had advanced over a mile along the whole length of the attack front, and with their covering barrage then stationary for twenty minutes, the men re-formed behind it, eager to press onwards, excited and confident. Behind them some hundred tanks were out of action, a few with bullets through engines or with tracks blown off, but many solely as a result of engine failure. And shortly after the advance began again, many more tanks broke down, while the remainder were running short of fuel.

On the northern flank of the advance, the American 1st Division endeavoured to reach the village of Breuil as their second objective, but were almost immediately blocked by the Missy ravine – a deep cleft on the earth nearly a kilometre long, with marshes and a deep stream at the bottom. Here they were held up all day and well into the following night, and during these heroic hours four companies of American infantry were obliterated either by artillery as they dropped down the western face of the valley, or by machine-gun fire as they tried, in broad daylight, to force their way through the marsh. Only five tanks went into the valley to support them, and the two not blown to pieces by shell-fire were engulfed by the swamp.

To the south, the Moroccans and the American 2nd Division were by evening farther ahead – but very tired and with sadly depleted ranks. There were no tanks now, too many of those Americans who had learned wisdom in Belleau Wood were nursing their wounds in hospital, and the new drafts were still inculcated with the doctrine of advance in line. By evening many of the companies were commanded by sergeants, a breed quicker to jettison Staff theories than are those holding commissioned rank. The Americans on the division's left flank were also troubled in mind by the barbaric savagery with which their Moroccan and Senegalese neighbours fought.

Then in the late evening, they were treated to a spectacle which did nothing to raise their morale, but reduced many of them to an impotent and soul-shaking anger.

From the Retz Forest behind them debouched suddenly columns of French cavalry, lined out as on parade. They were picturesque indeed, with crested helmets, lances and flashing sabres, and to an eye unsophisticated by that day's battle they would have been an inspiring sight. As it was, a hush of horror descended upon the scene: and from accounts written afterwards, it seems that even the German machine-gunners did not relish their task, simple though they knew it would be. The Light Brigade at Balaclava faced no more certain ruin.

The charge began slowly and with all the panoply of bugle-call and dipping pennants, and the ground rumbled evenly and sonorously under the hooves. Onwards they came, gathering speed, an occasional shell-burst among the ranks adding colour, but as yet little reality, to the scene. The drumming built up, the ground began to shake, the infantry cowered into the ground, and then with an enormous, thunderous clangour, the charge passed over them. But the glory of shouting men and creaking leather, of hoof-beat and clashing sabre was already laced with the dry rattle of machine-guns, and riderless horses were already neighing and plunging; screams of agony came back to the soldiers lying in the rifle-pits, and shells were bursting now with dreadful effect in the packed and smoking scene ahead. Abruptly it seemed, the charge halted, while every second saddle emptied and every third horse crashed to the ground – and all the time above the screams and neighing of terrified animals, came the steady, murderous crackle of rifle and machine-gun fire.

Three minutes after the infantry had lain beneath the charge, they were cowering again under the far more dangerous rout of red-eyed, riderless and bolting horses, quitting the scene of one of the more criminal stupidities of the war, leaving, as usual, the infantry of both sides to clear up the mess. This they did during the last of the daylight, ignoring each other to a great extent, more concerned with putting the animals (and some of the men) out of their misery, than with the prosecution of the battle. That could wait until the morrow.

By which time, Ludendorff had returned post-haste from the north, having postponed yet again his offensive in Flanders against the British.

As a learned and assimilated technique will enable an artist to continue working during the periods when inspiration is lacking, so a competent general can conduct efficient defensive operations even after he has lost the initiative. He may, if he is fortunate, even conduct them until such time as his opponent, in turn, either tires or mistakes the opportunity: the chance of victory then goes to whoever grasps it firmest.

The news of the Franco–American counterattack on the western flank of the Marne bulge reached Ludendorff as he sat in conference at the headquarters of the Army Group of Crown Prince Rupprecht. 'I concluded the conference . . .,' he wrote later '. . . (naturally in a state of the greatest nervous tension) and then returned to Avesnes.'

But the situation which there confronted him was by no means beyond his powers to resist, so long as he acted quickly – and this the admirable (and almost automatic) work of his Staff allowed him to do. By the morning of July 20th, there was little doubt as to Allied intentions, and none at all as their condition, for the tanks which had made the breach on the morning of the 18th were now almost all out of action (temporarily at least), the element of surprise had gone, and the attacking infantry were beyond the protection of their artillery.

That morning, German reserves were hurried westwards to guard the vital Soissons–Château Thierry road, while immediate measures were taken for the withdrawal along it of as much of the strength and material in the south as could be spared. In front of Rheims, too, the defence was stiffened so that no lateral thrust towards Fismes could threaten to close the mouth of the sack, and with the two jaws thus wedged apart, the gradual and systematic withdrawal of troops in the bottom of the sack could begin. And because they were not deeply committed to action with Pétain's reserves – as he had intended that they should be at this juncture – their successful extrication from what could have been a disastrous situation was commenced.

It can be argued that from a strategic point of view, Ludendorff was aided at this point by Foch, who, scorning all subtleties of luring his prey forward and then pouncing to cut off his retreat, and obsessed as ever with pure and unadulterated frontal attack, ordered advances by every Allied force surrounding the salient, thus forcing the Germans by convergent pressure, back towards the base of the salient and their own escape route.

This would not present a true picture from a tactical point of view however, for retreat under pressure is invariably a costly operation, and before the German line was stabilized again Ludendorff had lost 25,000 men as prisoners alone, and much irreplaceable material. But although Pétain's plan if followed completely would almost certainly have yielded even greater results for the Allies, it is unlikely that Mangin's thrust would have reached right across the base of the salient, as the armoured weapon had not yet reached the state of mechanical reliability – or mobility – for such a long, and indeed tenuous, advance.

On the morning of July 20th, the Allied line from Château Thierry to Rheims was held by the French Ninth Army under General de

Mitry (which had taken over this part of the front from the right-hand divisions of Degoutte's army), and the replenished divisions of Berthelot's Fifth Army. At dawn, these two armies struck along the whole line together, and in the south the American 3rd Division walked into a similar trap to that in which Gouraud had enticed the German First and Third Armies five days before.

Allied artillery had bombarded all the positions thought to be occupied by the enemy south of the Marne, but when the infantry advanced they found only empty trenches – and with the optimism and confidence of youth the Doughboys swarmed forward, rushing in frontal attacks the isolated machine-gun posts, uncaring of the fact that every German they killed or captured had cost them ten of their own lives; there were so many of them when they started out – and there was still a large number left when they reached the south bank of the Marne and met the artillery fire and solid infantry positions established by the Germans on the north bank.

All through the afternoon the Americans sought to throw a bridgehead across the river east of Château Thierry, while the French 30th Division on their left attacked the town itself – but it was as useless as all other frontal attacks undertaken by the other Allied armies during the war – and when, the following day, both divisions crossed the Marne, it was solely because the Germans allowed them to do so. Ludendorff was shortening his line and during the night the main defending force had slipped away.

Along the whole eastern flank of the Marne bulge, this was happening. The reserve British divisions behind Berthelot's army were ordered to relieve the Italian divisions 'on the move', but the 'move' stopped as soon as the forward positions were reached for there was no armour, no cloak of darkness, no surprise of attack to dislocate the impregnable defence. So long as frontal assault was used – and there could be no other method once Foch had scorned Pétain's plan for enticement and then counterstroke – the only ground which the Allies could win was that which Ludendorff was prepared to yield. And he was yielding only because of the overall strategic position, not because of the gallantry of the attacking troops.

By July 27th, the German line had systematically withdrawn ten miles in the centre, as far as Fère-en-Tardenois, retiring in seven days over ground they had captured in one on May 30th. The

American 1st Division on the left of Mangin's army had by now suffered seven thousand casualties and Soissons was still a mile ahead, while de Mitry's Ninth Army had been so severely handled that it had been completely withdrawn. Fortunately, the front had shortened sufficiently for Degoutte's right flank once more to link with Berthelot's left.

And here, it seemed, Ludendorff had decided to remain, for when at noon on July 28th a strong Allied attack was mounted along the fifteen miles between Fère-en-Tardenois and Ville-en-Tardenois, it was flung back with a series of fierce counterattacks, and an American corps which captured the village of Sergy was practically annihilated by a division of Prussian Guards obviously fighting with a spirit of grim purpose. In a forty-mile curve from Soissons to Rheims, the Allied advance lost momentum as – extended too far – the armies grew tired and weak.

So Pétain, without seeking guidance from Foch, imposed his own will upon the battlefield.

Forces were concentrated in the centre, and on July 30th, the American 32nd and 42nd Divisions (with MacArthur still scorning a steel helmet) attacked along a five-mile front at dawn, with their own 4th and 28th Divisions in close support. They gained, as was foreseen, but little ground, but their ferocity and determination ensured that every reserve of German strength in the neighbourhood was drawn into the battle. All that day, and the next, the battle raged with almost unprecedented fury in what one American historian (presumably referring only to events affecting his own country's forces) has called 'the dirtiest days of infantry slaughter since Grant lost his head at Cold Harbor' – and by the evening of July 31st, the Americans had gained perhaps a mile at the point of their deepest penetration.

But when the next morning, the right flank of Mangin's army struck at a point to the west of Fère-en-Tardenois, aiming at an indirect sweep around Soissons, it advanced nearly five miles against thin (but heroic) resistance, and captured the high ground overlooking the Vesle: and on August 2nd all three Franco–American armies faced a void. Out-manœuvred, Ludendorff had hastily withdrawn yet another eight miles to behind the Vesle along the whole front between Soissons and Rheims, and both Soissons and Fismes were bloodlessly occupied that evening.

191

Pétain had thus good cause for satisfaction, for not only had his own subtlety triumphed against the enemy where Foch's 'Spirit of the Offensive' had shown at least signs of failure, but he had done so at remarkably little cost in French casualties.

American casualties, of course, were their own business.

At the close of every battle, they lay upon the ground in evenly spaced, regular lines, like fallen bean-poles, or corn-stooks blown over by the wind. Or like the British dead on the Somme, in the hot, summer sunlight of July 1st, 1916.

9. Allied Advance

'IT was an anxious and intricate business to marshal fourteen divisions of infantry, three divisions of cavalry, more than two thousand guns and some four hundred and fifty tanks, on a front of ten miles, without giving to the enemy an inkling of what was afoot.'*

It was indeed, and the key to its success on this occasion lay in the character of one of the men who conceived the idea, and who commanded the army in whose area this concentration of force occurred. Sir Henry Rawlinson was disliked and distrusted by the Regular Army, who suspected him of harbouring ambitions, and worse still of possessing the brains to achieve them. This last quality had been demonstrated at an early age, for young Rawlinson had gained nearly double the necessary marks at the qualifying examination for Sandhurst – an achievement which failed to endear him to any of his contemporaries, who watched his inexorable rise to Army command with much moustache-chewing and dismissed his talents with the time-honoured idiocy of 'In the Army we want men of character: men who ride straight at their fences, dammit! Rawlinson's too clever by half!'

Being aware of this, Rawlinson in turn showed some disdain for many military codes of behaviour, thus enabling his rivals to point condemnatory fingers at him, to warn all forms of Authority against further promotions for him, and to nickname him 'Rawlinson, the Cad'.

Possibly by 1918 and judged by the peculiar military tenets of the time, he deserved – and relished – the epithet. Certainly Haig distrusted him, as many entries in the Commander-in-Chief's diaries show – but Rawlinson was nevertheless kept in high-level employment, and Haig had been quite agreeable to Wilson's suggestion that Rawlinson should take over Gough's command after St. Quentin. But then, Haig, as has been shown, was quite capable of guile himself when he felt that occasion demanded it: the great pity was

* *Life of Lord Rawlinson of Trent.* Ed. Sir Frederick Maurice.

that nearly four years of warfare had to pass before he realized that the battlefield was as good a place as any other upon which to display this aspect of his talents.

It is possible that Rawlinson sensed at this time that Haig had reached the point when he would appreciate intelligence and some degree of subtlety in the prosecution of the war, since he could hardly have chosen a better moment than the one he did for the presentation to the Commander-in-Chief of his ideas for an attack.

On July 12th, as part of Foch's never-ending campaign for the offensive, the Supreme Commander had written to Haig suggesting that the British should anticipate the threatening German offensive in Flanders by mounting an attack along the southern edge of the Lys battlefield between Festubert and Rebecq, aimed north-eastwards towards Estaires. Whether Haig's opposition to this scheme was an automatic reaction against the prospect of another nightmare in the Flanders mud, or whether he appreciated clearly the dangers of being caught in mid-attack by a counter-blow from Prince Rupprecht's Army Group is uncertain, but on July 17th he replied to Foch to the effect that he considered a far more advantageous operation to be one aimed at freeing Amiens from the menace of German artillery, by an attack east of Villers-Bretonneux.

'The best way to carry out this object is to make a combined Franco–British operation, the French attacking south of Moreuil and the British north of the Luce.' In other words, on either side of the tip of the Amiens Salient.

On the following day (July 18th, the day of Mangin's attack), Rawlinson lunched with Haig and suggested to him, with becoming diffidence, that if his Fourth Army could be reinforced with the Canadian Corps (still guarding the Vimy Ridge and the Béthune coalfields), it should be possible to mount a profitable attack driving eastwards towards Péronne – from Villers-Bretonneux: and with so large a measure of agreement between the two men, it needed little discussion to decide the limits of the assault, or the best ways to bring it to a successful conclusion.

When informed of the new proposals, Foch – who didn't care *where* an offensive was launched so long as it was *soon* – immediately agreed, but urged strongly that the date proposed by Haig for the attack should be advanced by two days to August 8th. This was in itself a most unusual modification, for other attacks on the Western Front had almost all suffered from at least one postponement.

Whether Rawlinson possessed the capacity for original thought or not is an open question which is unlikely at this date to be resolved: but in addition to his adaptability, which had always been evident, he exhibited now a refreshing ability to learn. From the accounts of every successful attack which had been delivered on any part of the front since the beginning of the year, Rawlinson and his Staff drew useful conclusions; and now set about putting them into practice.

The first and most vital task (and recognized as such at last behind the British front) was the manufacture of a cloak of secrecy under which to shelter the assault forces until the moment of attack. Its operation began at the highest level – where, it is reasonable to suggest, it would have been dismissed a year before as a lot of 'totally unnecessary fuss'.

But not in July 1918 – and every conference called to discuss operational plans was held in a different place, in order that no suspicions should be raised in any locality by too many meetings of too many red-tabbed officers. Moreover, only those whose presence was absolutely essential were called to each meeting, with the result that there was none of that happy chatter about the operation throughout the vast grapevine of the Staff society which had preceded almost every previous Allied offensive on the Western Front. Even the divisional commanders concerned knew nothing of their forthcoming activities until eight days before the attack, and as for the fighting troops themselves, they received no warning until thirty-six hours before zero hour: moreover, with a respect for their intelligence which was entirely new, especial measures were taken to see that they were given no evidence from which to draw correct conclusions.

One of the first phases of the preparations, in fact, did much to deceive them (and the enemy) into the belief that the section of the front between Albert and Moreuil was about to enjoy a period of comparative peace and quiet, for in late July, the British III Corps below Albert took over an extra mile and a half of front from the Australians – so that the British right flank extended to the banks of the Somme – while on their part the Australians under the suddenly inscrutable General Monash, edged farther southwards and took over another four miles of front down as far as the Amiens–Roye road – thus releasing French troops, apparently to join the battle still in progress between the Marne and the Vesle. In fact, the French merely concentrated more thickly along their own front.

So far as additional strength was concerned, the movement into the area of the Canadian Corps (who would take over half of the Australian front just before zero hour) was carried out entirely during the hours of darkness, and to divert attention and suspicion, two Canadian battalions, two casualty clearing stations and a wireless section were detached from the Corps and sent to positions north of Mont Kemmel. Here no attempt was made to disguise their presence, from which, in due course, the Germans drew the desired conclusion that this was to be the scene of the next British assault. They were aided in reaching this conclusion by an increase in the local wireless traffic and the observations of their scout planes, who reported the newly begun construction of extra aerodromes between Hazebrouck and Ypres.

Meanwhile the Canadians and the 1st Australian Division (who had shielded Hazebrouck during the battle of the Lys) were billeted as inconspicuously as possible behind Amiens, where their presence could, if necessary, be explained away as replacement for the divisions which had guarded the Franco–British juncture. In the event, they were not in the area long enough for their presence to be realized by the Germans.

Over a thousand extra guns were carefully smuggled into position (with their ammunition, this feat necessitated sixty extra trains), all movement taking place again at night, and the guns being efficiently camouflaged by daybreak. Once in position, each battery was given its opportunity for 'registering', but under such strict control that there was no increase in the number of shells fired daily along the whole length of the front, or even in one particular sector. The allotted targets for at least two thirds of the newly-arrived heavy artillery were the known enemy gun-positions, for recent events had shown that shell-fire alone possessed the power of stopping tanks – apart from their own mechanical fallibility – and this hazard must be reduced to a minimum.

For it was upon the combination of armour and the fighting

spirit of the Dominion troops in the centre that Rawlinson was relying for success.

In all, six hundred and four tanks were assembled behind the fourteen miles of the attack front – almost the whole available strength of the British Tank Corps. Nine tank battalions (three hundred and twenty-four fighting tanks) would lead the attack, while two light battalions of ninety-six Whippet tanks would wait to exploit the breakthrough, with – ominously – the Cavalry Corps; for even Rawlinson, infantryman though he was, could not dispense completely with the horse. One hundred and twenty supply tanks, twenty-two gun-carriers and the mechanical reserve made up the number, and the inevitable clatter and rumble occasioned by the arrival and assembly of this vast concourse of armoured vehicles was covered, as at Vaire Wood and Hamel, by a noise barrage created by Royal Air Force squadrons attached to the Fourth Army. In addition, these planes not only denied the air above the concentration area to enemy scouts, but also kept a very close check upon all matters of camouflage and security from observation of troops or supply movements.

It is curious how often Fortune favours the Brave, when once they have shown that they are capable of achieving some degree of success without her favours. On this occasion, the German troops in the line opposite heard rumbles of heavy transport many days before the arrival of the tanks, and so plagued the Corps Staffs with warnings of their presence in the area that the Staff attitude hardened into indifference, and all further reports were dismissed as phantoms of the imagination caused by feelings of panic and an unsoldierly nervousness.

The night of August 7th/8th was moonless and fine, after a hot, cloudless day; and towards 3 a.m. – as on the night of March 21st – a ground mist began to form in the river valleys, gradually thickening and spreading out over the whole plateau. Under its cloak, the eastward movement of the spearhead force into their final positions was concluded, and by 3 a.m., from the banks of the Ancre in the north down across the Somme and past Villers-Bretonneux to the Luce, waited the British and Dominion troops, with the tanks a thousand yards to the rear. South of the Luce were the troops of the French First Army under General Debeney, who despite orders from Foch that his whole army was to advance frontally with the main attack,

Battle of
AMIENS, Aug. 1918

Line morning Aug. 8
Line evening Aug. 8
Line morning Aug. 15
Line Aug. 26
Line Aug. 29

had decided that protection of the Canadians' right flank by his own left-hand divisions was the maximum role it could play. In view of the total absence of tanks on the French sector, this decision was wise.

Twelve minutes before zero hour, the tanks began rumbling forward, guided through the thick mist by white marker tapes laid out to direct them through the infantry positions, while above, the air squadrons circled and swooped, roaring low over the German lines, effectively deafening the troops and diverting their attention.

At 4.20 a.m. – with still an hour to go before dawn – the artillery opened fire, a creeping barrage crashed down two hundred yards in front of the attack infantry, while steel and high explosive shattered known German gun-positions further afield. After two minutes, the barrage lifted forward another hundred yards, and after another two minutes, a further hundred yards.

Behind the barrage, the Canadians on the right, the Australians in the centre and the British on the left moved forward, the ranks of the Dominion troops dotted along the whole length of their line by the squat, frightening, mastodon shapes of the fighting tanks.

The Allied advance to the Rhine had begun.

As with Mangin's attack on July 18th, the initial thrust forward was successful along its entire length. Shaken by the sudden impact of the assault, blinded by the fog, and panic-stricken by the sounds of clanking armour which seemed to come from everywhere in front, the German troops were ripe for surrender or flight many minutes before the Dominion infantry came storming at them out of the murky, flame-shot darkness. Even the German machine-gunners – deservedly recognized as some of the toughest-minded troops of any army – succumbed to an understandable psychological reaction, and wasted precious time and ammunition in vain attempts to stop the tanks, upon whose armour their bullets rained with tremendous clatter but small effect, while the Australians and Canadians closed in from uncovered angles.

The fog also caused confusion among the attackers, and for the first two hours they fought their way forward more as isolated units – like the fingers of many hands – than as a broad, co-ordinated fighting front, and if this was unintended it was also successful, and when light came, the sections of the attack soon linked up again.

By 8 a.m., the first objectives along the whole length of the front between the Somme and the Amiens–Roye road had been obtained, and on the left flank the Australian 4th and 5th Divisions came up, passed through the positions already gained by their 2nd and 3rd Divisions, and pressed forward towards the second objective.

'When a machine-gun post gave trouble,' wrote the Official Historian, 'the infantry lay down whilst a tank tackled it; in most cases the crew surrendered as the machine came near, or fled.'

Not always, however, and in the village of Marcelcave, six machine-gun posts so enfiladed the flank of the Australian advance that they were held up for some time. It took one of the Male Mark V tanks nearly half an hour to eliminate these posts, each one of which fought until it was either crushed beneath the tank tracks or received a direct hit from one of the tank's six-pounder guns: after which the tank commander handed over the village to the accompanying infantry, having duly received from them an authorized receipt.

In the centre, the Canadian 4th Division passed through the positions of their 3rd Division on the line of their second objective – which had been reached by 11 a.m. – and as they advanced, they were overtaken by thirty Mark V Star Tanks, each of which carried two infantry machine-gun sections in addition to their crews. These tanks in turn passed through the infantry with the idea of pressing immediately forward to the third objective, dropping the machine-gun sections and then returning to aid the general advance – but unfortunately for this otherwise far-seeing project, the tanks ran into the fire of an unscathed and heroically manned German battery, and as by this time there was neither surprise nor darkness to aid them, only eleven of the tanks reached their objective. Here – as on the Australian front where a similar experiment was being tried out – it was found that the machine-gunners were so exhausted by the heat and fumes inside the tank that they were in no state to take full advantage of their positions behind the enemy lines.

Another operation of enterprise and initiative, however, had been crowned with the success it deserved. Shortly before the 4th Australian Division had reached its second objective, an armoured-car battalion came up and its endeavours to assist the infantry revealed a weak patch in the German defence. Probing forward, the sixteen cars passed rapidly through a light artillery barrage, and before its commander could be assailed by doubts as to his orthodoxy of

200

behaviour, he found his command rapidly approaching a convoy of enemy horse-drawn transport. The leading cars immediately opened fire, causing the head of the column to try to turn about, with the result that confusion and at the end chaos, engulfed the convoy. The armoured-cars swept down, their machine-guns raking the blocked and tangled traffic, killing the drivers and causing the horses to rear and bolt across country with their wrecked and disintegrating waggons bumping and crashing behind them.

Soon afterwards the cars reached a crossroads where they diverged right and left, those to the left racing into the village of Proyart where they shot up more enemy transport, set supply and ammunition waggons alight and left a trail of dead and wounded behind when they vacated the village ten minutes later.

The cars that had gone south were even luckier. They reached the village of Framerville where they surprised a German Corps Headquarters at lunch in one of the houses. A fusillade of machine-gun bullets brought the meal to a hasty end, and as the Staff ran in panic from the building, they were hunted through the village and shot down like coursed hares: while this happened, the crew of one of the cars ransacked the headquarters building and removed all interesting-looking documents, including a detailed plan of the Hindenburg defence system which was to prove extremely useful in the relatively near future.

The cars patrolled the area for the remaining hours of daylight and then returned to their own lines, having at last been given the opportunity to justify their existence on the Western Front. For many of their critics this was indeed an unhappy day, for these vehicles needed only lower reduction gears and wide pneumatic tyres to be enabled to take over completely all duties hitherto carried out on the field of battle by the Cavalry Corps.

That this arm had become obsolete on the day the first efficient machine-gun was manufactured, had been once more convincingly demonstrated. Its role, in theory, had been to pour through the gaps torn in the enemy defences by the infantry and tanks, exploiting the breakthrough by wrecking the enemy's rear communications. This they attempted to do when the Australians and Canadians reached their second objectives – and in those places where they found gaps between isolated machine-gun posts, they undoubtedly made satisfactory progress. But this progress became increasingly disjointed – for the horsemen were completely helpless against any form of concentrated fire which could be directed at them from as much as a quarter of a mile away, and a platoon of riflemen could bar the road to a cavalry brigade, if necessary, so long as daylight lasted and their flanks remained secure.

Thus on this occasion, the only progress the cavalry could make in any specific direction was that across country cleared for them by the attached Whippet tank companies, a co-operation which proved wholly unsatisfactory as the Whippets could only move at eight miles an hour. When there was no opposition, therefore, the cavalry raced ahead, but the moment fire from emplacements was opened upon them they had perforce to retire until Whippets came up to clear the way – and in the meantime, their situation was uncomfortable to a degree, because horsemen, unlike infantry, cannot lie down under cover. One would have thought that from four years' experience of modern warfare, this fact could have been previously appreciated.

By the time the Cavalry Corps reached the third objective – which they did, in general, just before the infantry arrived – it was obvious that only total failure confronted them if they tried to press further forward against a noticeably hardening defence. Despite their orders to advance to a line some seven miles ahead, one divisional commander now claimed that he had not received confirmation of those orders, and the other declared loyally that he could not advance on his own – although whether his loyalty was to his men or to his fellow member of the Cavalry Club is uncertain.

It cannot, in all frankness, be said that these men were anything but wise – and it must have been a great disappointment to them that, after sitting on their horses for four years bemoaning the lack of that open warfare in which they had thought to distinguish themselves and bring added glories to their arm, they found themselves unable to do so when opportunity apparently presented itself.

The commanders of the Whippet tanks were even more furious, as they had been held back near Amiens with the cavalry until well after zero hour, and not all were able to catch up with the main battle. One did, however, the somewhat winsomely named 'Musical Box', and its story has passed into Tank Corps history.

Some two hours after watching the cavalry unit he was supposed to be escorting gallop bravely off into the distance, and shortly after he had overtaken the infantry and passed through them, the attention of the Whippet commander, Lieutenant Arnold, was drawn to a battle raging between some Mark V tanks and a German artillery unit. Two Mark Vs were already out of action, one with tracks blown off, the other holed and burning, and in order to divert a similar fate from the others, Arnold drove at full speed diagonally across the front of the German battery, spraying the gun-positions liberally from his machine-guns as he did so. He reached the sanctuary of a small belt of trees, doubled back behind them and attacked the battery from the rear, killing the gun-crews and thus releasing the heavier and slower-moving tanks for action further afield.

He then found two cavalry patrols held up by rifle-fire on the edge of a cornfield, and removed their opposition for them by driving over the rifle-pits, after which he ran along the southern bank of the Amiens–Chaulnes railway until he found yet another cavalry patrol, this time blocked by a machine-gun post firing over the parapet of one of the bridges. He drove his Whippet up the bank and on to the line, clearing the gun-post from the bridge as he crossed it.

He was by now completely alone, and, one gathers, enjoying himself hugely. According to his map, he was only a mile or so from a small valley reputed to contain huts in which were billeted a substantial number of German troops, and when a few minutes later he arrived there, he found many of these hastily packing their kits preparatory to evacuation. Those not immediately killed were pursued until completely dispersed, after which Arnold pressed on eastwards, undaunted but extremely uncomfortable, for he carried spare petrol in tins lashed to the tank's roof and these had now been perforated. Petrol ran down inside the tank, flooding the floor, and filling the constricted space with fumes to such an extent that Arnold and his driver and gunner were all compelled to breathe through their box respirators. As the heat inside the tank was increasing all the time, there must have been some speculation in their minds as to the growing fire risk.

By 2 p.m., 'Musical Box' was some way in advance of all except the armoured-car units, (operating some two miles away to the north) and Arnold was now presented with the same type of targets as those which had first attracted the attention of the armoured-car commander – roads packed with transport.

For almost another hour, he cruised along the roadsides, shooting up lorries, killing or so frightening the horses that they bolted, killing the packed infantry – but his tank was itself the target of such concentrated rifle-fire that the spare petrol-tanks were riddled, the tank itself so swamped inside and out with petrol, that it was only a matter of time before a spark ignited it.

The end came just before 3 p.m. – by which time Arnold and his crew had spent nearly ten hours inside the torrid confines of their tank. A light field-gun opened fire upon them, and a glancing blow from one of the shells was all that was required; the Whippet became a flaming cauldron. Arnold managed to force the door open and drag out the other two members of his crew, who were practically unconscious, but as they recovered in the fresh air, they became aware that their clothing was alight, that they stood in the middle of a growing pool of flaming petrol, and that they were still under fire.

As they staggered out of immediate danger and began rolling on the ground to extinguish the flames from their clothing, they were surrounded by infuriated Germans, who killed the driver, kicked the other two unmercifully as they lay on the ground, and subjected them to considerable brutality until they were taken over by other authorities. Even then Arnold's treatment did not improve, as he refused to answer questions, and was struck in the face for his recalcitrance and then imprisoned in solitary confinement for five days before being taken to a properly organized prison camp.

This in itself was a revealing piece of evidence of the decline of enemy morale, for such treatment is usually the result of anger and hatred, which in turn is caused by fear. There were many more instances of unusually harsh treatment of Allied prisoners taken about this time, giving good grounds for believing that by now confidence throughout the armies of the Central Powers was on the wane.

Certainly Ludendorff was shocked when on the following day he appraised the results of the fighting of August 8th.

Fifteen miles of his front had been stove in, with a maximum penetration of seven miles in the centre along the whole ten-mile stretch from Proyart in the north down to the Amiens–Roye road, while to the north and south the flanks sloped evenly back to the original start-line. In all, some hundred and ten square miles of country had changed hands, while thirteen thousand prisoners and three hundred and thirty-four guns had fallen to the Australians and Canadians. North of the Somme and south of the Amiens–Roye road, the British and the French had done little more than keep pace on their inner wings with the Dominion troops in the centre, in both cases possibly owing to lack of tanks, but on the British front owing also to organizational confusion at the beginning, plus a pronounced lack of ardour among the troops. These had been savagely mauled during the retreat from St. Quentin, and had as a result of their experiences even less faith in their command staffs than was usual; a condition possibly not unconnected with the discovery, on one of those disastrous days in March, of a divisional commander weeping disconsolately in a ditch.

But however the British troops felt about conditions, the Germans felt far worse. Eight months had now passed since the first mass onslaught by tanks had fallen upon them at Cambrai, and their re-appearance upon the field had had the maximum psychological effect of a long-feared weapon suddenly wielded. The German troops were only too well aware of the fact that they had virtually no armoured vehicles themselves, and the sudden appearance in two different sectors of the front of hundreds of the dreaded machines, caused morale – already sagging as a result of the obvious failure of the 'Friedensturm' – to plummet.

Mr. Churchill chose the day after the opening of the Amiens battle to visit his old friend Rawlinson, and two sentences of his account reveal a significant change of attitude on the part of the German soldier. Mr. Churchill had been delayed in his arrival at Fourth Army Headquarters by the endless streams of German prisoners trailing by on the hot and dusty roads.

'No one who has been a prisoner of war himself', he wrote, 'can be indifferent to the lot of the soldier whom the fortunes of war condemn to this plight. The woe-begone expression of the officers contrasted sharply with the almost cheerful countenances of the rank and file.'

There were, of course, many more rank and file than officers, and troops glad to fall into enemy hands belong to a losing army. This was a point which was already impressing itself deeply into

Ludendorff's mind as he read, with growing horror, of various events which had taken place during that epochal first day of the Amiens battle. It was not so much the loss of territory, of material, or even of men, which worried him; the Allies had lost far more in all these categories every day for over a week during the March retreat, but they had not lost the war. It was an entirely different type of loss which spelt out to him the presage of doom. It was the loss of spirit.

According to reports which reached him, six German divisions had collapsed that day in scenes unprecedented in German military legend. Companies had surrendered to single tanks, platoons to single infantrymen, and on one occasion retreating troops had hurled abuse at a division going forward resolutely to buttress the sagging line, accusing them of blacklegging and of 'toadying to the Junkers'. These were, indeed, ominous happenings, and they sounded in Ludendorff's already melancholy mind uncommonly like the first warning notes of disaster.

'August 8th was the Black Day of the German Army . . .,' he wrote afterwards. 'It put the decline of our fighting powers beyond all doubt. The Army had ceased to be a perfect fighting instrument.'

There is a wealth of significance in that last sentence. To a Commander capable of believing that any Army could be a 'perfect instrument' – composed as it is of frail humanity – the first signs of serious infirmity in his own, will come as a considerable shock: and possibly owing to the narrowness of Ludendorff's knowledge and experience, he lacked mental resilience. That the German Army had suffered a defeat and that some of its elements had failed to uphold its highest military traditions were undoubtedly facts of high importance: but their effect upon Ludendorff was infinitely more so.

This was the crisis.

The most significant event of 1918 did not occur on the field of battle. It occurred in Ludendorff's office – for as he read the reports of the fighting of August 8th, he began to believe that his Army was breaking up from within.

And history is made in men's minds.

It was not, of course, very long after the conclusion of his lunch with Rawlinson that Mr. Churchill was making his way across the newly captured ground in order to observe the battle at closer quarters. ('Cavalry cantered as gaily over the reconquered territory,' he remarks with scathing innocence, 'as if they were themselves the cause of victory.') In the late afternoon he reached the scene of what was, in fact, a dying battle.

Only one hundred and forty-five tanks had been found to be still serviceable on the morning of August 9th, and although the crews of these were just as keen to push forward as were the Dominion infantry who accompanied them, they were to do so under two major handicaps. Firstly, there was no carefully prepared and beautifully dovetailed plan for the second day's fighting as there had been for the first, and secondly, the tanks very soon found themselves upon the edge of the torn and devastated area of the old Somme battlefields, with its maze of derelict trenches and its forests of rusty wire, which if no handicap to the tanks would still delay the supporting infantry. Moreover, it must be remembered that the tank crews had no body of past experience upon which to draw: they were, in fact, the men making the mistakes from which others might reap benefit.

As a result, the progress on the second day of the battle was spasmodic and uneven, and in the face of the German reaction to the previous day's fighting it is a matter for wonder that any occurred at all. Three German divisions had arrived to hold the rear defence line by the evening of August 8th, three more came up during the night and three more by mid-afternoon of the 9th – while the only force attacking them was still the one which had begun moving forward thirty-six hours before, and its members were by now very short of sleep. They were also outnumbered, and their superiority thus lay solely with the diminishing tank force.

In all, an average advance of three miles was made on this second day of the attack by the British and Dominion troops, but further south, the French General Debeney now threw his right-hand divisions into action, thus widening the front by some fifteen miles. The French troops also made some advance – of varying depth – together with the delightful (and illuminating, if only they had realized its implications) discovery that Ludendorff had evacuated Montdidier during the previous night. Examination of the map, and a comparison with the events of the July 31st and August 1st between Soissons and Fère-en-Tardenois, would have been revealing had anyone cared to make it.

And on the third day of the attack (August 10th) although a

fresh British division was brought up through the tired but still aggressive Australians and Canadians, there was an advance of rather less than a mile – and that only in the centre, for there were but sixty-seven tanks now left in action, and the immutable laws of the Western Front applied to British advances just as much as to those of Germany.

These laws were not, of course, ones of which Foch was prepared to take cognizance. At 11 a.m. on this third day of the attack, he met Haig in order to urge further reinforcement of that section of the front which was already close up against an almost rock-hard defence, while he for his part ordered Debeney to continue to attack on the right, with an even further extension of the front by Humbert's French Third Army (still in the Noyon cleft). Haig countered – possibly through force of habit – with a suggestion that, instead, the British Third and First Armies to the north should take up the offensive, to which Foch enthusiastically agreed – so long as Rawlinson's Fourth Army kept up the pressure as well in order to force the Germans back across the upper Somme, and thus recapture Péronne. Constant frontal attacks everywhere would seem to have been the limit of Foch's military imagination, and the idea of turning a line, rather than steamrollering over it, seems never to have occurred to him.

But by August 11th, Rawlinson knew that so far as his own front was concerned, the law of diminishing returns was in operation, and he managed to persuade Haig – who visited him that morning – of the realities of the situation; not, in fairness to Haig, that much persuasion was needed.

That evening, the battle of Amiens came officially to its end from the point of view of the British Fourth Army – and as Debeney's French First Army was short of ammunition for its artillery, the fighting stopped on the right flank as well. The tanks were withdrawn, the Australians began to dig in, and the Canadians – as a result of orders issued by Haig before he left Rawlinson's Headquarters – to withdraw.

For at last it had been realized – by some of the Allied commanders at least – that to continue an attack when once resistance had hardened, was a useless waste of lives.

There ensued during the next few days between Foch and Haig, the most serious difference of opinion of the whole period of their co-operation. The fact that acrimony was never exchanged between them might possibly have been due to the fact that neither spoke the other's language sufficiently well – but despite the urbanity of the exchanges, Haig remained so inflexibly opposed to an immediate renewal of attack by Rawlinson's Army, that Foch was in the end forced to give way.

This Foch did the more gracefully, because on August 12th Sir Julian Byng reported that opposite the front of his British Third Army, it would seem that the Germans were thinning out and actually in the process of a limited withdrawal. There seemed, therefore, to be excellent prospects for another offensive between Albert and Arras, directed towards Bapaume, but Byng insisted that despite the Supreme Commander's wishes, the attack could not be delivered before August 21st. So Foch, unwilling to wait but unable to stampede the stubborn British, issued orders direct to the one man of whom he could be confident of prompt obedience – Mangin.

As a result, on August 18th, the French Tenth Army carried out a local operation immediately north of Soissons – which did little, in fact, but send the opposing German troops to their battle positions. But on the 20th, the Butcher drove his armies two miles forward to capture eight thousand prisoners and two hundred guns, and to establish themselves on the heights between the Aisne and the Oise – from which position they constituted a distinct menace to the whole of Ludendorff's position along the north bank of the Vesle.

One of the chief objections to the philosophy which holds that the end justifies the means, is that so often they bear such little relationship to each other. Foch's doctrine that everyone should attack everywhere all the time, appears so fatuous that only its complete impracticability could have prevented disaster, especially in view of the history of previous battles on the Western Front. It is thus with some chagrin that one is forced to accept that on this occasion, the happiest ends resulted from unpromising means.

From a study of the August battles, one could easily assume that at last the value of time in military affairs had been fully appreciated. On August 8th, the Fourth Army had attacked at Villers-Bretonneux and advanced ten miles before the battle ended on the 11th. On August 9th, Debeney's right wing had attacked and taken Montdidier, while the following day Humbert's French Third Army – one stage further south – advanced towards Noyon and succeeded in liberating Lassigny in fighting which lasted until the 16th. And on the 18th, Mangin struck on Humbert's right – and took the Aisne heights on the 20th.

Each attack had been broken off as soon as it had lost its initial impetus, by which time another attack had been launched near enough in location to the one preceding it to profit from its successes – and again continued only until resistance stiffened to such a point that further attacks would be unprofitable. Had this series of operations been carefully prepared and guided throughout by a shrewd directing brain, it could not have presented a more perfect picture of the only technique which was practicable in the conditions which reigned, and with the weapons which were available, on the Western Front in 1918.

Yet although every one of these attacks – even Rawlinson's – had been launched largely on Foch's insistence, every one had been broken off in spite of it, that of the French Armies usually through lack of ammunition. Poor logistics had thus combined with poorer tactics to produce gratifying success – and as, while Mangin's army fortified itself in its new positions on the Aisne, Byng's British Third Army was making ready to attack north of Albert (on August 21st), the impetus was being maintained, the ball – to use a simile frequently on Foch's lips, although usually with singular irrelevance – was being kept rolling.

To give added weight to Byng's thrust towards Bapaume, nearly two hundred tanks had been hastily assembled – a total only achieved by the re-issue of Mark IVs to battalions whose Mark Vs had been destroyed in front of Amiens. Once again, there was no warning bombardment, only a creeping barrage behind which tanks and infantry advanced, and their task to begin with was so easy that one historian has described progress as an 'amble forward', while another states that their only hindrance was provided by the early morning mist.

But when the mist lifted, the situation changed considerably. The attackers then found themselves close up against the main resistance line to which Ludendorff had withdrawn his troops during the previous fortnight, and they suffered accordingly during the remainder of the day. As a result, there was little sign of aggression from the British on the following morning, for they had wisely decided to await the arrival into new positions of their field artillery, before attempting further progress. And in his attempts to discover the reason for the lull in the attack, the local German commander made a curious, and to him heartening, discovery: fifty per cent of Byng's infantry could well be described as 'boys' – and undernourished ones at that, for they consisted largely of those troops hastily rushed out to France after a most inadequate training in Britain, in response to the emergencies created by the St. Quentin and Lys battles. For many of them this was, in fact, their first taste of action.

Thus encouraged, the Germans brought up close reserves and launched one of their more aggressive counterattacks – which ran headlong into point-blank fire from the field artillery, then arriving on the scene with a fortunate but unusual timeliness. Despite heavy casualties, the counterattack was pressed until it was finally broken – and indeed, flung back – by the unyielding defence of the 'boys', who had had time by now to dig themselves in and who were armed, not only with an adequate supply of machine-guns, but also with their own ignorance augmented by an as yet unshaken faith in their leaders. By nightfall the Germans were back in their own lines, leaving their dead to litter the battlefield, and feelings of considerable satisfaction to hearten their enemies.

And while counterattack and repulse had raged along a fifteen-mile front *north* of Albert, Rawlinson had moved his left flank forward *south* of Albert – between Albert and the Somme – thus straightening the line between the advanced positions reached by the Canadians and Australians in the centre of his front, and the new positions reached on his left by Byng's army, recapturing Albert at the same time.

Thus the front line of the two armies was made continuous – running on the evening of August 22nd along the edge of the old Somme battlefield, upon which had fallen two years before the elder brothers, the uncles, and often the fathers of those boys who now lay waiting to attack across it once more. Thiepval, Pozières, Martinpuich, High Wood and Delville Wood, Bazentin and Mametz

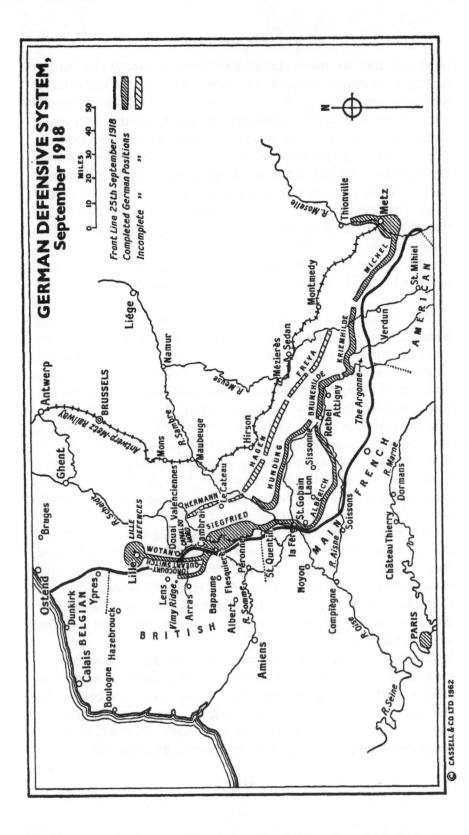

GERMAN DEFENSIVE SYSTEM, September 1918

Front Line 25th September 1918
Completed German Positions
Incomplete " "

MILES
0 10 20 30 40 50

N

© CASSELL & CO LTD 1962

– all those places whose names had passed into British history during the summer of 1916 were now again to be the scene of a British assault.

There were, however, important differences between the prospects then and now. If time and occasion had reduced many of the villages in the Somme Valley to little but rubble-strewn and cratered wildernesses, they had also affected the morale and calibre of the German troops who sought to defend themselves there – and their numbers had been drastically reduced by the abortive counterattacks they had just been called upon to deliver. So when the 'boys' of the Third Army rose from their trenches at 4.45 a.m. on the morning of August 23rd – still triumphant from their success of the previous afternoon – they faced an opposition far less grimly determined than that which had shot down 60,000 of their predecessors in a single hour two years before. All day long the pressure on the German line kept up, and by evening, the twelve divisions of Byng's army had advanced in places as much as three miles – taking over five thousand prisoners in the process – whilst Rawlinson's Australian divisions had attacked south of the Somme again, and were punching forward towards Chaulnes and the river line beyond, where it ran south from Péronne. Everywhere the Germans had gone back, and no counter-attack by them had been attempted.

August 23rd was thus another 'Black Day' for the German Army, during which, according to Ludendorff, one division completely disintegrated, while the effect upon several others he considered to have been disastrous. Nevertheless, neither that day nor later did the German line break, and once well within the web of trenches of the old battlefields the veteran infantry, stiffened as usual by their machine-gunners, fought with great skill until either overrun or out-manœuvred.

Usually they were out-manœuvred – for if the British army commanders were learning the value of outflanking techniques on a large scale, the infantry were just as quick to apply them in a hundred tiny, individual instances. The web of trenches which sheltered enemy posts also surrounded them, and during the days following August 23rd, the entire British line from the Amiens-Roye road in the south up as far as the bastion of Arras in the north, edged inexorably forward, as the young soldiers of Byng's Army cannily threaded their way between the strongpoints. Those German troops who would not retreat were surrounded and either killed or captured – and a significantly large fraction now preferred to surrender than to die an heroic death for a failing Fatherland.

Then on August 26th, the line of attack was further lengthened as the British First Army - with the Canadian Corps once more lining the Vimy Ridge – joined in the battle, extending it northward to beyond Arras, driving forward until it reached the northern hinge of the Siegfried Position. And here, for the moment, it paused, for the onslaught upon this deep system of fortifications, stretching from Arras right the way down past the Flesquières Salient and St. Quentin to la Fère, was not one to be undertaken without much thought and considerable preparation. There were many men in London and in France who thought that it should not be undertaken at all, but that some method of outflanking even this barrier could be found.

But although the Siegfried Position was over fifty miles long, it was itself only a part of a much longer defensive system. Northwards for thirty miles as far as Lille, it was extended by the Wotan Position (known to the British as the Drocourt–Quéant Switch) while to the south, the Alberich, Brunehilde, Kriemhilde and Michel Positions took it in varying degrees of apparent impregnability right down as far as Metz.

On the face of it, it would seem that outflanking sweeps could only be made through the narrow gap between the Ypres front and the sea in the north, or between the St. Mihiel Salient and the Swiss border in the south, and neither of these fronts was wide enough to permit the passage of sufficient troops to encircle a defensive system some hundred and eighty miles long, at a time when the speed of advance was still dictated by the rate at which the infantry could march.

Even Haig's newly acquired instinct for economy of force could inspire at the moment no better plan for future operations than that of an attempt to smash a way directly through the Siegfried Line – and his appreciation of the time values (also newly acquired, or at least lately renewed) told him that it must be quickly mounted if the enemy were not to be given the chance of consolidating the line once they reached it.

Except opposite Arras, however, the Germans were still falling back on the Line, as the British Third and Fourth Armies slowly forced shut the door which had been flung open by Ludendorff's Michael attacks in March; and during the last week in August the pressure was maintained, heavy and unrelenting. From German accounts, each day was 'spent in bloody fighting against an ever and again on-storming enemy, and nights passed without sleep in retirements to new lines'. By August 29th, Byng's Army was past Bapaume to both north and south – with the result that the town was evacuated during the night – and Rawlinson's Australians reached the Somme below Péronne. Further south still, the French First Army under Debeney was only slightly behind Rawlinson's right wing, and beyond them again, Humbert's French Third Army hinged forward, its own right wing resting on the advanced positions of Mangin's army, the whole front slowly levering the Germans backwards.

From Arras in the north to Noyon in the south the battle raged as day succeeded day; and just south of the mid-point of this straight, seventy-mile long line lay Péronne, guarded from the Australians by the right-angle made by the Somme as it curved through the town.

On the evening of August 30th began the Australian assault across the Somme, directed at Péronne and the Mont St. Quentin heights which dominated the town from the north. This has been hailed as one of the most brilliant epics of the war: it was certainly one of the bloodiest, for the positions were defended by elements of five German divisions, including the 2nd Guards Division, which had been given instructions that Mont St. Quentin was not to fall.

All the Somme bridges in the immediate vicinity of the town had been destroyed, but in the village of Feuilleres, some four miles west of Péronne, was found a railway bridge which could be repaired sufficiently to allow the passage of troops. As this village was already behind the British III Corps front, two brigades of Australians passed over on to the north bank of the river, and immediately pushed eastwards to form bridgeheads from which the main assaults could be launched. By midnight of the 30th, the bridgeheads had been formed, one due west of Mont St. Quentin, and one south-west from it and north-west from Péronne itself.

Supported by five brigades of field artillery and one brigade of heavy artillery firing from the Australian positions south of the river or from behind the British III Corps lines, the attack started at 5 a.m. on the morning of the 31st. By 7 a.m., solely as a result of the surprise occasioned by the direction of the attack, Mont St. Quentin village fell to the Australians of the 17th Battalion, but unfortunately flanking attacks on each side had broken down, having lost direction in the maze of trenches which seamed the entire locality. Thus at 7.30 a.m. when the Germans counterattacked with every man they could bring to the area, they killed the majority of the Australians in the village, and drove the survivors back down the hill into a trench system running along the strip of land between the base of the hill and the river.

And for the rest of that first day, a vicious battle was fought from trench to trench – an affair mostly of bombing attacks along the trench lines, or of gallant, heart-breaking attempts to charge along lanes through the enormous, man-high wire belts, against machine-gun fire aimed directly down them. With Mont St. Quentin still in enemy hands, no attempt could be made to capture Péronne from the bridgehead between the two objectives, so the troops there were gradually drawn upon to replace casualties lost in the battle to their left.

But there was no attempt at secrecy or at surprise, and there were no tanks to aid the infantry – so at nightfall the Germans still held the hill-top, and the Australian dead were strewn around the foot. The exhausted survivors of the attacking battalions, grim, bitter, their courage sustained mostly by their reputation, held a line which meandered between the bridgeheads, made up of trenches unpromisingly named Florina Trench, Gott Mit Uns Trench, Deus Trench, Elsa Trench and Oder Trench.

It cannot be said to have been a satisfactory day's battle, especially in comparison with those which had immediately preceded it – which possibly accounts for the defiant air about the paragraph in the Fourth Army history which sums it up: 'The attack on Mont St. Quentin by the 5th Brigade, with only hastily arranged artillery support and without a creeping barrage, ranks as one of the most notable examples of pluck and enterprise during the war.'

Unfortunately, pluck and enterprise are not enough in battle.

During the night, more troops were fed into the bridgeheads, and as dawn broke violent attacks were launched up the slopes of Mont St. Quentin – and owing to the ferocity with which the battle was fought, the enemy's attention became gradually concentrated there. Australians of the 54th Battalion thus found their way into Péronne practically unimpeded, and by 8.40 a.m. they were established in the centre of the town, having cleared all points of resistance in the southern and western quarters. As they pressed on, attempting to clear the garrison out of the north-eastern districts, they in turn distracted the enemy's attention from the fighting on Mont St. Quentin – with the result that the German commander was caught off balance and, uncertain as to which of the two positions was the more important, he suffered a moment's indecision which gave rise to a fatal mistake. In order to recover a position he had lost, he weakened one he was holding – and when the Australians of the 6th Brigade next attacked up the face of the hill, they took the uppermost system of trenches, and from there quickly overran Mont St. Quentin village itself.

For the remainder of that day (September 1st) the German troops counterattacked both positions fiercely, but were unable to beat the Australians out of the positions they had already won – although they kept them, in turn, out of the north-east corner of Péronne. Casualties were high on both sides, for both, despite the lessons of the last months, were relying upon direct assault to win for them the desired positions.

But next morning, well to the south of Péronne, the Australian 15th Brigade crossed the Somme and advanced due west, thus outflanking the remnants of the German 2nd Guards Division still striving valiantly to redeem its prestige by beating the Australians back out of the positions between Péronne and Mont St. Quentin, and those infantry units still clinging to the Péronne ramparts. All these were thus forced to withdraw: and the names of Péronne and of Mont St. Quentin passed into the history of the Australian Army.

The Dominion troops certainly fought with all the dash and resolution which had come to be expected of them; and their casualty list reflected this, for on one of the minor attacks of the first day, of twelve hundred men who advanced, only six hundred were still alive an hour later – and many of these were to fall before the end of the day. Such slaughter had not been unusual.

But one cannot avoid wondering whether it was all necessary. During the actual progress of the Mont St. Quentin Battle, Byng's

Third Army advanced well beyond Bapaume, thus outflanking the entire position in the north as the Australians of the 15th Brigade were to do in the south. Possibly these two advances would not have been so easy had it not been for the fierce battle between them, but even this can be doubted, for the country on either side of Péronne was far more vulnerable to attack than the walled town, or the heights which dominated it.

It is said that during the first day of the landings on the Gallipoli Peninsula in 1915, the Admiral in command of the Royal Naval units taking the troops ashore, watched the bitter struggle on the beaches for some time and then remarked reflectively to his Chief-of-Staff: 'Gallant fellows, these soldiers; they always go for the thickest place in the fence.'

Apparently even a combination of brains of the calibre of those of Rawlinson and Sir John Monash is not enough to resist the dreadful fascination of directing men engaged upon an almost impossible task.

10. The Grand Assault

AN even more cogent reason for questioning the necessity for the Australian attack upon Péronne and Mont St. Quentin is provided by the activities of the Canadian Corps opposite Arras during almost the same period. Their pause on the northern hinge of the Hindenburg Line had not been of long duration, and as a result of their progress since, it seemed likely that the envisaged frontal attack on the main defensive position might receive, if not modification, at least support from a less obvious angle of attack than a right angle.

That portion of the Line known to the Germans as the Siegfried Position ran north from St. Quentin to a point not far past a line drawn between Bapaume and Cambrai – facing the whole of the front of Rawlinson's Fourth Army and that of the southern half of Byng's Third Army. From this point northwards, three strong defence lines diverged, the most westerly one hingeing on the main German front line opposite Arras, the middle and perhaps most formidable one running north from Quéant up to the anchor-point of the Lille defences (the 'Wotan Position'), while the most easterly line followed the east bank of the Canal du Nord as far as Douai on the Scarpe, thereafter continuing on up to Lille.

These three lines lacked the deep concrete fortifications and subterranean tunnels of the main Siegfried Position, but they were nevertheless well-constructed trench systems, all protected by wire belts at least twenty yards wide, and according to Churchill (who inspected it the morning after it fell) that of the Drocourt–Quéant Switch by a belt a hundred yards wide. Machine-gun posts covered the most likely lanes of approach to the belts, and dug-outs in the trench system, although not so bomb-proof as those to the south, nevertheless gave considerably more protection to their occupants than the majority of those built by the Allies.

It is possible that this strength of fortification led to the loss of the lines, for if the finest elements of Ludendorff's infantry had led the main attacks of the last few months, its most competent residue

219

was still fighting in the remains of the salients formed by those attacks. This left only the barest minimum, in both quantity and quality, to hold what was, after all, almost the only section of the German front facing the British not to have moved forward during the recent battles. First-class fighting material would long since have been drained from it and thrown into the attack.

But the defence of even the strongest positions relies upon the men behind the guns, and during the days immediately following the arrival of the Canadians on the northern hinge of the Line, opposite Arras, it became increasingly evident that morale was not very high amongst the Germans holding it. Artillery bombardments from the guns still in position 'to guard the coalfields behind Béthune' caused a certain amount of damage to the wire belts, but even more to the fighting spirit of the defenders, for during August 28th the Canadians broke through the belts and into the line, and by the 29th they had killed or captured the majority of the occupants and driven the survivors either south into the main Siegfried Position or straight back into the Drocourt–Quéant Switch.

During August 30th, the massed artillery was thus able to devote its attention to the wire belts guarding this second position, and the following day – the day of the first attack on Mont St. Quentin – the infantry started moving up for the assault.

It began at dawn on September 2nd. Led by fifty-nine tanks (almost the total remaining strength of the Tank Corps) two Canadian divisions advanced on a five-mile wide front, running northwards from a position some two miles north of Quéant and the junction of the lines. The attack was successful everywhere except on an unimportant section of the left flank, the tanks trundling massively through the wire, the infantry following close and then taking the trench line in a storming rush. Once the Canadians had broken into the line, the British 57th Division followed through the wire, turned south and bombed their way down the defensive positions towards Quéant itself, while the Canadians pressed directly on east of the line, and the 63rd Royal Naval Division came through, fanned south-eastwards between the Canadians and the 57th, and raced down to cut the Quéant–Cambrai railway line, filling the fork between the Switch Line and the Canal du Nord.

Truly the day of trench warfare was over – and the fact that this complicated series of manœuvres was carried out with complete success can be attributed almost as much to growing efficiency and imagination among the British as to failing strength among the enemy. In seven hours a defence system long considered near-impregnable by both its builders and their enemies had been completely ruptured, with the result that Allied soldiers were in country which had been behind German lines since 1914.

Even more important, the famed Siegfried Position was within measurable distance of being completely turned from the north, while as a secondary and almost unforeseen profit, the whole of the salient of the Lys basin, won by the Germans at such enormous expense in April, had become untenable.

That evening, Ludendorff accepted the fact that the time had come for him to cut his losses. Orders were issued to the troops in the south – already retreating from in front of Rawlinson's and Byng's armies as a result of the losses of Péronne and Bapaume – to withdraw right back to the old British defences from which Byng's and Gough's armies had faced the onslaught of March 21st; there the German troops were to begin immediately to prepare the strongest possible fortified screen as a crush barrier in front of the main Siegfried Position. And in the north, from the ravaged countryside south of Ypres, from Mont Kemmel and Bailleul, Estaires and Merville, the bitter and despondent German infantry were systematically drawn back to a line east of the Lys.

By September 9th, Armentières and Neuve Chapelle had been lost, and from the Sensée river down to la Fère the forward German screening positions were not far in advance of those from which their Storm Troops had advanced, so victoriously, only five and a half months before.

Almost the entire territorial gains of the Ludendorff Spring Offensive had now been lost, the majority in fighting which had taken place in the thirty-two days since August 8th. Since then, too, a hundred thousand German soldiers had gone into Allied prison-camps – seventy thousand captured by the British and the remainder by the Franco–American Armies; and to Ludendorff the most ominous note about the German casualty lists was that the combined figures for dead and wounded did not make a total large enough to exceed that of those missing – of whom he had good reason to believe a substantial proportion had surrendered to the enemy.

There had also been reported to him many more instances of local collapse and insubordination, of the type which had plunged him into gloom after the events of August 8th. 'Stop prolonging the war!' was a cry often heard from the wayside by marching German troops, and a troop train had been seen in Nuremberg bearing the inscription 'Slaughter cattle for Wilhelm and Sons' chalked upon a carriage side.

If such episodes truly reflected the morale of his army, it was no wonder that the nine under-strength divisions holding the Drocourt–Quéant Switch had broken before the six full-strength Canadian and British divisions who, between August 30th and September 3rd, cleared the whole of the Arras front and established themselves against the line of the Canal du Nord. Not that all the German units were so badly affected, for those which still contained a high proportion of veterans of the Western Front were yet to prove themselves capable of resolute defence and even of counterattack; but where heavy casualties had been replaced by men combed out from industry or released as a result of the Treaty of Brest-Litovsk from Russian prison camps, disaffection and even mutiny were rife. Officers commanding loyal battalions often preferred, in the circumstances, to carry on with greatly reduced numerical strength rather than to accept the disruptive elements which threatened to undermine morale.

Ludendorff was therefore faced with the prospect of continuing the war with an army in which all the fighting units were either undependable or weak – and by the end of September the average field strength of his trustworthy battalions was to be reduced to less than six hundred, a number only maintained by breaking up fifteen divisions and re-allocating the men.

He had good cause for depression – if not dismay.

Haig, on the other hand, had ample cause for satisfaction – yet there is a waspish note about some of his diary entries at this time, surprising in view of the situation, and also of the stolidity with which he had appeared to accept the violent criticisms levelled at him from some quarters during the disasters of the Passchendaele period. On September 1st, he had received a note from the Chief of the Imperial General Staff which included the passage, 'Just a word of caution in regard to incurring heavy losses in attack on

Hindenburg Line, as opposed to losses when driving enemy back to that line. I do not mean that you have incurred such losses, but I know that the War Cabinet would become anxious if we received heavy punishment in attacking the Hindenburg Line without success.'

This can hardly be deemed an unreasonable attitude for a Government to take with regard to the lives of its countrymen – especially in view of recent history – and one would have thought that in the atmosphere of victory and confidence which the events since July should surely have engendered at GHQ, Haig could have accepted this missive with good humour. Instead: 'What a wretched lot of weaklings we have in high places at the present time', his diary reads, and later, 'How ignorant our present Statesmen are of the first principles of war!'

In view of the economies of force which he had practised with such success of late, one would expect a more sympathetic reception to what was little more than a friendly warning; but perhaps he suspected friendly warnings from that particular quarter. Possibly too, the warning came at an unfortunate psychological moment, for a vision had just been vouchsafed to Haig of victory in 1918, instead of a long, hard-fought but triumphant campaign in 1919, which was the course of war predicted by practically everybody else in the Allied Governments and High Commands.

There had been many occasions during the previous years when Haig's optimism strikes the historian as fatuous. At last it was to be justified, although whether this was owing to a genuine intuition of the state of enemy morale or merely the result of Haig's continually chanting the same refrain until at last circumstances conformed to give it a truth which it had lacked before, is difficult to decide. But whatever the cause – wishful thinking or genuine insight – Haig believed by the end of August that continued pressure on the enemy would break them before the turn of the year, whereas a slackening of effort now would give to Ludendorff the breathing space he needed for withdrawal to shorter lines of defence and consolidation within them. In these circumstances, it can be seen that Wilson's note must have been extremely irritating – especially as there was no chance now of making up numerical deficiencies on the British front with American troops.

For with the end of the immediate and urgent dangers caused by the spring retreats, Pershing had insisted upon the withdrawal of American divisions from British and French command, and their formation into an American army under his own. From the point of view of the United States – and there was not the slightest reason why Pershing should have paid attention to any other country's – there were several excellent reasons for him to follow this course of action. It was thus somewhat ungracious of him to insist upon every occasion when opportunity offered, that his main reason for doing so was that his officers and men were refusing to participate in battle with troops of other nations. It was also untrue, for in Rawlinson's army the Americans had made firm friends with the Australians, and if they never developed a taste for British Army tea, they at least accorded unqualified admiration to the British Tank Corps. In the event and despite Pershing's wishes, two American divisions – the 27th and the 30th – remained with the Fourth Army to participate in the attack on the Siegfried Position.

But these divisions were the exceptions, for Pershing – who was a man accustomed to getting his own way – was intent upon commanding a separate American army in a separate American sector of the front; and as such a wish fitted, at this time, rather neatly into Foch's plans for the autumn fighting, it received what support was necessary to make it a reality.

For many years, the existence of the St. Mihiel Salient immediately below Verdun had been a painful thorn in France's side. It was not only an affront to her pride, but also a curb upon her freedom of action, as it blocked the main supply route to the Lorraine front. Thus the salient had not only precluded an attack along the shortest line leading to the enemy homeland, but during the Verdun battles of 1916 it had been such a serious menace to the supply lines leading to the front that a secondary road had perforce to be widened and strengthened during the height of the battle, occupying the attention of many men whose endeavours were urgently needed elsewhere.

The Salient also guarded Germany at her most vulnerable point.

Fifteen miles behind the eastern shoulder of the Salient was Metz – itself a city of historic significance to both French and Germans, and from a strategic point of view vital to the German cause. It was the eastern terminus of the Antwerp–Metz railway system which fed the German fighting front, and once in Allied hands would give them a nodal point from which to turn every defence line to which the Germans might retreat until such time as they were back across their own frontier.

That no major attempt to capture Metz had been mounted by the Allies during the previous four years is in itself a reflection upon the poverty of strategic insight with which the war had been waged. Granted that the Flanders front was more convenient to the British lines of communication, and that the French had been naturally zealous at all times to protect Paris -- but if Passchendaele or the Somme battles had been attended by ten times the success they had each achieved, they could not have threatened Germany so shrewdly as an advance in this sector. If previous Allied offensives be compared to attempts to knock out a boxer by heavy punches to the chin and under the heart, an assault towards Metz would be a kick in the stomach: and war in this century is too bloody an affair to be regarded as a sporting contest.

In late July, Foch had issued a memorandum in which he had suggested that, as soon as conditions allowed the release of forces from other sectors, the American army should pinch out the Salient in order to accomplish 'The clearing of the Paris–Avricourt railway around Commercy.' Even now, Foch appears to have possessed no appreciation of the threat which might be developed there, but when, after the Amiens battle, the staff of the American First Army moved into the area south of the Salient in order to draw up the necessary plans, they quickly produced a paper urging that their attack should not be limited by the bounds of the Salient itself. Whether ambition or genuine strategic sense prompted their vision is difficult to decide, but their suggestion was that after reaching the base-line of the Salient (formed by the Michel Position) the Americans should press on at least as far as the railway opposite the centre of the baseline, possibly then extending eastwards along it to attack Metz itself.

The plan called for the use of fifteen American divisions to attack the sides of the Salient, while four French divisions occupied the attention of the Germans at the tip. Pershing approved the plan on August 15th, while two days later, Foch – characteristically – endorsed it heartily, increased the French contribution to ten divisions, and suggested an extension of the frontage of the attack to a width which would most probably have wrecked its chances of

225

success. But it would have made a nice, wide frontal attack, of the kind which he thoroughly understood . . . and Pershing agreed.

Haig didn't.

With all the singlemindedness of a convert to a new religion, Haig now saw 'convergent attack' as the golden means to victory – and if this was a narrow and limited view of the wide field of strategy, it should be appreciated that it was nevertheless a considerable intellectual advance upon the doctrines of either attrition or the 'Spirit of the Offensive, direct and brutal', which had previously obsessed those in High Command. Moreover, there appeared to Haig to be an excellent opportunity for a convergent attack on a hitherto unprecedented scale, in connection with his forthcoming assault on the Siegfried Position. While the British attacked towards Cambrai from the west at the northern end of the Line, the Americans should attack St. Quentin from the south at the southern end; thus each attack would help the other, and another heavy punch would be delivered to Germany's ribs.

This was far better, in Haig's opinion, than allowing the Americans to go far off to the remote corners of the country, delivering attacks which so far from following his lately accepted creed, actually *diverged* from his own line of attack: and if they were already in that remote area and it was not to be thought of to bring them all the way back, then a compromise should be reached. If Pershing wanted the American armies to attack Metz while Haig wanted them to attack St. Quentin, then the reasonable and amicable course to follow was for an objective to be chosen halfway between the two places. Haig therefore suggested to Foch that Mézières, north of the Argonne Forest, should provide the line of attack of the American armies, should Pershing refuse to co-operate in a closer assault on the Siegfried Position.

Foch might have refused to consider this strategy had not Haig at the same time given him a glimpse of the vision of victory in 1918. To one of Foch's enthusiastic temperament, this prospect was too glorious to deny – and possibly the fact that the two main subjects of Haig's thesis were not necessarily inseparable, escaped him. Moreover, when Foch consulted Pétain on the subject of an American attack towards Mézières instead of towards Metz, he found that cool and lucid individual unexpectedly agreeable. For to Pétain, the advantages of a British attack eastwards from the area of

Bapaume together with an American attack northwards from any-where between Rheims and Verdun, were obvious: French forces between the two attacks would hold the curve of the bulge, and by advancing always one step in rear of the two flank offensives, carry out their part without undue exertion or expense in lives.

So on August 30th, Foch visited Pershing at the American's headquarters at Ligny-en-Barrois. If he had merely presented Pershing with the change in strategic objective, it is probable that the latter – who on principle always suspected his Allies – would have withstood him completely; and as a result the Americans might have collapsed the St. Mihiel Salient, breached the Michel Position, and then advanced at least halfway to Metz before their supply problems overwhelmed them. What the tactical developments would have been after that it is impossible to say, but it is evident that the attention of the German High Command would have been jerked violently away from the more western theatres, in order to concentrate upon the immediate protection of the Fatherland – or at least that portion of the Imperial Lands which since 1870 had been graciously allowed to call itself 'Lothringen' instead of by the effeminate and surely too beguiling name of 'Lorraine'.

This could hardly have been to Haig's disadvantage.

But Foch elaborated the plan. He suggested not only the substitution of Mézières for Metz as the prime objective for the Americans (the St. Mihiel Salient to be merely eliminated so as to free lines of communication) but that this larger attack should be mounted by two armies, one wholly American under Pershing, and one *Franco–American under the command of a French General.* Moreover, with a tactfulness which must have been the more infuriating for its transparency, he proposed that General Degoutte should join Pershing's Staff in order 'to guide his tactical decisions'.

It must have made a memorable scene.

From the historical point of view it is also of considerable importance, for by now – either by accident or design – all Pershing's native antagonism was directed against the relatively unimportant issues of French control of American troops, and in his emphatic and categorical rejection of this part of Foch's suggestions, he accepted without argument Foch's right to dictate to him where his army should fight. Thus if all Americans fought under American commanders (and Degoutte was eventually foisted off as military

227

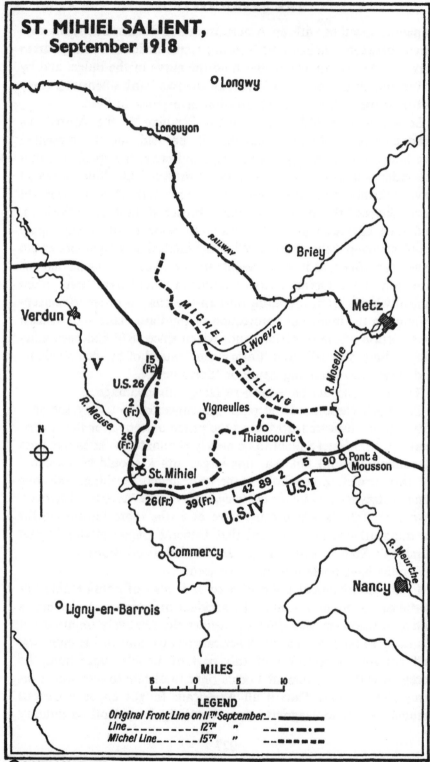

ST. MIHIEL SALIENT,
September 1918

Longwy

Longuyon

RAILWAY

Briey

MICHEL STELLUNG

Metz

Verdun

V

R. Woevre

15 (Fr)

U.S. 26

2 (Fr)

R. Meuse

Vigneulles

Thiaucourt

R. Moselle

26 (Fr)

N

St. Mihiel

5   90   Pont à Mousson

2

1   42   89

U.S. I

26 (Fr.)   39 (Fr.)

U.S. IV

Commercy

R. Meurthe

Nancy

Ligny-en-Barrois

MILES

5   0   5   10

LEGEND

Original Front Line on 11ᵀᴴ September ____

Line _____ 12ᵀᴴ "   ___·___·___

Michel Line ____ 15ᵀᴴ "   ___ ___ ___

© CASSELL & CO. LTD. 1962.

adviser to the King of the Belgians) the American First Army was still committed to an attack up through the Argonne – which bore striking resemblance to Belleau Wood but was far more extensive – instead of across the relatively open and level plains of the Woevre and the Moselle.

This was not only to prove unfortunate for the Americans, but was not to contribute very largely to Allied victory.

It was raining on the evening of September 11th – and it was to continue raining almost all night. As light faded, the dripping darkness was filled with men, the roads leading to the chosen sectors of the St. Mihiel front rumbled dully under the wheels of the transport, and under the tracks of the light French tanks which were all that could be spared for this now relatively unimportant operation. Six American divisions only would now attack along the southern face of the Salient, while only one (the 26th Yankee) would attempt to break through the western face to meet the others at the village of Vigneulles, just short of the centre-point of the Salient baseline. Five French divisions would participate in the operation, three pressing gently against the opposition in the nose of the Salient, in order to occupy their attention until the Americans had cut the lines of retreat. The other two would accompany the Yankee Division through the western flank.

The remainder of the American divisions which should have been participating in the operation were already moving towards their attack positions east of Verdun, facing the ominous height of Montfaucon and the gloomy menace of the Argonne Forest.

At 1 a.m. on September 12th, the artillery bombardment began, ploughing through the enemy wire belts, pulverizing their trenches, plastering the road-junctions and identified control centres in the rear areas. For four hours this bombardment was maintained – from 2,971 French or British guns – and when at 5 a.m. it was suddenly shortened and concentrated into a creeping barrage, the tanks moved forward, the infantry rose to their feet, and along a twelve-mile stretch of the southern flank the advance began.

It met virtually no opposition until after midday, as the German commander in the neighbourhood had begun the withdrawal of his troops from the Salient the previous evening. As well aware of the impending attack as any other European newspaper reader – and one Swiss paper had even published the time of the bombardment and its intended duration – he had appreciated the enormous difference in men, material and morale between his own force and the attackers, and rightly decided that the time for sacrifice on a large scale was over. Leaving behind them the inevitable machine-gun posts, the mass of the German army in the Salient had quietly departed by the time the Allied bombardment began. An earlier departure would, in fact, have been more beneficial, for the longer-range Allied artillery caught some of the last of the retiring units, but in general the Allied bombardment had been wasted and the Americans advanced at first across virtually deserted country. The isolated machine-gun posts took their inevitable toll before they were crushed, and when on occasion contact was made with the retreating German infantry, there were many short and sometimes brisk actions; but in the main, the Germans marched stolidly towards the Michel Position and the Americans followed them. On one section, an over-enthusiastic American commander authorized a probe forward by a cavalry patrol – a piece of impertinence which was summarily dealt with – and on another it seemed at first that the men of an Austro–Hungarian division preferred death to dishonour, for instead of retreating they advanced in formation towards the Americans. Before much damage had been done to them, however, it was seen that those who had brought their weapons had not bothered to unsling them and the division in fact merely wished to be shown the quickest route to the nearest American prison-cage.

By evening, a gap of only ten miles separated the leading troops of the American 1st Division from those of the Yankee Division advancing from the west, and in response to urgent telephone calls from Pershing, aided by the competitive spirit of the New World, one battalion of National Guardsmen from the 26th Division abandoned its attack formation and marched into Vigneulles in column of route. By 6 a.m. on September 13th – Pershing's birthday – the American line was thus continuous across the Salient, some 14,500 prisoners and 443 guns had been captured, at a cost of less than 8,000 casualties; from their forward positions, American observers could watch small, ant-like figures digging furiously in the positions of the Michel Stellung – which had, apparently, never been completed. An American attack now would undoubtedly have ruptured the line, though whether it would have penetrated far beyond is questionable, for there were reasons other than Foch's orders for it not being undertaken.

When the war was over, both Pershing and the Commander of the American IV Corps, General Dickman, proclaimed vociferously that Foch's limiting directive had kept the Americans out of Metz. But General Liggett, commanding the I Corps, nearer the baseline, has pointed out that such an advance would only have been possible had the American Army been a well-oiled, fully co-ordinated machine, 'which', he remarks sadly, 'it was not as yet.'

There had been considerable organizational chaos.

But the American First Army had carried out its first operation with marked success – and if it had been so easy that afterwards the St. Mihiel Salient was referred to as the sector in which the Americans relieved the Germans, it is fair to say that such a victory might not have been accorded to any other army. To frighten the enemy out of his positions is just as valid a tactic as to bomb him out, and infinitely more economical – and those Americans who had not been killed in the Salient were now available for the slaughter of the Argonne.

The American sector of the vast offensive which Foch now planned to deliver against the Germans, lay between the Meuse and the Aisne where the two rivers, flowing northwards, cut the front line at points respectively five and twenty-seven miles west of the corner of the Verdun fortress position. The Argonne Forest lay across the western-most ten miles of this sector – between the Aisne and the Aire – and in view of the difficulties of the ground, Foch had offered Pershing an easier sector between the Argonne and Rheims.

Possibly because to fight on this more westerly sector would complicate his supplies, and possibly also because to do so would come perilously near to falling in completely with Haig's first suggestion of an attack towards St. Quentin, Pershing chose, instead, to fight 'east of the Argonne' – a decision which was to cost his army dear.

It was originally intended that this Meuse–Argonne attack should be the right-hand curving pincer of a vast encircling movement, of which the British attack through the Siegfried Position should be the left-hand arm, and the bulge held by Pétain's armies the sack in which the Germans should be caught. Ignoring such factors as the inexperience of some troops in open fighting, the inexperience of all Staffs in supplying a lengthy advance across the chaos and desolation of the battlefields, and the still potent menace of the German machine-gunners – for there were comparatively few tanks available for such an extended front – there was really very little chance of this scheme of operations ever being put into effect. Although Foch was delighted to pay lip service to the virtues of the plan, he was totally incapable of leaving it alone – and the army commanders had hardly had time to appreciate their own parts in it before Foch was, once more, urging everyone to attack everywhere.

'Tout le monde à la bataille!' was his continual chant, and if Pétain was prepared to hang back, Mangin certainly wasn't, and neither – once Foch had visited him – was Gouraud. With all armies attacking on a curving front, it should have been obvious that a repetition of the assault on the Marne Salient would occur – an immensely long frontal attack, endeavouring to push the Germans by main force back out of France and Belgium and over their own frontiers. By itself, this was doomed to failure; but in default of a completely successful thrust towards Metz – which would have needed the close co-operation of all three Allies – it is by no means certain that this was not the only plan. Mobility is an essential for encircling movements: and by 1918, the machine-gun had precluded the successful use of cavalry, while armoured vehicles were not yet fast or reliable enough to take their place to the necessary extent.

So during the middle fortnight of September, the plans were laid, the armies assembled. In the south, from Verdun to the Aisne, the Americans were hastily – too hastily for their inexperienced Staff – packed into the line facing Montfaucon and the Argonne, with the unknown strength of the Kriemhilde Position awaiting them eight miles further back. Supporting them on their left flank was the eager Gouraud with the French Fourth Army, and beyond him Berthelot and the French Fifth Army lining the Vesle; then Mangin's French Tenth Army still holding the Aisne heights above Soissons which they had taken on August 20th; then Debeney's First French Army along a line from below la Fère to above St. Quentin – the scene of the defeat of Gough's Army five months before.

Four miles north of St. Quentin lay the boundary between the French and British commands.

232

Three days after the German retirement to screening positions in front of the Siegfried Line, Rawlinson's Fourth and Byng's Third Armies had come up, re-established contact and continued, with dogged persistence, the wearing away of German strength. At Havrincourt (in the base of the old Flesquières Salient) on September 12th, and further south at Epéhy on the 18th, pitched battles had been fought of a dour and grim brutality, which spoke of the weariness of soul of all participants. In both cases the German positions had been pierced and the defences to north and south turned; and as a result Ludendorff's armies were now completely back in the Siegfried Line and General von der Marwitz had lost his command.

From just above St. Quentin up as far as the area which had been the southern haunch of the Flesquières Salient, lay Rawlinson's Fourth Army, while beyond them Byng's Third Army continued up across the Hirondelle and Sensée valleys of grim and bloody memories, until its northern flank curled around the newly won positions above Quéant. Then came the Canadians of the First Army, with the Wotan Position behind them and the line of the Canal du Nord in front.

Above Arras was the Lys basin, held now by the reconstituted Fifth Army under the command of General Birdwood (a previous commander of the Australian Corps), thus allowing Plumer to shorten his Second Army Front, though not as yet to escape from his wardenship of the Ypres Salient. And from north of Ypres to the coast, still lay the Belgian Army, with the six divisions of the French Sixth Army in reserve.

Of all these armies, only Birdwood's British Fifth in the north, and Barthelot's French Fifth and Mangin's French Tenth Armies in the central sectors, were not immediately to attack as a part of Foch's Grand Assault: they were to await developments.

The opening blows of the Grand Assault were to be delivered at twenty-four hour intervals, beginning at dawn on September 26th with the assault towards Mézières by the Americans and Gouraud's Fourth Army. Twenty-four hours later, the British First and Third were to break through the Canal du Nord line and down into the Siegfried Position from the north, while on September 28th, Plumer's army, together with the Belgians and French, were to burst out of the Ypres Salient and drive along the Belgian coast, later diverging in order (it was piously hoped) to free both Bruges and Brussels.

And on September 29th, Rawlinson's British Fourth and Debeney's French First Armies would smash their way by frontal assault through the Siegfried Position.

It is incredible that any man could believe – after the experiences of the last four years and especially of the last six months – that success could be achieved by such an assault. Even during the collapse of the Marne Salient, where the Germans were driven from the sketchiest of defences, the only progress made by the Allies until Pétain imposed his will upon the battlefield, had been by Ludendorff's permission – and Pétain was a subordinate commander these days, his interests and activities rigidly limited to his own front.

That the assault did succeed is even more incredible.

It did so because it was aided by factors external to the battle; and all of History's irony is epitomized in the fact that to his dying day, Foch remained resolutely unaware of the vital part played in his own success by the more important of them. The British Navy, he had claimed in 1912, would not be worth a single bayonet to the Allied cause – and nothing he said between then and his death indicates that he ever changed his mind: yet the naval effort was fundamental to Allied victory.

It was the Blockade – and the Blockade alone – which so weakened German resistance that Foch's Grand Assault could win some measure of success. Since two days before the expiration of Britain's ultimatum to Germany on August 4th, 1914, the Royal Navy had been exerting an inexorable and slowly tightening throttle-hold upon the Central Powers, and once America joined the Allies, the hold became surer, the grip tighter. If conditions in Germany had been bad at the end of 1917, by the summer of 1918 they were so appalling that the prospect of the approaching winter was enough to cause a wave of suicides among the civilians, which grew in size as every day went by; and in Hungary and Austria, conditions were even worse. Mere hunger was almost a forgotten luxury. Stark famine gripped Central Europe.

Nothing could stop conditions at home affecting the troops at the front, especially once the casualty rate necessitated a shortening of the time available for training recruits, and men arrived in the front line who had been civilians only weeks before. These confirmed the details in the soldiers' mail, without cushioning their impact with familial affection. Even the most honourable soldier will hesitate when he knows that if he dies, his family will starve – and starve to death: and when his own boots are repaired with cardboard, his own rations reduced to the bare minimum necessary to maintain life, his arms old and irreplaceable, his ammunition short, and only paper dressings exist with which to bandage his wounds, then hope sinks low indeed.

Chiefly, however, it was the letters from home – lying heavily on empty stomachs.

But in the discipline and common danger of the front line, German training and efficiency were such that the soldiers fought well. They had, indeed, little choice but to do so, for once the armies were back within the complex of the defensive systems, it became much easier for the Command Staffs to administer stern discipline than had been the case during the fighting in the open. Thus the Allies ran into fierce opposition.

The Americans suffered first – and indeed most – for, owing to the use of their experienced divisions during the St. Mihiel operation, many of those which opened the Meuse-Argonne offensive were going into battle for the first time – a condition which has led to their collective appellation of 'the thin green line'. Nine full-strength American divisions attacked on the morning of September 26th – assisted by one hundred and eighty-nine light tanks and preceded by a bombardment which had lasted three hours – along a front of twenty-two miles defended by five German divisions, four of which were officially described as 'low grade'.

The rifle-strength preponderance of the attackers over the defenders was therefore very close to eight to one, but it is quite easy for one man lying in a rifle-pit to shoot eight men when they walk towards him from three hundred yards away, across open ground in broad daylight. It is even easier in forested areas, as the defenders can be more cunningly concealed – and if the attacking troops are so inexperienced that they continually call out to each other in order to maintain contact, then the task of the defenders is simple indeed.

By the end of the first day, the Americans – who Pershing had confidently expected to reach and breach the Kriemhilde Position, eight miles distant, within twenty-four hours – had advanced an average of three miles, and this only as a result of their enormous numerical superiority, their youth and the luck which accompanies it, and their limitless courage, firmly based as it was upon a massive ignorance of the dangers they faced. During the following day Montfaucon was taken as the result of flanking movements on each side – both of which bear every indication of being accidentally performed – but after that the organizational chaos which had snarled the St. Mihiel offensive reappeared along the entire front, and the advance faltered. Guns failed to move up in support, units became hopelessly lost, supplies failed – and Pershing had no alternative but to call a halt. While order was being restored, more German divisions moved into the Kriemhilde Position to await the next stage of the American advance, and to prepare – with Teutonic efficiency – as warm a reception for it as their arms and ammunition would allow.

In the meantime, Byng's army had attacked the line of the Canal du Nord defences north of Quéant in an assault along a six-mile front. Owing to lack of large numbers of tanks – and opportunity to use them until the problem of crossing the canal had been solved – there had been a partial return to the bombardment methods of 1917. Throughout the previous night a crushing barrage had pulverized the eastern bank of the canal, and when the infantry attacked at 5 a.m., a crossing was achieved in one sector which was quickly and imaginatively exploited. While machine-gun fire was maintained along the whole length of the attack front, riflemen were quickly transported to the crossing point, where they pushed the bridgehead eastwards until it burst through the defence lines, after which they fanned out in both directions, bearing down on both sides of the breach until they broke away. Machine-gun teams followed through from reserve and from the west bank as soon as the canal bank opposite them was cleared of the enemy, and by nightfall, the British were through the main defences and completely past the width of the main Siegfried Position at its northern end, thus turning it.

Promptly to time the following morning, Plumer's army attacked up the slopes of the ridge which encircled the Ypres Salient in a blood-drenched arc from the Houthulst Forest in the north, down to Messines in the south: and if the spirit of victory was in the air, it must have wilted in the driving rain which, once again on the eve of an Allied offensive, turned the ground to mud and congealed the hearts of many soldiers with bitter memories. But even the rain could not help Ludendorff now, for the troops of the German Fourth Army holding what has become known as the Passchendaele Ridge would, in the words of their own commander, 'no longer stand up to a serious attack'. By evening the ridge was in British hands, and British soldiers stared unbelievingly eastwards across Flanders with something of the feelings experienced by the Israelites when they viewed the Promised Land. Behind them lay the graveyard of nearly half a million of their compatriots, all of whom had died to take or to hold the derisory crest upon which they now stood, and which they had taken that day for little more than the trouble of wading through the mud. But there seems to have been little feeling of triumph abroad that evening: only an air of immense desolation, a deep sense of vast, irretrievable waste.

And away to the south for the past forty-four hours, 1,600 guns on Rawlinson's front had been methodically smashing the frontal defences of the main Siegfried Position, having first deluged them with a new type of mustard gas, which drove the defenders deep into their subterranean tunnels. The bombardment was to continue for another twelve hours. Then at dawn on September 29th, five divisions attacked on a nine-mile front, the American 30th Division in the centre, with the American 27th Division on their left flank and the British 46th Division on their right. Two more British divisions flanked the attack.

It was thought that the best chance of breakthrough lay with the Americans, owing both to their extra strength and to the ground across which they must advance – for the British 46th Division was blocked by the St. Quentin Canal, which in the American sector ran through a subterranean tunnel. Fortune, however, confounded expectations.

Two nights before the main attack, the American 27th Division, in a praiseworthy attempt to clear its front for what its commander called 'a clean jump on the day', attacked three enemy posts lying between the American positions and their main objective. They reported success, with the result that the protecting barrage was dropped beyond the positions in order not to harm the occupants – and when the main American advance began on the morning of the 29th, wide swathes were cut in the attacking infantry by German machine-gunners, who had either never been dislodged or who had counterattacked and retaken the positions. All day long the Americans of the 27th Division remained pinned to the ground in front of their own trenches, and not until evening did attached tanks manage to eliminate the posts and let the infantry through – and in the meantime the stalemate on this sector had reacted upon the left flank of the Americans of the 30th Division in the centre, who were held up by emplaced machine-guns firing on their open flank when they tried to advance.

Further south, the right flank of the 30th American Division had better luck – at first. They had crossed their 'Start Line' at 9 a.m. under cover of a smoke screen, and two hours later were over the long canal tunnel and breaking into the main positions of the Siegfried Position with immense gallantry and complete success. Unfortunately their success was too great, and heartened by it, they pressed forward instead of abiding by the timetable and waiting for the Australians to come up and pass through them. This would not have mattered except that once the Americans had passed over the canal tunnel, German machine-gun teams emerged from it and set up their posts, thus barring the way to the Australians and cutting off the Americans who, unknowingly, were pushing forward into ever-increasing danger.

The Americans – and the day – were saved by the British 46th Division. In war it seems best not to expect too much, and with the deep chasm of the St. Quentin Canal in front of them, the British considered that they would do well to reach the far side with as much as half their strength still alive. In view of the difficulty of the task, they had made meticulous preparations: life-belts were borrowed from cross-Channel steamers, the Royal Engineers brought up pontoons and rafts – and as had happened before when it had been made quite clear to her that her help was not essential, Nature came so bountifully to their aid as to render their efforts almost unnecessary. So thick a mist cloaked the canal on the morning of the attack that when the British infantry reached the west bank, there was nothing to stop those who could swim dropping down the bank, crossing the canal and climbing the far side.

Still cloaked by mist, they formed a bridgehead into which their non-swimming compatriots were quickly ferried, and from which they launched an attack on the main Siegfried Position. They had all the advantages which had helped the Storm Troops on the morning of March 21st, plus the experience which had been gained since then – and as, inevitably, their ranks thinned, another division came up, leapfrogged through them, and drove even deeper into the complex of trenches and dug-outs, wire-belts and tunnels which Ludendorff – and indeed all Germany – had confidently expected to withstand any onslaught which might be launched upon it.

This deep penetration aided the Americans on their left who managed to link up, and as more reserves followed into the wedge, the base was widened until at last it could exert leverage on the defensive positions holding up the Australians. As they in turn came through, the last of the machine-gun posts pinning down the American 27th Division in the north was eliminated and so the whole attack front began to draw up – and by evening a deep block had been bitten into the German line.

All day long the German troops had fought from the defences of their famous line with much of the skill and ardour which had distinguished them in the past – their defeat was due mainly to fog, to the offensive spirit of the Americans and the Australians, and to the spirit of victory which animated the British: and possibly to German luck, which had changed.

For although no one completely realized it at the time, that afternoon Germany had lost the war.

Under the accumulating strain, Ludendorff's nerve had cracked.

11. Breaking Point

FOR many years Ludendorff had borne immense responsibilities, but throughout 1915 and 1916 he had been upheld by personal triumphs in the east, and in 1917 by appreciable success – if only in defence – in the west. But 1918 had apparently brought him failure. Few men appreciated more clearly than he had done the hollowness of his Spring victories, and now it seemed that evidence of outright defeat was growing apace in front of his troubled gaze.

July had seen the first weakening of his grip upon immediate events, for there had been many egregious errors in the mounting and launching of the offensives on each side of Rheims. Perhaps Ludendorff had felt this himself, for although he had not in the end been greatly perturbed by the loss of the Marne Salient, he nevertheless admitted that when the first news of Mangin's counter-thrust had reached him at Crown Prince Rupprecht's headquarters, it had precipitated his return south 'in a state of the greatest nervous tension'.

Such tension fatigues the strongest man if it continues for an extended period, and as almost everything that had occurred since then had served to increase – and nothing to relieve – the strain upon Ludendorff's nervous system, it is no wonder that in two months it approached the breaking strain.

The greatest single shock to Ludendorff's composure had undoubtedly been contributed by the events of August 8th. These had shaken the foundations of his staple faith – belief in the reliability and strength of his Army, and with that gone or at least severely impaired, he saw himself defenceless in a hostile world. It had so affected him that on the following day, either as a test of his own standing or as a genuinely sincere wish not to embarrass his nominal superiors, Ludendorff had suggested to Hindenburg that perhaps it was time for him to be superseded; and when Hindenburg had refused the suggestion, he repeated it to the Head of the Military Cabinet, who passed it on to the Kaiser.

Although His Imperial Majesty, in turn, declined Ludendorff's

resignation – showing him, indeed, 'especial favours at this time' –
there was no doubt that he shared Ludendorff's view of the developing situation. After hearing his Quartermaster-General's reasons for
suggesting his own replacement, the Kaiser had remarked, 'I see
that it is necessary to review conditions. We have come to the limit.
The war must be brought to an end. Accordingly, I shall expect the
Commanders-in-Chief at Spa in the course of the next few days.'

As it happened, no particular new threat to the German line
developed before the conference at Spa – which took place on August
13th and 14th – and so Ludendorff was given a period of a few days
in which to recover his spirit, but not sufficient, apparently, for him
to regain any form of mental or moral initiative, for during the
meetings of the first day (with the German Chancellor von Hertling
and the Secretary of State for Foreign Affairs, von Hintze) he
announced bleakly and with only the harshness of his voice to
remind them of his authority, that 'we can no longer hope to break
the war-will of our enemies by military operations' and that 'the
object of future strategy must be to paralyse the enemy's war-will
by a strategic defence.' These could hardly be deemed reassuring
statements from the Fatherland's foremost soldier.

And the following day, although Hindenburg repeatedly pointed
out that much of France and almost all of Belgium still lay behind
German lines while no hostile troops stood in arms on German soil,
there was still an ominous lack of constructive thought from Ludendorff. His chief contributions to the discourse, in fact, were concerned
with complaint of the deteriorating morale of the Home Front,
coupled with dour announcements that everywhere stricter discipline
was needed and that many more young men should be combed out
from soft jobs at home and sent to serve with the colours.

Throughout the centuries, soldiers of many lands have chanted
this refrain – as they felt power slipping from their hands.

After listening to his chief military adviser, the Kaiser could
thus hardly be blamed for pessimism, and his suggestion that either
the King of Spain or the Queen of Holland should be asked to act
as mediator for an approach to the Allies, was the only positive
idea to emerge from two days' rather uncongenial wrangling. It
was a pity that this idea was marred by the almost incredible naïvety
of the soldiers – and possibly the Kaiser as well – as to the terms
upon which the approach should be made, for they were thinking

of an armistice that would allow them to withdraw their armies to shorter lines of defence, and there to reorganize them. If, during the armistice period, satisfactory terms for peace could be agreed – all well and good. If not, the fighting should then recommence.

It is inconceivable that Ludendorff would have allowed the Allies such a breathing space had the positions been reversed, for he was above all a practical soldier; yet he experienced no difficulty in believing that such a respite was almost a right which Germany could not be denied. He also considered that Germany's sufferings throughout the war had been such that no other country would refuse her the right to occupy Belgium upon such a basis as to give Germany full control of the Flemish coast, and that even the King of the Belgians could be brought to see the necessity for the city and fortress of Liège becoming an inalienable German possession.

So invincibly set upon these two last points was Ludendorff, that during the first day of the Spa Conference he had abruptly cut short discussion on the Belgian question. 'Why bring up Belgium?' he demanded curtly. 'That question is settled and is laid down in black and white!' – and no further mention was made, that day, of the country for whose freedom the British Nation and Empire had gone to war.

With an outlook of such political unreality, it can be seen that Ludendorff was soon to experience many more rude shocks; and he was to be given no chance of recovery between them, for as day followed day, the strain increased. During the remainder of August – while his armies were being subjected to the tattoo which Foch (and Fortune) were beating on the German line from Soissons to Arras – Ludendorff was beset to extreme aggravation by both politicians and soldiers who visited him at his headquarters. The former inquired with plaintive but nerve-wracking monotony if the situation were really as serious as it looked; the latter suggested, with varying degrees of formality, alternative strategies to his own.

The politicians were of small account to Ludendorff at this stage – especially those who could not appreciate that control of Belgium was the least reparation the German Army and Nation should expect as recompense for all the suffering they had endured during the war – but the soldiers were important. They were also dangerous, for Ludendorff was perfectly well aware that even in the Fatherland's present somewhat parlous condition, military

242

ambition would still drive some of his co-evals to intrigue for his position. Both Generals von Böhn and von der Schulenberg considered that a retirement right back to the Antwerp–Meuse Line was advisable, and said so in no uncertain terms – and Ludendorff's testy rejoinder that this line hardly existed except on paper could have done little to re-establish his own reputation for far-seeing efficiency. The fact that he had never had the labour to complete this line was of small account to those who wished, however obliquely, to undermine his authority.

It is by no means impossible that one of the most serious obstacles to Ludendorff's return to equanimity of mind – so far as military criticism was concerned – was his mental image of the man who now commanded the armies in the east. Major-General Max Hoffmann had at one time been Ludendorff's most important Staff officer, and it is true to say that since they parted, Ludendorff's victories had been neither so economically gained nor so clearly triumphant: and the thought of that ungainly individual watching Ludendorff's discomforture with his usual expression of sardonic amusement must have been exasperating in the extreme. Ludendorff had already had occasion to press the Kaiser for Hoffmann's instant dismissal when, as early as January 2nd, the two had violently disagreed over the question of German annexations in the east, and since then, Hoffmann had impertinently suggested that Ludendorff's fixed determination to cling fast to Belgium would in the end cause the downfall of them all. But the Kaiser had failed to respond, and Hoffmann remained in office. After the war, Hoffmann was to write of the Ludendorff Spring Offensive:

The first attempt, undertaken with all the means at our disposal, had failed, so that it was certain *a fortiori* that further attacks undertaken with diminishing resources could not hope for success. On the day that Ludendorff broke off the first offensive before Amiens, it would have been his duty to draw the attention of the Government to the desirability of opening peace negotiations.

If Hoffmann, thinking this, was many miles away, there were some who thought it close at hand. One of these was General von Kuhl, Chief-of-Staff to Prince Rupprecht of Bavaria and one of Ludendorff's chief assistants before the opening of the offensive.

As the other had been von der Schulenberg – who was now pressing for a retirement to the Antwerp–Meuse Line – Ludendorff had become isolated: and it was becoming increasingly obvious that owing to clear-cut differences of opinion between them, Ludendorff would shortly be forced to dispense with the services of the Chief of his Operations Section, Lieutenant-Colonel Wetzell – and another prop to his sense of security would fall away.

Against the vast and sombre background of the retreat to the Hindenburg Line, all this may seem trivial, but a speck of grit in the eye of a surgeon can divert attention and cause the death of the patient; and (to labour the simile) Ludendorff was not only suffering from impaired vision. His hand was beginning to shake.

An army reacts with surprising speed and sensitivity to weakening control, and if nothing could be now expected of the poorer elements in Ludendorff's command, there is much evidence that frustration and concern were affecting its finest. About this time, one young officer – with a most distinguished record – became so infuriated with conditions in a comparatively quiet sector, that he noted savagely in his diary:

One is able to shake one's head between two shellbursts over many matters of grave importance, such as that the Town Major of X has lost a terrier with black spots answering to the name of Zippi, and to follow with fascination the suit for maintenance of the servant-girl Makeben against Corporal Meger. The pro formas and returns, too, provide us with needful distraction. One is kept so fully occupied with the inner organization that time is scarcely left over for the little affair of holding the line. Indeed one is asked little about it. It often appears that collecting empty cartridge cases is of far greater importance.

Ludendorff's grip was indeed slipping – with results which would, in turn, plague him further. And so the endless, enervating circle would revolve.

On August 22nd, Albert fell to the Allies; the 23rd was the day upon which the youngsters of Byng's army had annihilated one German division and ruined six more; and on the 26th, the Canadians drove forward from Vimy Ridge to the northern hinge of the Siegfried Position, to smash through it on the 28th and reach the Wotan Position on the 30th: during which crucial period Ludendorff had been compelled to devote much of his time to discussions with the Spokesman of the Reichstag, Herr von Payer – yet another politician congenitally incapable of appreciating the reasons why Germany should retain control of Belgium. Von Payer was quickly dispatched back to Berlin, but Ludendorff's blood-pressure, his temper – and of course, his nerves – had all suffered as a result of the rages precipitated by the arguments, and when, every evening, he read the military reports, they contained nothing but further severe shocks to his peace of mind.

Then on August 30th, all these troubles – and the Australian attack at Péronne – paled into insignificance before a series of developing catastrophes which threatened the German Cause to an infinitely greater degree. The Quadruple Alliance of the Central Powers began to break up, as a first token of which the Austrian Ambassador, Prince Hohenlohe-Langenburg, announced that his country intended to sue for a separate peace.

This was of such serious import that for the moment Ludendorff and the politicians acted in concert, and diplomatic telegrams shuttled between Spa and Berlin and Berlin and Vienna in frantic attempts to avert the defection of the closest, in blood and space, of Germany's allies. On September 6th, word was at last received that the Austrian Baron Burian had agreed to withhold his appeal for peace for the time being, but only on the condition that Berlin took serious steps to persuade the Queen of the Netherlands to act as mediator with the Allies – and if this move had already been in the minds of Germany's rulers, it can have been no balm to Ludendorff's temper that they were now being forced into it by an ally for whom he had long felt little but contempt.

In the meantime, the Canadians had broken through the Wotan Position.

From then on, hardly a day passed without some military or diplomatic defeat for Germany, which to Ludendorff's heightened sensitivity meant a humiliation for himself. Twenty-four hours after the agreement with Baron Burian, Austria changed her mind again and only a direct appeal to the Emperor Karl – whom Ludendorff loathed and distrusted – stopped an immediate appeal for peace.

Then on September 9th, after being forced both to authorize the evacuation of the Lys basin and finally to remove Lieutenant-Colonel Wetzell from his position, Ludendorff was called to yet another conference at Spa to endeavour to answer a string of

questions directed at him by von Hintze, obviously acting as spokesman for a number of disgruntled politicians. As Ludendorff's only
answer to these questions was 'The general idea of the defence is
to remain where we are', his authority in the eyes of those present
could have been in no way increased, and his statement 'I cannot
agree that Austria may launch her "Universal Appeal for Peace" '
must have been followed, in many minds, by the unspoken question
as to how he intended to stop her. He could not even indulge in the
emotional release of a fit of temper on this occasion, for the Kaiser
was present.

On September 12th came the American elimination of the St.
Mihiel Salient, followed three days later – in flat contradiction to
Ludendorff's wishes – by Austria's appeal for peace, together with
news which portended collapse of another of Germany's allies –
Bulgaria. That morning the Allied 'Army of the Orient' had attacked
the Bulgarian front in Macedonia and there were already strong
indications of the collapse which would in the end allow the Allies
to drive forward twenty-five miles in three days, and break open the
shield to the Danubian Basin. On the 19th, the whole of the Bulgar
Army began to disintegrate – and then news arrived that the army
of the only remaining German ally, Turkey, had been decisively
beaten by the British in Palestine.

No peace, no rest, no gleam of hope on any horizon: in truth
the trials of the First Quartermaster-General were numerous and
intense. As he lacked genius, they were also insoluble.

Within a week, the first blow of Foch's Grand Assault fell, and
if first reports of the fighting in the Argonne were not indicative of
disaster, any dawning hope Ludendorff may have felt as a result
was quickly crushed by a telegram from von Hintze to the effect that
Austria's complete secession from the Quadruple Alliance was now
considered certain and imminent. The following day brought the
destruction of the Canal du Nord Line and the consequent turning
of the Siegfried Position, the opening bombardment of the main
fortifications to the south and the developing menace in the north,
coupled with the warning from the local commander that the German
troops opposite Ypres were unlikely to resist a determined attack.
And as he watched – helplessly and with anguished gaze – the
apparently inexorable disintegration of his Army, his ambitions and
his professional reputation, Ludendorff received word that von

246

Hintze was once more *en route* for Spa, in order to demand from Headquarters an open and unequivocal declaration of military possibilities. Would the First Quartermaster-General please attend?

Ludendorff travelled to Spa during the morning of September 28th and occupied his usual suite on these occasions, on the second floor of the Hotel Britannique. When he had first stayed there, he could afford to be amused by the name of his accommodation: now, no Fates would be propitiated by his staying elsewhere. The first news to greet him upon his arrival was of the opening of Plumer's attack on the Passchendaele Ridge, and the obviously impending loss of positions held by the German armies, despite tremendous attempts to dislodge them, for the past four years.

In the early afternoon, he attempted the composition of the declaration of strategical aims for the morrow's conference – a task akin to that given to the Israelites in the brickfields of Egypt. Wherever he looked, the armies of the Central Powers were in retreat, the fruits of their glorious victories despoiled, their strength wasted away; everywhere the enemy, grown immense in size and strength, crowded in towards the Fatherland, trampling into dust the results of his own ability and life-long industry, and of the valour and spirit of countless thousands of his gallant compatriots.

Now that spirit was gone. Mutiny at home; feebleness, irresolution and stupidity among the politicians; jealousy in the High Command; weakness in the Imperial Ruler. All these had served to undermine the noble power of the German Army, to whittle away their confidence in both his leadership and their own true purpose, and thus rob the German Nation of its Destiny.

And he himself was helpless, the instrument of power broken in his hand. Even as he strove to find some saving factor which might for the moment deflect the spite and envy of those whom he would face tomorrow, his personal staff brought him further news of encroaching defeat in the west – and disaster in the east, for Bulgaria had requested an armistice from the victorious Allied Army of the Orient. This indeed was a further blow, for the six divisions he had recently demanded from Hoffmann's eastern command in order to help absorb the shock of the Grand Assault, must now be diverted to form some frail defence in Serbia.

There was no end to the labours expected of his Army, but only too evident an end to its strength.

And to his own. Helpless in the face of enormous difficulties, unable to find a loophole of escape because to his clouded vision none existed, fears for the future and the passions of the past combined to bring to a climax the strains and tensions of the past weeks, the past months, the past years. Railing at his staff, accusing all around him of deceit and treachery, accusing those at home of cowardice, the Kaiser of weakness and the Imperial Navy of blind arrogance in their belief in the efficacy of the over-rated submarine, he began to lose the last control of all – of himself.

With rising rage, the nerves grew ever tenser, the lungs, the veins, the arteries more congested, the heart overworked, and the speech thicker and more incoherent. Fists clenched in fury, blood-vessels pulsing visibly at temple and brow, voice hoarse and mouth twisting with fury, he grew paler and paler as hysteria gripped him.

Shortly before four o'clock foam spluttered from his mouth, and he fell to the floor with a crash which shook the room – and was to re-echo through the corridors of the world.

That evening, pale and shaken, Ludendorff visited Hindenburg in the suite below and admitted that he could see no way out of the impasse into which Germany had been manœuvred; and sadly, Hindenburg – as ever – agreed with his chief subordinate. An armistice must be asked for, with all the loss of prestige and territory, honour and influence, which this would entail. In view of the Fourteen Points in the American President's Peace Proposals – which would serve at any rate as a basis for discussion – it seemed likely that Germany's aspirations in Belgium must be forgone, and quite possibly the fruits of the 1870 campaign in Alsace-Lorraine yielded up to French demands. Western fears of Bolshevism, however, should at least negate the demand for withdrawal in the east, so some recompense for all their sufferings would be saved from the wreckage of their hopes.

The Staff, they decided, must immediately commence drawing up movement orders for a planned withdrawal of the Army, together with as much of the heavy materials of war as could be moved, back to the western frontier of Germany. There they would present to the world the spectacle of a proud and united force, worn down by their struggles against immense odds – *but unbeaten* – and still capable of defending their honour and the Fatherland. The troops would probably be glad to be home again.

Power had not corrupted these two old men. It had merely isolated them from reality.

There were still a few more weeks left for the five hundred and seven year reign of the House of Hohenzollern to run its dying course, but the moment of Ludendorff's collapse marked its end. The following morning, Wilhelm II – the nineteenth member of his family to rule – came to Spa to be greeted by two sombre and depressed soldiers and a politician worried to desperation.

Von Hintze had had a thoroughly frightening morning. To begin with, he had arrived in a chastened frame of mind, for the imperious mood in which he had requested the presence of the two soldiers at the conference in order for them to deliver the 'unequivocal declaration of military possibilities' had not lasted long. The nearer his train brought him to the formidable pair, the more despondent he had become, particularly because, if in return for a statement on the military situation, Hindenburg requested from him an account of conditions at home, von Hintze would have an alarming picture to present.

Von Hintze feared revolution. There had been many signs of it before – there had even been a mutiny in the Fleet in 1917 – and since the crushing of the big strike in January last, there had been a continual agitation among the Social Democrats, fed and increased by the 'Spartacus' movement which seemed to draw much of its strength from soldiers and deserters who had been in contact with the Bolshevik revolutionaries in Russia. There had been many ominous incidents of late, upon which von Hintze felt he should report. Nonetheless, he had considered that despite appalling hardships, the vast majority of the German Nation were still loyal, mainly because of their innate discipline, their intense patriotism, and their belief that in the foreseeable future all their sufferings would be rewarded by the glorious victory which the Kaiser, Hindenburg, Ludendorff, and the entire structure of the High Command had continuously and vociferously promised them. The news of the Austrian treachery had come as a jolt to their equanimity, but on the whole, confidence in the iron strength of Prussian leadership had been maintained.

249

Now, it seemed, there was to be no victory – and the thought of the effect upon the German people of the rapid transition from paeans of glory to dirges of defeat, was so disturbing to von Hintze that as soon as he decently could after the beginning of the conference, he offered his resignation to the Kaiser. This, His Majesty coldly declined to accept.

The Kaiser then listened with bleak reserve to the reports and suggestions of his soldiers, agreed with the necessity for an armistice, and also that there would be no need to approach a third party in this respect, but that von Hintze in his capacity of Foreign Secretary should make a direct approach to President Wilson signifying Germany's willingness to discuss peace terms on the basis of the Fourteen Points, and suggesting the immediate conclusion of an armistice.

At noon, the elderly Chancellor von Hertling arrived, to have his life-long belief in the invincibility of the German Army and the integrity of the Prussian Command abruptly shattered by the curt announcement that they were losing the war – a shock which so unnerved him that he too immediately offered his resignation to the Kaiser. In view of the unlikelihood of Wilson – or any other Allied statesman – being willing to treat with the present German Government, von Hertling's resignation was accepted, and the search for someone to take his place ended with the suggestion that Prince Max of Baden, a relative of the Kaiser but a man of well-known liberal views with an international reputation for moderation, should be appointed.

One more significant event was to take place that day.

If an approach were to be made to the American President, it was obvious that far more sympathetic consideration would be given to Germany if there were signs that she was abandoning her centuries-old system of government by monarchical decree, and at least going through the motions of establishing some form of popular government. This was a suggestion which had to be phrased with particular delicacy by von Hintze, and at first the Kaiser was so upset that he left his seat and made for the door. He was persuaded back, however, and with marked distaste – and to the disgust of Hindenburg and Ludendorff – signed a proclamation which, if put into effect, would allow a somewhat rudimentary form of government through an elected parliament to be established.

The members of the conference then dispersed to their separate zones of activity, the soldiers feeling manfully that they were discharging their painful duties with honour, the politicians with the doleful conviction that they carried with them the detonator of an explosion which would spread immeasurable chaos and disaster. This conviction they quickly transmitted to Prince Max by informing him of his appointment as Chancellor, an announcement which made him feel 'like a man awakened, who has been condemned to death but had forgotten it in his sleep.'

The position in which Prince Max found himself casts an illuminating light upon the almost feudal system of government which, in the twentieth century, still existed in one of the most powerful of European states. He had been summoned from private life, appointed as political head of his country, instructed to form a government of an entirely new type and possibly revolutionary outlook, and to sue his country's enemies for peace. Protests and requests for extra time received summary refusal, and his actual position was clearly indicated on October 1st, even before he had formed his government, by the receipt of a telegram (actually addressed to von Hintze) from Hindenburg which read:

If by seven or eight o'clock this evening it is certain that Prince Max of Baden will form a Government, I agree to a postponement [of the appeal for an armistice] till tomorrow afternoon.

If, on the contrary, the formation of the Government should be in any way doubtful, I consider it desirable that the declaration should be issued to foreign Governments tonight.

By what body, did not apparently concern Hindenburg, who was to be astonished the following day, when it was revealed at a Crown Council that Prince Max had failed to obey what had surely been a clearly worded instruction. The new Chancellor, moreover, voiced strong opinions to the effect that such a precipitate appeal to the enemy was the most certain way to invite the severest possible conditions of peace, and in any case was probably unnecessary. He was abruptly silenced by the Kaiser who coldly informed him that whatever his own opinions, the Supreme Command considered an immediate appeal for peace absolutely essential, a statement which was confirmed the following day (October 3rd) by another telegram from Hindenburg which brusquely announced:

The Supreme Command insists on its demand of Sunday 29th September that a peace offer to our enemies be issued at once.

In view of the increasingly indignant tones in which the Supreme Command addressed messages to the Chancellor, until he finally acceded to their demands on October 4th and telegraphed President Wilson, it will always remain a matter of speculation whether outraged authority played as large a part in the collapse of the German war machine as did unfounded panic. Panic, or at least failure of will on Ludendorff's part, was certainly the prime factor – and that it was unfounded became evident during the ensuing days.

The vast size of modern armies, their complexities of organization and their diversity of arms, have all contributed to specialization of role, and comparative isolation within it. One of these roles is that of command, and the danger of its losing touch with actuality is common to all armies.

Haig was virtually unknown to his troops, except by photograph or recruiting poster; so was Foch, so had been Gough. So was Ludendorff – for the industry and competence which had qualified him for command had also kept him at his desk. He had therefore seen events through the reports which arrived on it, and interpreted them in the light of his own knowledge, experience, intuition or imagination. From these he had drawn, during September, the conclusion that his country's forces were on the brink of defeat, and so he had insisted that an armistice be asked for.

He had been considerably mistaken.

Although the Allied armies had jumped forward along almost the entire length of the most fiercely contested sector of the Western Front, this jump was to be followed by no vast flooding of Allied troops across liberated country, no annihilation of the German armies. These were, in fact, to be guarded from further Allied onslaught by a combination of three factors which between them gave greater protection than that of the Hindenburg Line. In the north, the Belgians, the French Sixth Army and Plumer's British Second Army were held up by much the same obstacles as had brought every Allied attack in that area to a halt – rain, mud, and the consequent impossibility of supplying the forward troops with food, ammunition or reinforcement, and although the Passchendaele Ridge had been in British hands by the evening of September 29th, no further progress was made before October 14th, as until then all available labour was needed to build roads through swamps. There was also a disinclination on the part of troops of all nations present to get themselves killed when the war might soon be over.

Further south, Horne's, Byng's and Rawlinson's armies had by a combination of concentrated onslaughts on narrow sectors of the Siegfried Position followed by leverage to widen the penetrations and so link up, smashed through the entire width of the main German fortifications by October 6th. Their success had been extraordinary and only achieved by considerable skill and determination ... plus mist – which if not so thick as upon the first morning of the British crossing of the canal, or upon the morning of March 21st, had nevertheless made their progress possible. Even so, the Siegfried Line had been won only at immense cost, and by the time the Fourth Army had breached the final defences – the Beaurevoir Line – they had exhausted their strength. They were like the man who battled his way home through snow and ice, but when he reached his front door was so exhausted that he lacked the strength to turn the key and push it open. They could not, therefore, follow up the dislodged German armies and so turn their retreat into a rout.

In the Argonne the Americans were blocked by their own vast numerical superiority. It is an excellent thing in war to possess many more divisions than your enemy, especially if they are twice their size and composed of younger and fitter men – but only if you can deploy them to advantage. In an effort to break the deadlock which existed in front of the Kriemhilde Position, Pershing had brought up more and more strength, packing it tighter and tighter behind a front of fixed length, until his entire army area became choked.

Foch had made plans to clear the traffic jam in the Argonne as soon as it became apparent, but despite his experiences in the past, his suggestions entailed withdrawing American troops from the sector and employing them in others under French generals. They were therefore curtly rejected by Pershing on October 2nd and the blockage remained.

Between the two stalled offensives which had been intended as the converging pincer arms, waited the French, patiently and with what has been delicately called 'perhaps too acute a strategic sense'. They knew their part in the plan, and appreciated its significance: if and when the British and Americans drove forward to close the neck of the sack, they would exert their gentle pressure to occupy the attention of the enemy – for Marshal Foch was surely far too much of a patriot to intend his aggressive exhortations to apply to his own countrymen. In the meantime, the news was far better than it had been for years.

To the Allied leaders the news of the pause after the opening leap forward was at first disappointing, and when they learned of its causes, alarming, so the news that President Wilson had received peace overtures from Germany, came to Lloyd George and Clemenceau as an immense relief. Upon reflection however, this relief became alloyed with considerable anxiety, for unless terms were very quickly agreed, it seemed by no means unlikely that events might serve to restore Germany's confidence in her ability to win the war – confidence which her requests for an immediate armistice indicated that she had lost. Speed in concluding the arrangements was obviously essential. Unfortunately, speed was also impossible, for the simple reason that even if Germany were prepared to agree to the Fourteen Points of the American Peace Proposals, Britain certainly wasn't and there were many aspects of them about which France held strong doubts.

Both countries had been too busy fighting the war and too eager to gain American support to raise the matters of disagreement beforehand – in any case, why waste time and energy arguing on matters which may never pass beyond the stage of abstract principle? Now, suddenly, these matters were of vital and urgent importance – and their urgency was lessened in no degree by the passing of time, which to President Wilson was apparently of no particular account: although he had received the German Note on October 4th, he made no attempt to open formal discussions with his allies, or even to inform them officially of its contents. They waited, therefore, with varying degrees of impatience, and growing concern, for the inscrutable but immensely powerful man in the White House to give some indication of his intentions.

President Wilson was a man of many parts. He had such a degree of political realism as to enable him, on the turbulent scene of American party politics, to achieve leadership of one party and thus to assume the position of America's Chief Executive. Notwithstanding this, he was, on the international scene, an idealist of high principle and rigid convictions, thus displaying a dichotomy of thought that would do justice to an Irish pacifist.

Clemenceau, who admired America but wished to live in Europe, summed up European bewilderment at the difference between Wilson's expressed Utopianism and his practised diplomacy, with the caustic comment that no man should talk like Lord God if he was going to behave the next day like Lloyd George: but then, Clemenceau was an agnostic who distrusted the British Prime Minister.

The Fourteen Points of Wilson's Peace Proposals were, in their content and phrasing, typical of the best qualities and the highest principles to emerge from the United States. It is a great pity that human nature is so weak that it cannot live up to them, for they would undoubtedly have led to peace on earth had they been interpreted as Wilson intended. They read:

1. Open covenants of peace, openly arrived at, after which there shall be no private international understandings of any kind, but diplomacy shall proceed always frankly and in public view.

2. Absolute freedom of navigation upon the seas, outside territorial waters, alike in peace and in war, except as the seas may be closed in whole or in part by international action for the enforcements of international covenants.

3. The removal, so far as possible, of all economic barriers, and the establishment of an equality of trade conditions among all the nations consenting to the peace and associating themselves for its maintenance.

4. Adequate guarantees given and taken that national armaments will be reduced to the lowest point consistent with domestic safety.

5. A free, open-minded and absolutely impartial adjustment of all colonial claims based upon a strict observance of the principle that in determining all such questions of sovereignty the interests of the populations concerned must have equal weight with the equitable claims of the Government whose title is to be determined.

6. The evacuation of all Russian territory and such a settlement of all questions affecting Russia as will secure the best and freest co-operation of the other nations of the world in obtaining for her an unhampered and

255

unembarrassed opportunity for the independent determination of her own political development and national policy, and assure her of a sincere welcome into the society of free nations under institutions of her own choosing, and more than a welcome, assistance also of every kind that she may need and may herself desire. The treatment accorded Russia by her sister nations in the months to come will be the acid test of their goodwill, of their comprehension of her needs as distinguished from their own interests, and of their intelligent and unselfish sympathy.

7. Belgium, the whole world will agree, must be evacuated and restored without any attempt to limit the sovereignty which she enjoys in common with all other free nations. No other single act will serve to restore confidence among the nations in the laws which they have themselves set and determined for the government of their relations with one another. Without this healing act the whole structure and validity of international law is forever impaired.

8. All French territory should be freed, and the invaded portions restored, and the wrong done to France by Prussia in 1871, in the matter of Alsace-Lorraine, which has unsettled the peace of the world for nearly fifty years, should be righted in order that peace may once more be made secure in the interest of all.

9. A readjustment of the frontiers of Italy should be effected along clearly recognizable lines of nationality.

10. The peoples of Austro-Hungary, whose place among the nations we wish to see safeguarded and assured, should be accorded first opportunity of autonomous development.

11. Roumania, Serbia and Montenegro should be evacuated; occupied territories restored; Serbia accorded free and secure access to the sea; and the relations of the several Balkan States to one another determined by friendly counsel along historically established lines of allegiance and nationality; and the international guarantees of the political and economic independence and territorial integrity of the several Balkan States should be entered into.

12. The Turkish portions of the present Ottoman Empire should be assured a secure sovereignty, but the other nationalities which are now under Turkish rule should be assured an undoubted security of life and an absolutely unmolested opportunity of autonomous development, and the Dardanelles should be permanently opened as a free passage to the ships and commerce of all nations under international guarantees.

13. An independent Polish state should be erected which should include the territories inhabited by indisputably Polish populations, which should be assured a free and secure access to the sea, and whose political and economic independence should be guaranteed by international covenant.

14. A general association of nations must be formed under specific covenants for the purpose of affording mutual guarantees of political independence and territorial integrity to great and small states alike.

If these terms do credit to President Wilson's heart, they do not reflect a sound historical sense, or even a very profound knowledge of human nature. At least four of the clauses relied for their interpretation upon opinion as to what constituted the limits within which each clause should operate: and although President Wilson might have been clear in his own mind as to the limits he intended, others might read into them an entirely different significance. There was also implicit in every line of Wilson's propositions, the pure ideal of freedom which they were obviously intended to breathe through the world like a healing zephyr. Unfortunately, as perhaps the statesmen of the older nations realized more clearly, human nature is so constituted that the only freedom it seems to value is that to enforce its will upon others.

In view of the position to which Wilson had risen, it is unlikely that he was entirely free from this trait himself, and as the clauses of his Fourteen Points would all have to be agreed and put into operation by men who had themselves risen to the leadership of nations by the exercise of similar qualities, it can be seen that a fruitful source of misunderstanding – some sincere and some deliberate – would exist in a peace based upon them.

One clause, however, permitted a minimum of misunderstanding and Britain categorically rejected it. This was the second clause, guaranteeing freedom of the seas in peace *and in war*, and it is a measure of Wilson's diplomatic impracticability that he had failed to appreciate that American troops fought on European soil simply because Britain had kept the Imperial German Navy from the seas. The war itself was being won by the Allies largely as a result of the weapon of Blockade, which Wilson now proposed that Britain should deny herself in future times of national danger. There would have been no point in Lloyd George agreeing to such a limitation of his country's power of self-protection – even for the sake of finishing the war – as he would inevitably have been toppled from office by the War Cabinet, and another Prime Minister installed who would immediately repudiate the point.

Not that Lloyd George had any intention of agreeing. Later in the month, he crisply informed President Wilson's representative that if as a result of their disagreement upon the matter, America chose to make a separate peace with Germany, Britain would regret it: but in order to protect their future, the British Nation would be forced to continue the war themselves. As Clemenceau for France and Sonnino for Italy both ranged themselves unhesitatingly alongside Lloyd George, the point was brought home to both the representative and to President Wilson that there were factors in European politics of which they were unaware, and that consultation with allies upon their requirements for peace instead of a bland assumption that one's own were the best for everyone, might secure more satisfactory results. It was about this time that Clemenceau began referring to President Wilson as 'Jupiter'.

But for the moment there were to be no consultations – and in the absence of any word from Wilson, the Allies in France had no choice but to continue the war.

In this they were aided by events. Either through lack of control or as a result of a not untypical insensitivity to political atmosphere, the retirement of the German armies immediately after the dispatch of the appeal for peace, was accompanied by havoc and destruction of property far exceeding anything that military expediency could warrant. Houses were wrecked, villages mined, even gardens despoiled and fruit trees ringed; and as, slowly, the Allied armies began to creep forward again, the anger and hatred which had been swamped by feelings of relief when first news of the peace move had been circulated, renewed themselves at such useless and wanton destruction, and rose indeed to greater heights. In the centre, the British First, Third and Fourth Armies gathered their strength, picked up their arms and began again to drive forward with a grim determination which astonished all observers, and reminded one of them of the warning uttered by Bugeaud after he had had time to appreciate the lessons of Waterloo: 'The British infantry, sire, are the finest in the world. Fortunately there are not many of them.'

There were enough of them now, however, and what they lacked in physical height, breadth of shoulder or depth of chest, they made up for in cunning, whilst nerves stretched beyond recovery by years of danger received at least a temporary revival from anger and a fierce resolve to finish for ever with an opponent capable of such brutal vandalism. On October 8th, Cambrai was taken, the Germans opposite forced back behind the river Selle, and the front cleared from the Sensée in the north to a point east of St. Quentin in the south. Since September 26th, the British had taken nearly fifty thousand prisoners and captured a thousand guns.

Prisoners were being captured farther south, too, as the Americans gradually sorted out the chaos behind their front and began inexorably to press forward through the Argonne towards Mézières and Sedan.

On October 8th, a patrol of twenty men under a sergeant were probing forward to find and eliminate some machine-gun posts holding up the general advance, when they came to a dell containing some seventy-five German troops. Either through immediate shock of surprise or recent disintegration of morale, the Germans promptly surrendered, but the Americans were now observed by the machine-gunners they had been sent out to find: these swung their guns around and with their customary efficiency, shot down the members of the patrol until there were only eight Americans left.

Fortunately, one of these was a Corporal York, a large man from Tennessee, who had passed his formative years shooting for the pot in countryside not dissimilar from that in which he now found himself. From a kneeling position, he shot the machine-gunners – all of them – and when a German infantry lieutenant led a charge of half a platoon along the edge of the dell towards him, York continued to pick them off one by one until his rifle ammunition was gone, whereupon he drew his ·45 automatic and continued a deliberate and accurate fire until the survivors of the charge threw down their arms and joined their compatriots already lying flat in order to avoid the stray bullets.

Action now ceased, and York marched his prisoners back towards American lines where, after a certain unavoidable misunderstanding over identity, he handed them over to a lieutenant who asked how many there were.

'Jesus, Lieutenant,' said York in one of the classic replies of military legend, 'I ain't had time to count them yet!'

He must have been an excellent soldier, possessing not only a remarkable degree of markmanship, but also a lot of luck. Had he endeavoured to execute his feat of arms at any previous time during the war, all the world would ever have known of Alvin York would have been his name on a cross.

Upon the same day that York won his Congressional Medal, Wilson at last dispatched his reply to Germany's peace move – still without consulting his allies. Possibly this lack of contact is justifiable on the grounds that upon two matters Wilson was asking for clarification of the original German Note: he asked if Germany herself fully accepted all of the Fourteen Points, and also – pointedly, and with true democratic fervour – whether the Chancellor was speaking 'merely for the constituted authorities of the Empire who have so far conducted the War'?

But he also stated categorically that he would not feel at liberty to approach his allies on Germany's behalf whilst troops of the Central Powers still stood upon the soil of France, Belgium, Italy or Luxembourg. This on the face of it appeared much to the point but in the slippery world of European diplomacy, it could well have been adroitly interpreted by Germany as a pledge that once behind their own frontiers, their armies would be given the armistice they required – and thus the time needed – for reorganization and defiance in the face of further Allied demands.

Something very like this did, in fact, occur. The Germans replied on October 12th to the effect that they accepted the Fourteen Points, they took it that America's allies accepted them as well, and they were ready to evacuate occupied territory as a condition of an armistice. They also assured Wilson that the offer was made by the German Government representing the views of the majority of the Reichstag, and as such speaking for the German people.

Unfortunately for the German leaders – and by now the Supreme Command was back in control – the smoothness of this reply was marred by the news that on October 10th a passenger steamer had been torpedoed off the Irish coast with a loss of nearly three hundred of her passengers' lives, followed shortly by the sinking of the Irish Mail Boat *Leinster* – torpedoed a second time as she was going down – with a reported loss of five hundred and twenty passengers, mostly women and children. In addition, more and more instances of wanton destruction and a barbaric disregard of human life by the German troops were reported as the Allied armies advanced.

By this time, too, Wilson had received a number of telegrams from Lloyd George and Clemenceau suggesting that there were one or two matters of policy which should be cleared up between them, before he committed them all to terms with which they might not be in full agreement. As a result of these and the public outcry caused by the sinkings, Wilson dispatched a second Note to the German Government on October 14th, phrased rather more tersely than the almost courtly wording of the first. He stated flatly that for armistice conditions the Germans would have to deal solely with the Allied military authorities – who in any case would insist upon conditions ensuring the maintenance of present Allied supremacy in the field – that none of the Allied Governments, including his own, would wish to treat with one whose armed forces continued in the illegal and inhuman practices still followed by those of Germany, and that the continuance of these practices seemed to indicate – despite the assurances received – that the same powers which had ruled Germany in the past, ruled them now.

In this, Wilson was quite correct, for Ludendorff had recovered his nerve.

Perhaps the physical collapse on September 28th, followed the next day by the confessions to the politicians and the Kaiser that the military position was far more serious than he had previously allowed them to realize, had acted as a psychological catharsis upon Ludendorff, during which he sloughed off his despondency. The brisk and victorious argument with Prince Max regarding the dispatch of the peace offer would then have acted as an emotional – although highly irrational – tonic to a convalescent nervous system, after which Ludendorff could turn his mind to the military situation and find that it was far better than he had imagined.

Something like this must have occurred, for by October 7th Ludendorff's authority had been miraculously reasserted at headquarters, the armies nearest to him felt again the firm grip of control, and although they continued to retreat they made the British fight every step of the way, while the previously haphazard destruction and havoc wracked by the troops became a systematic devastation of the countryside second only to the one they had perpetrated during the 1917 retreat to the Hindenburg Line. When the first of President Wilson's Notes arrived on October 8th, Ludendorff immediately appreciated the advantages to be reaped by Germany from it: his armies, if unmolested by the enemy under armistice terms, could cause such a devastation of the occupied territory as they retreated, that it would take the Allies six months to follow them across it to the German frontier, during which time he could carry out a complete reorganization. His front would be reduced from four hundred kilometres to one of two hundred and forty-five, seventy divisions could be broken up to rebuild the remainder, and in their new defensive positions the German armies would be fed entirely by domestic lines of communication. Here they would surely prove invincible, and it was unlikely that the Allies would even attempt to prove otherwise, preferring instead to conclude the war with a negotiated peace.

No one could then say that the German Army had been beaten, the gains in the east would be secure, and – who knows – in time they might be able so to threaten the Belgian coast again as to retrieve some margin of profit in the west.

President Wilson's second and terser Note was therefore received on October 15th with some scorn at Supreme Headquarters, and the reply which Prince Max first drafted was rejected as too abject in tone. The one finally dispatched to Wilson on October 20th denied the charge of inhumanity although it agreed that the practice of torpedoing passenger ships should cease; it accepted that armistice conditions should be agreed between military leaders but pointed out that if the Allies wanted guarantees that their military supremacy would be maintained, Germany was entitled to guarantees that it would not be increased, and that President Wilson should approve no demand 'that would be irreconcilable with the honour of the German people and with paving the way to a peace of justice.' In conclusion, it asserted that the new Government involved a fundamental change in the German constitution – which would take time – and that a Bill had to be passed to make the decision on war or peace subject to approval by the Reichstag.

All this, of course, was little more than an astute move to gain time in which to rebuild strength, and would have been much to the point if military morale had been all that mattered – but if Ludendorff was now again in touch with his armies, he was utterly devoid of contact with the atmosphere at home.

The news which von Hintze had taken back with him to Berlin on September 29th had served completely to destroy all confidence in Ludendorff and in the entire German High Command. To members of the Cabinet, of the Reichstag and to the whole German

Nation, the revelation of the military situation as seen by Ludendorff on that fatal day had come as an overwhelming shock, and in the same degree as the High Command had previously enjoyed trust and confidence, now, with disillusion, it was the object of abuse and condemnation. 'We have been betrayed' echoed through the corridors of the Reichstag and across Germany: and everywhere the forces of revolution gathered strength and attempted to take control of the German Nation, 'suddenly blinded', as Liddell Hart was to write, 'by too much light after too long a darkness.' The fact that the light had not the pure clarity of complete truth did not affect its strength, and while the armies in the field began again to believe in their invincibility, those at home were assuming that the defeat and ruin of the Nation was imminent.

Like all peoples throughout history in such a situation, they turned to rend their leaders – a condition of mind which was nursed by revolutionaries and received an enormous impetus from the hint contained in the concluding passage of Wilson's second Note.

When Wilson's third Note arrived – in crushing reply to the bravado of the German communication of October 20th – then the fate of the Kaiser and his military advisers was practically sealed in the eyes of the German people at home, for it concluded with the statement that if the United States had to deal 'with the military masters and the monarchial autocrats of Germany now, or if it is likely to have to deal with them later in regard to the international obligations of the German Empire, it must demand, not peace negotiations but surrender.'

This Note – received in Berlin on October 23rd – announced also that the only armistice terms which Germany would be offered were those which would leave her virtually defenceless, and so brought the whole situation to a climax. Ludendorff's confidence was by now so restored that he called upon the nation to reject the terms and the Army to continue the war; but if the Army still believed itself capable of doing so, the nation did not, as only three weeks before Ludendorff had insisted to von Hintze and the Chancellor that the Army was almost broken. Riots broke out all over Germany, instigated by revolutionaries and augmented by deserters from both eastern and western fronts, and tension increased as hours and then days went by with no sign whatever of either dismissal of the key figures of the Supreme Command, or abdication of the Kaiser, both of which conditions were obviously required by Wilson.

But as it happened, the Kaiser was in Germany at this time, not at the front, and his somewhat malleable personality was thus more influenced by the Chancellor than by his First Quartermaster-General. With the excuse that Ludendorff's appeal for the continuance of the war was a breach of privilege, Prince Max announced that there was no longer room at the head of the German Nation for both Ludendorff and himself: and with the unfeeling ingratitude of the essentially shallow personality, the Kaiser sent for Ludendorff on October 26th and curtly indicated that his resignation would be acceptable.

Thus after a lifetime of service to the German Nation, Ludendorff was dismissed, and it is doubtful whether he ever realized that the cruelty of his own fate was overshadowed by that of his country – for which he was himself largely responsible. That Germany would have been beaten militarily in the end there is little doubt, for her armies were by now greatly outnumbered – but even had they been pressed right back behind their own frontiers, Germany might still have secured relatively satisfactory peace terms, as four at least of the Allies were very tired. But when the Nation behind the Army disintegrated, then all was lost and Germany's enemies could impose what terms they liked. This was a direct result of Ludendorff's collapse on September 28th. Germany's complete ruin was brought about because, at a crucial moment, Ludendorff thought that her armies were beaten; and by the time he had discovered his mistake, it was too late.

With Ludendorff gone, the clamour rose for the abdication of the Kaiser, but this event was to be postponed for a few days by the return to Supreme Headquarters of the Imperial War Lord, and also by the fact that at this moment, Prince Max was stricken by the Spanish influenza. He took to his bed, endeavoured to continue from there with his ministerial duties, but either by accident or design took an overdose of sleeping-draught which gave him a doubtless blissful release from strain for thirty-six hours. When he returned to his desk on November 3rd it was to discover that both Austria and Turkey had completed their armistice terms with the

Allies, and there was no doubt that Germany was looking to him to complete hers.

As he hesitated, Admiral von Scheer attempted to take the High Seas Fleet to sea in a last bid for glory by the Imperial Navy. The crews mutinied, killed some of their officers, brought the ships back into port with red flags flying from the gaffs, and then deserted their ships to flood through the ports spreading revolution, which quickly spread to Berlin, its flames fanned by the reported reluctance of the Kaiser to abdicate.

To Prince Max and the Government it now became obvious that if they were to save anything of the old order, the war must quickly be brought to an end so that they might retain some form of control within the country. On November 6th therefore, delegates left Berlin for Supreme Headquarters, whence, half an hour after midnight, a wireless message was sent to Foch asking him to name a meeting place at which the armistice terms might be agreed. Names of the delegates were given, and at seven o'clock on the morning of November 8th they arrived by train at a siding in Compiègne Forest. There they were greeted by Foch who, after examining their credentials, asked brusquely, 'What is the purpose of your visit? What do you want of me?'

Prince Max's representative, Erzberger, replied that they had come to receive 'the proposals of the Allied Powers towards the conclusion of an armistice . . .' and was accordingly disconcerted when Foch announced blandly 'I have no proposals to make', and indicated that the Allies were quite willing to continue the war.

During the silence which followed, some inkling of the utterly powerless condition to which Germany had been reduced must have permeated the consciousness of the delegates and banished from their minds any hopes of retrieval from disaster. With a voice far gone in humility, Count Oberndorff then asked, 'How do you wish us to express ourselves? We are not standing on any form of words. We are ready to say that we ask the conditions of an armistice.'

'I have no conditions to give you,' replied Foch.

There was another pause, and Erzberger began, hesitantly, to read out President Wilson's third Note. He was abruptly silenced.

'Do you wish to ask for an armistice?' asked Foch, who was not particularly concerned to spare anyone's feelings. 'If so, say so – formally.'

'Yes, that is what we are asking.'

'Good. Then we'll read out to you the conditions on which it can be obtained.'

There were no points which the Allies had overlooked in their determination to ensure that Germany would be unable to re-commence the conflict after an armistice period, and few that Germany would be left so defenceless that she could not resist whatever demands the Allies chose to make at a Peace Conference. As the clauses were read out, the countenance of another of the delegates, Major-General von Winterfeldt, became increasingly crestfallen, although the other members retained expressions of blank immobility. When Weygand (Foch's aide) finished reading the terms, there was silence for a moment and then questions were asked in order to clarify certain points. Erzberger also asked that hostilities should cease forthwith in order to save lives – a request which was refused – and Winterfeldt asked for time and facilities with which to com-municate with the Government in Berlin. This was granted, but the time limit for agreement to the armistice conditions was fixed to expire at 11 a.m. on the following Monday morning, November 11th.

There followed a dispatch of signals, the departure of one of the Germans, Captain von Helldorf, back to headquarters at Spa, a flurry of telegrams between Foch and Clemenceau and between the British representative, Admiral Sir Rosslyn Wemyss (the First Sea Lord), and the British Government in London ... and what must have seemed an endless wait. Then at eight o'clock on the evening of November 10th, a wireless message was intercepted reading 'The German Government to the plenipotentiaries at the Allied Headquarters: The German Government accepts the con-ditions of the Armistice communicated to it on November 8th ... The Imperial Chancellor – 3,084.'

The number was merely a code to establish authenticity, and the main terms which Germany accepted were as follows:

Immediate evacuation of all occupied territory – including that of Alsace-Lorraine.

Evacuation of the western bank of the Rhine by all form of German military force, and also of bridgeheads on the east bank of the Rhine at Mainz, Coblenz and Cologne, these bridgeheads to be as much as thirty kilometres radius.

Repatriation of all Allied prisoners of war, without immediate recipro-city, and repatriation of all civilians of Allied nations.

Surrender, in good condition, of the following materials of war:

5,000 guns (2,500 heavy, 2,500 field).

25,000 machine-guns.

3,000 trench mortars.

1,700 aeroplanes, including all night-bombing machines in the possession of the German forces.

All German submarines.

The internment in British ports with only German care and maintenance parties on board, of the following German Naval vessels:

6 Battle-cruisers.

10 Battleships.

8 Light cruisers (including two mine-layers).

50 destroyers of the most modern types.

There were numerous other minor clauses which regulated such matters as movement of troops during the armistice period and the charge upon the German Government of the upkeep of the occupation forces, and in Clause XIX nestled a time-bomb inserted with considerable cunning but unforeseen consequences by Clemenceau, which read:

With the reservation that any subsequent concessions and claims by the Allies and United States remain unaffected, the following financial conditions are imposed:

Reparation for damage done. . . .

This would in the end prove a highly efficient rod with which the mess of European politics could be vigorously stirred until it was finally whipped up once again into an explosion of national hysteria and war: but that was twenty years ahead.

This war was to end with the expiry of the period for armistice agreement, at 11 a.m. on Monday November 11th.

12. Epilogue and Aftermath

At 6.50 a.m. on the morning of November 11th, the following message was sent out to the British armies:

'Hostilities will cease at 11 hours today, November 11th. Troops will stand fast on the line reached at that hour, which will be reported by wire to Advanced GHQ. Defensive precautions will be maintained. There will be no intercourse of any description with the enemy until receipt of instructions from GHQ.'

In fine, cold, but misty weather along almost the whole of the fronts as far south as Le Câteau and between the Argonne and the Meuse, the Allied advance therefore continued against varying resistance – and during the closing hours of the war occurred minor actions which typified national mentalities, and pointed an unerring finger at the future.

German fanaticism and ruthlessness, for instance, were clearly demonstrated in a small village east of Valenciennes. A British battalion had reached the edge of a plantation and saw across open fields a small and apparently unoccupied cluster of houses some five hundred yards away. A patrol probing forward found a young German lieutenant, wounded by shell-fire in the thigh and left propped against a wall, presumably for the better medical attention the Allies could give him. The village was empty, he told them in educated English, the last German rearguards having left two hours before – and as a result, the British battalion emerged from the plantation, formed up and marched into the village.

As it halted in the village square, machine-guns opened up from well-sited vantage points all around – including the church tower – and killed or wounded over a hundred of the massed men before the square emptied and the enraged British stormed through the buildings to attack the machine-gun crews. These, during the brief seconds left to them, concentrated on finishing off the wounded lying in the square, and then fought coldly and skilfully when the moment

268

of their own deaths approached, intent only upon taking as many as possible of their attackers with them.

In the meantime, the corporal of the scouting party had run back through the village to find the wounded lieutenant, who was obviously expecting him and watched his approach with an amused and scornful look; he did not flinch as the bayonet descended. Later, the same corporal discovered in a barn the naked and mutilated body of a young girl, obviously dead only a matter of hours, victim of the strange Teutonic lust to take the whole world with them to their own destruction.

The British managed to finish the war as so many of them would have liked to conduct it, with a cavalry charge.

At 10.50 a.m. and with only minutes to go, a squadron of the 7th Dragoons was sent forward to capture a bridge over the river Dendre at Lessines, the official reason given being that a bridgehead was required over the river in case the Germans chose to violate the terms of the armistice. Along a straight road lined with trees, and in perfect formation, the squadron galloped forward – and even had the war been over, they would have presented to the German machine-gunners a most tempting target. But the war was not over and the machine-guns were manned by the toughest and now bitterest of the German troops. These opened fire – together with some like-minded riflemen – and although the impetus of the charge carried some of the horsemen on to the bridge, the position was not taken until 11 a.m., when the machine-gunners ceased fire in accordance with their instructions. During the closing minutes of the action, the Germans were attacked with sticks and stones by released British prisoners of war who, fighting as unarmed infantry, proved more effective at hampering the enemy than the galloping Dragoons. Over one hundred German officers and men were captured as a result of this action – although to what Allied profit is difficult to see – but according to one observer, Allied losses were remarkably light. Except, of course, to those who were killed, and their families.

On the American front, the Germans would appear to have had large stocks of artillery ammunition which they had no desire to see wasted, and throughout the whole of the morning they shelled the positions in front with a prodigality which was as haphazard as

German innate efficiency would allow. Not unnaturally the Americans replied, but as eleven o'clock drew nearer, the feeling apparently spread through the gun-teams that as American artillery had not been present to fire the first shell of the war, they could at least make certain of firing the last.

This might not have mattered had it not been for the American national trait of competition, for each gun-team wanted the doubtful honour for itself alone – and it is fatally easy, while ammunition lasts, to fire 'just one more shot'. The war therefore did not end at 11 a.m. on the front between the Argonne and the Meuse, and it needed several orders from increasingly high-ranking sources before the shelling finally ceased.

And with Gallic logic and reasonableness which compels admiration and strikes the happiest notes in the sorry tale of the morning's innumerable, wasteful tragedies, the French troops – once the news of the signing of the Armistice reached them – did nothing but post their sentries and stand ready to defend their positions against any sudden, suicidal attacks which the local German troops might, in the madness of despair, attempt to launch.

None occurred, and it would appear that the only Frenchmen killed that morning lost their lives as the results of accidents. It is said that if one maintains a consistent attitude towards life's larger problems, circumstances will in the end conform to give the attitude validity: certainly on the morning of November 11th, Pétain's view of the value of French lives was justified.

By midday, silence lay across the battlefields like a blessing. Men climbed out of their rifle-pits or shallow ditches – for the elaborate trench systems were miles away to the westward – stood erect in open country with feelings of apprehension and uncomfortable nakedness, and then, as the wonder and release from danger took hold of their minds, they became excited. They formed groups and stared at other groups forming not so far away in space, but until that moment divided from them by hatred and the bar of war. Slowly, almost shyly, the groups approached each other, but often they would halt some few yards apart, while each member of each group scanned the faces of the men opposite, watching for the flash of ferocity which they had learned by precept or experience to

270

associate with the alien uniform. Then some movement or expression by one of them would break the tension and the groups would mingle, shaking hands, all talking excitedly in an effort to break the incomprehension, exchanging souvenirs, the British and Americans forcing cigarettes on the Germans who, pathetically, had little to offer in exchange.

Wine was produced and in some places the men managed to get drunk together, but not often, for only too soon came the stern, forbidding order against fraternization: by mid-afternoon an Allied picket was posted between the lines along almost the entire front.

After all, something might still have happened to wreck the negotiations, and then these men would have to start killing each other again: it would not do for them to become too friendly.

But officialdom was not completely successful, and where the lines were close, shouted messages and singing celebrated the spiritual release from enforced animosity, and when night fell each side treated the other to fantastic firework displays of rockets, flares, signal lights and burning explosive. The morrow would bring a million problems of withdrawal and reparation, of occupation and control: but for the moment, hatred could be forgotten.

If silence greeted the end of the war on the battlefronts, the centre of London greeted it with a poignant explosion of joy and grief which grew from nothing to near pandemonium in the time taken by Big Ben to chime the momentous hour. According to Sir Winston Churchill, on the first stroke of the clock Trafalgar Square and Whitehall were deserted: by the eleventh stroke, the whole area was choked with a sea of people, dancing, laughing, singing and cheering, while from the office windows above, waste paper, official forms, carbons, dockets and leaflets floated down as the clerks abandoned their desks and flung the symbols of war-straightened economy into the street before flooding down to join the tumult themselves.

Flags appeared, the bells of all the city began to peal, from heaven alone knows what dusty shrines were produced tarnished bugles and hunting-horns green with verdigris, and to the accompaniment of their unmusical blasts augmented by those from taxicabs and military lorries, the crowd swarmed through the Park towards Buckingham Palace and sang 'God Save the King' until at last he appeared on the balcony, and tried, ineffectually, to speak through the uproar. Nobody heard him: nobody minded – and when at last after many re-appearances to stand waving to the crowd acknowledging their loyal demonstrances, the Royal Family disappeared and the tall windows were closed, the crowds still stayed, singing and cheering outside the forecourt. A thin, cold rain fell on them, but no one seemed to notice and when dusk came and the Palace lights remained unscreened, all were reminded of other forgotten joys which now they could taste again.

They dispersed through the Park and filled the streets, living again the wonderment of children as they wandered between walls of brilliantly lighted shop fronts, unable after four years to compare the poverty of the wares now on show with pre-war abundance. When pubs and restaurants opened, the crowds packed in and although food ran out quickly there was plenty to drink and an apparently unlimited supply of money to pay for it: no one's glass remained empty for long, and who paid for the filling was of little concern. As the evening wore on, alcohol enabled many to forget their past losses, and even to ignore the almost continual stream of funerals passing along the streets – even at this hour – bearing the victims of the latest wave of Spanish influenza.

Pickpockets had the best haul of the century.

In Paris the joy-making was neither so spontaneous nor so concentrated, for there was no monarchical figure around which it could focus at its outset, and the guiding spirits in what celebrations developed were usually British or American servicemen. The French themselves were in general too tired and too war-weary to do much more than remain at home, mourning their losses or celebrating their deliverance in quiet domesticity, or if their calling demanded, assisting the public revelry in a professional capacity.

New York slept for some hours after the end of the war, for it was 2.45 a.m. when the State Department announced to the nation that the fighting had ceased. A searchlight on Times Tower was switched on, a few nightbirds celebrated in Times Square, but until breakfast time the streets remained comparatively empty and quiet. But after that, the crowds began to form and the tumult to build up, until by mid-morning, Broadway was witnessing the scenes which

272

had enlivened Trafalgar Square eight hours before. Ticker tape floated in the concrete canyon of Wall Street, Times Square became packed and remained so all day, an English girl sang 'Praise God from whom all blessings flow' to a silent and apparently deeply impressed crowd on Broadway, following it with 'America', 'God Save the King' and 'La Marseillaise' – and with all their native illogicality, the Irish joined in with such enthusiasm that an uninformed observer might well have deduced that England had suffered a major defeat.

Large department stores announced Victory Sales.

But in the capitals of the Central Powers, the scene was sombre indeed. The misery in the towns had been of soul-destroying proportions when there had still been the prospect of victory to offer a glimmer of hope – but now, the news of defeat opened vistas of degradation and physical hardship which struck terror into many hearts. Winter was upon them and it seemed extremely probable that in the very near future there would be no food at all. There was only an uncertain supply of potatoes now – no meat, no fat, no bread – and when the meagre ration of tasteless vegetables was obtained there was often an insurmountable problem in finding fuel with which to cook it. The uncertain joy with which the return home of the soldiers could have been greeted was offset by the problems of more mouths to feed, and the Spanish influenza was regarded by many as providing the only solution to multitudinous problems. In Berlin alone thousands died of the illness every day during November, through a lack of resistance both physical and spiritual, while throughout the ruins of the Austro-Hungarian Empire the epidemic raged with a fury and fatality unsurpassed since the days of the Black Death.

But in Germany, illness and lack of food were not the only worries – indeed many found them almost subsidiary problems. To men and women grown to maturity in a way of life whose basic creed was one of unquestioning obedience to Established Authority, the sudden eclipse of the House of Hohenzollern, to say nothing of that of Wittelsbach and half a score others of historic tradition, plus the destruction of the Army, was enough to reduce to tatters the very fabric of their lives. They felt as a man might who had been deprived of his old and now comfortable strait-jacket, and left naked in the Arctic winds: neither the temperature nor the unnatural freedom appealed to them at all, and the chaos to which their lives had been reduced held more terror for them in its lack of control and direction, than in its lack of physical necessities.

The proclamation of the Republic upon the Kaiser's abdication did little to assuage the sense of loss, for there was no dominant figure in the new Government to take the place of the absent Hohenzollern, who, whatever his personal shortcomings, embodied the spirit of over half a millennium's autocratic rule. A significant portion of the framework of many people's lives had therefore been permanently detached to Holland where the Kaiser had found refuge, an even more significant portion had vanished with the acceptance of the defeat of the Army, and even the disappearance of Ludendorff (who had escaped from revolutionaries through Denmark to Sweden, wearing dark glasses and a false beard) added to the void which had suddenly appeared in the national life.

During the days which immediately followed the Armistice, the Social Democrats, the Spartacus Movement with its Workers' and Soldiers' Councils, a Bavarian Separatist Movement, all tried vociferously to stake their claims to the vacancies left by the Kaiser and the Supreme Command, but the very plurality of claims was enough to bewilder people used to a monolithic form of government, and in their unfamiliarity appeared none of the symbols of power which the German people had learned to love.

Anarchy, despair and hopelessness dominated the horizons of the German Nation at home; and for days, the vast non-political mass stayed indoors, numb in mind and body, awaiting death from starvation or disease, and prepared even to welcome it unless some sign of a return to the old order could be vouchsafed to them.

The sign came – though not everyone recognized it – with news from the fronts, and the return to the Fatherland of the armies from the West – for those staunch elements of Ludendorff's armies who had not fallen in battle or in suicide at the end, formed themselves into groups which rejected the Republic, rebutted the facts of defeat, and vowed amongst themselves to devote their lives to the re-establishment of German domination.

Thus the Freikorps was born; and by the end of November, its units were already fighting in Latvia and Lithuania to hold some of the gains won in the east during the last four years – for they believed, mistakenly, that the Allies were not sufficiently interested in the territory to send troops into action for it.

So much for the Armistice conditions: so much for the hopes of the peoples of the Allied nations.

Among the politicians it is from Sir Winston Churchill that the most vivid picture of Germany's collapse is obtained, together with the most prescient conclusions from it:

The mighty framework of German Imperial Power, which a few days before had overshadowed the nations, shivered suddenly into a thousand individually disintegrating fragments. All her Allies whom she had so long sustained fell down broken and ruined, begging separately for peace. The faithful armies were beaten at the front and demoralized from the rear. The proud, efficient Navy mutinied. Revolution exploded in the most disciplined and docile of States. The Supreme War Lord fled.

Such a spectacle appals mankind; and a knell rang in the ears of the victors, even in their hour of triumph.

But not all would have appeared to have heard the knell, for Mr. Asquith in the House of Commons was to announce his opinion that the war had 'cleansed and purged the whole atmosphere of the world', Mr. Wilson in his address to Congress prophesied a new era of peace for the world under the aegis of the League of Nations (whose Covenant he was, at that very time, pondering in solitary muse), and even Lloyd George expressed the hope that at 11 a.m. on the morning of November 11th 'came to an end *all* wars.'

But at least Lloyd George had confined himself to a hope, whereas Wilson had committed himself to a prophecy, and further examples of the way in which the Prime Minister had retained a firm grasp upon realities while the President had allowed the Homeric sweep of recent events to weaken his own political judgement are found in their respective handlings of their own domestic policies. Lloyd George immediately called for a General Election which swept him back into power upon a wave of gratitude to the War Leaders, while Wilson – who was faced constitutionally with Congressional elections as the war ended – so mishandled his attempt to secure a Democratic majority that not only were Republicans returned in overwhelming numbers, but they did so upon a mandate which rendered

275

rejection of Wilson's proposals for peace and the League of Nations practically automatic.

The stability of a European peace based upon Wilson's preconceived ideas was thus further jeopardized by the repudiation of those ideas by his own country.

Six days had been given to the Germans by the Allied armies to allow them to get clear of the battle lines upon which the war had ended, and to organize their withdrawal to beyond the Rhine. On November 17th, Belgian, British, French and American troops destined for the occupation of Germany began an unhurried march forward.

They were held up at first by the inability of the Germans physically to keep to the time-scale arbitrarily decided upon in offices far from the operational zone, then by the difficulties of organizing their own supplies (and, additionally, supplies for the unfortunate people of the districts which had lain for so long under German domination), and finally by the necessity for locating and neutralizing mines and demolition charges which had been buried beneath the permanent way by the Germans before the Armistice. Location maps of these were provided under the Armistice agreements, but although these were accurate and detailed, it took many days for each stretch of the approaches to the Rhine to be cleared: it was December before Allied troops crossed the German frontier in strength and the middle of the month before the bridgeheads at Cologne, Mainz and Coblenz were occupied.

The reception of the occupying troops at German hands was at first cold and correct, and the troops found themselves initially in clean but none too comfortable billets. The speed at which their conditions improved depended greatly upon their individual attitudes, but in the British and American sectors, Christmas and New Year festivities were enough to melt all but the most fanatic hostility on the part of the Rhinelanders, for the troops themselves were incapable of eating well while children around them starved – especially at such a season. Wherever permitted, individual soldiers drew their rations and shared them with the families upon whom they were billeted – and a large percentage of the chocolate and sweet rations sold in the canteens found their way between the pinched but eager lips of the very young.

But the elders benefited too, and the story is told by C. E. Montague that on Christmas Eve, he witnessed in the moon-flooded Cathedral Square of Cologne, two slightly tipsy Highlanders offering consolation to one of the downcast inhabitants. They pressed whisky on him, which he accepted, he was smoking a cigar from a British canteen, and was probably surfeited with Army rations – but the consequences of his country's defeat still weighed upon him, and his reactions to their attempts to cheer him up were well-directed but pathetic.

'Och,' said one of the Highlanders, taking him by the arm. 'Dinna tak' it to hairt so, mon. I tell ye, your lads fought grand!'

During the eleven years the British stayed there – until December 1929 – only developing German politics could serve to disrupt the amity between victors and vanquished, and when the Americans left in January 1923, their departure caused more private tears than public celebration.

Only the French remained on inimical terms with their unwilling hosts, for the distrust between the two nations was too great for even the commonalty to break down, despite their shared misfortunes at the hands of the world's political and military leaders.

The cost to mankind of the conflict which had just ended was incalculable, and even the recorded totals of killed, wounded and missing can give but an indication of the heartbreak and broken lives caused by the ugly burgeoning of national ambition and military pride. For what the figures are worth, 9,998,771 men of all nations were killed in the fighting or as a direct result of it, and a further 6,295,512 had been sufficiently seriously wounded for their subsequent lives to be marred by physical suffering. What the cost was in mental and spiritual pain cannot be even imagined, for imagination loses its sensitivity when it attempts to encompass so vast a field.

That fear, chauvinism and a desire for increased security on the part of Europe's rulers were responsible for the outbreak of the war, seems now indisputable, although Wilson later claimed that it was fought solely for business interests. This may have been true in part of America's intervention, for the outbreak rescued her from a depression while the German submarine campaign of 1917 had nearly plunged her anew into a fresh one – but nevertheless, one senses that Wilson's claim is based upon a misunderstanding of

European affairs, and may indeed have been inspired by pique. When he made it, he had just been rejected by the American people.

But if failure of policy caused the war, failure on the part of the military leaders was responsible for its cost. The Allied generals especially seemed to measure the success of their own projects in terms of the size of their own casualty figures, and as late as October 1918, Foch endeavoured to answer Clemenceau's complaints of the slowness of the American advance through the Argonne with the simple statement that in four weeks, 54,158 Americans had been killed. This, apparently, was in Foch's view a criterion of excellence to silence all criticism, and such factors as progress made or enemy defence lines pierced were irrelevant. One cannot help wondering whether such a standard was in his mind when, upon receiving a post-war honour in London, he included in his speech of thanks the phrase 'I am conscious of having served England as I served my own Country.'

If so, it was unfortunate that the price was so high.

Foch had not been alone in prodigality with the lives of his soldiers. Haig too, had remained for far too long unaware of the value to his country of the men entrusted to his care. During the last year, some realization of the near-bankruptcy of England's manhood came to him, but it was not until he was compelled to practise it that he perceived that economy of force possesses an intrinsic value in itself. The smaller the military force, the greater the degree of control that can be exercised over it, and therefore the greater its efficiency – and once it has reached the optimum size to complete its task, additional numbers form dead weight. It is the mark of military greatness to gain success with the greatest possible skill and the smallest possible force – but such is the traditional pattern of the military hierarchy that the smaller the force, the lower the rank of its commander. All ambitious soldiers naturally wish, therefore, to command armies; and being given them, wish to command them in battle.

Thus the very size of the force under Haig's command in 1916 and 1917 had fascinated him into attempts to use it, while at the same time, its bulk had proved too great for him to employ anything but the battering-ram tactics of the Somme and Passchendaele; for Haig, in common with all the Allied generals who attempted the feat,

278

lacked the intellectual power – or genius – to handle so mighty a weapon as his army with any degree of subtlety.

If the mud of the Ypres Salient had engulfed Haig's force in 1917, it also swallowed his prospects of post-war employment. His conduct of the campaign had made him a bitter enemy in Lloyd George, whose re-election as Prime Minister spelled the end of Haig's professional career, for although honours and decorations were showered upon the Field-Marshal, directorships of large companies, an earldom, a parliamentary grant of £100,000 with which he bought his estate at Bemerside – he received no employment in either military or administrative capacity once he had relinquished command of the Rhine Army in early 1919, and returned to England. Even Lloyd George's fall from power in 1922 was not to change this state of affairs, and until the day of his death in 1928, the only contribution Haig was allowed to make to the national life of his country was as head of the British Legion – a body devoted to charity work for the survivors, the wounded, and the relatives of those killed in the war.

This must have been the more difficult for him to bear as most of his erstwhile juniors secured the prize Governorships of the British Empire. Byng became Governor-General of Canada, Rawlinson went to India as Commander-in-Chief, Plumer became Governor of Malta and later High Commissioner to Palestine, and even Sir Hubert Gough was named as Head of the British Mission to the Baltic States in some slight recognition of the injustice done to him in the early days of the retreat from St. Quentin. All these received honours and wealth, but also the satisfactions of high rank and further responsibility.

Haig received just the honours and the wealth; and he had been a rich man already when the war began.

America's reward to Pershing was the re-creation for him of the rank of General of the Armies, previously held only by George Washington, and his appointment in 1921 as Chief-of-Staff, during the tenure of which office he re-designed the United States Army. He lived in retirement after 1941 in the Walter Reed Hospital, where he died on July 15th, 1948, having lived to see the second army moulded to his design, fight its way into the enemy homeland in the manner in which he had wished to lead the first.

The French rewarded their military leaders in a manner similar to that in which the services of the bulk of the British leaders had been recognized, although with the devaluation of the franc which followed soon after the war's end, perhaps they did so more economically. Inspectorships of the French African Empire went to those whose physical strength was still sufficient to stand the rigours of the climate and the campaigning, the rest commanded the provincial garrisons at home.

Foch remained as Commander-in-Chief of the French Army, but his peace of mind in the years before his death was ruined by what he considered to be weak-mindedness on the part of the Allies in not ensuring Germany's permanent subjugation by extending the French frontier at least as far as the Rhine. His public life also, was marred by an unseemly display of discord between himself and Clemenceau. That he was hardly likely to come off best in a battle of words with so shrewd and ironical an opponent seemed not to daunt him – but then, Foch had ever proved incapable of envisaging failure or defeat, and perhaps the Allies should be thankful for it. It is difficult to find specific instances where his direction of military affairs revealed genius or even a very firm grasp of reality, yet it is undeniable that once his position as Supreme Commander was established, his own spirit of invincibility had permeated the Allied armies. Herein lies his claim to fame.

Clemenceau, for his part, dominated the proceedings of the Peace Conference. He had taken the measure of his colleagues and opponents – who were often embodied in the same person – and he had a definition of purpose and aim which gave him an immense advantage in that atmosphere of pious hope and mental confusion. J. M. Keynes was later to write the clearest exposition of Clemenceau's political attitude, and from it can be gained an insight into the reasons for the failure of the Treaty of Versailles to usher in the era of peace which Wilson had so confidently predicted.

Clemenceau, according to Keynes

... was a foremost believer in the view of German psychology that the German understands and can understand nothing but intimidation, that he is without generosity or remorse in negotiation, that there is no advantage that he will not take of you, and no extent to which he will demean himself for profit, that he is without honour, pride or mercy. ... But it is doubtful how far he thought these characteristics peculiar to Germany, or whether his candid view of other nations was fundamentally different. ... Nations are real things, of whom you love one and feel for the rest indifference – or hatred. The glory of the nation you love is a desirable end – but generally to be obtained at your neighbour's expense. The politics of power are inevitable, and there is nothing very new to learn about this war or the end it was fought for; England had destroyed a trade rival ... a mighty chapter had been closed in the secular struggle between the glories of Germany and of France. Prudence required some measure of lip service to the 'ideals' of foolish Americans and hypocritical Englishmen; but it would be stupid to believe that there is much room in the world, as it is, for such affairs as the League of Nations, or any sense in the principle of self-determination except as an ingenious formula for re-arranging the balance of power in one's own interest.

Upon the occasion of the signing of the Treaty, one of the German delegates turned to Clemenceau and said, 'I wonder what History will have to say about all this?'

There was a pause while Clemenceau eyed the speaker with cool deliberation.

'History', he replied, 'will not say that Belgium invaded Germany!'

As for the armies of the victorious powers, they were as quickly reduced to peacetime establishments as the exigencies of occupation and the processes of demobilization would allow – although units of both British and American armies were to fight for a few more dreary months in the Baltic States and in Russia. Once the civilian element had been sufficiently reduced, pre-war conditions and outlook returned, and those regular officers of the British Army who had risen to high rank in the divisional and army headquarters during the period from early 1915 until the Armistice, returned to their regiments as battalion officers, some of them with their pure, pristine, pre-war ideas still unsullied by close contact with reality.

'Thank Heavens the war is over,' one of them is reputed to have said, '. . . now we can get back to real soldiering.'

Most of the wartime regimental histories appear to have been written by regular officers, and it is revealing to note how many times the volume ends with a statement to the effect that such and such a battalion crossed the German frontier during December, settled quickly into its billets, after which *a sound programme of training was immediately commenced.*

To what end the training was directed is never explained, but some idea of its viewpoint and methods may be deduced from the fact that nearly ten years after the end of a war which had seen Britain introduce and lead the world in the use of mechanized armour, the British Defence Budget made provision of £607,000 for forage and stabling, while only £72,000 was set aside for petrol, of which a sizeable fraction was necessary for ordinary thin-skinned transport. In 1933, twenty cavalry regiments of the Regular Army still rode horses, sixteen regiments of the Territorial Army did so, twenty-one of the Indian Army, and there were only four tank regiments in existence in the entire Imperial Force. In 1937, mobilization orders for the 16th/15th Queens Royal Lancers instructed officers that upon the outbreak of hostilities all swords were to be sharpened, and as late as 1940 a candidate for a war-time commission was asked by the interviewing board at Cambridge three questions – and three only. What school did he attend? What was his father's income? Did he ride a horse?

It was apparently unnecessary for the ideas with which Britain's military leaders went to war in 1914 to be modified; after all, the Allies had won the war. They won the next one, too, and it is disturbing to find – even if horses are at last at a discount – evidence of little encouragement to men of imagination or high intellect to serve in the armed forces. On a Staff Course held by the Royal Air Force shortly after the war, one of the pupils wrote a paper in which he suggested that the day of the manned fighter was almost over, and that rockets would soon be developed to such a state that they would be able to deliver atomic weapons into the heart of an enemy country. He received the paper back with the word 'Poppycock' written large across it by the officer controlling the course, and was subjected to some heavy sarcasm during the following days. One would have thought that in this Service at least, new ideas would be welcome, and some appreciation exist of the fact that the fantasy of one year is the reality of the next.

Perhaps the British Public are to blame. The Headmaster of a famous English school wrote to the father of one of his pupils during the summer term of 1960, requesting the father's presence in order to discuss the boy's future. He assured the father that his was indeed a son to be proud of – good at games, extremely popular with his fellows, cheerful, of happy disposition and most attractive

personality. However, it was no good blinking the fact that the boy
was no mental prodigy – he would be extremely lucky to pass any
written examination for which he might enter . . . 'in which circumstances,' the headmaster continued smoothly, 'why not send him to
Sandhurst and let him become an Army officer? They don't worry
about such things there.'

It is easy to see how the cavalry mentality died hard, if this is
the public attitude to the army; but it remains a matter of speculation
as to which is the cause and which the effect.

The French Army never recovered from the twin disasters of
Verdun in 1916 and the Nivelle offensive of April 1917. The flower
of the nation had caught the force of the first onslaught of the German armies in 1914, held it, and then forced the Germans back to
what became the trench line. Then, while Britain's army expanded
during 1915 and the beginning of 1916, France had borne the burden
of the fighting on the Western Front until Ludendorff's predecessor
Falkenhayn commenced the conflict at Verdun. This battle devoured
with the appetite of Moloch the tough, belligerent 'grognards' of
Pétain's divisions, and so sucked the lifeblood from the French
Army; and although there was enough strength and spirit left in
the nation to respond to the eloquent and facile promises of General
Nivelle, when these proved empty – at a cost of 120,000 casualties –
despair and disillusion spread through the ranks.

Pétain managed to nurse the Army out of its despair, but he was
a realist at the head of an army of realists – and some degree of
optimism and illusion is necessary to make men in large numbers
climb out of trenches, and walk forward into a curtain of falling
steel and erupting flame. The most important illusion for a soldier
to believe in is that some good will come of his sacrifice – and when
the war ended, too many French homes were without fathers, too
many French farms without strong sons to work the land, and no
transfers of credit balances from German to French banks in the
form of reparations could fill the gaps.

During the inter-war years pressure of popular opinion reduced
the conscription period from two years to one year, and the French
Nation's pride in its Army dwindled to nothing. Only fools served
in the armed forces, for the war had proved that only fools commanded them – and with deep-rooted cynicism the French

congratulated themselves upon the fact that there were increasing numbers of idiotic foreigners to volunteer to serve in the Foreign Legion. This famous corps therefore grew to unprecedented size, its battalions manned at full strength by Germans, Russians, and the nationals of half a dozen new Central European States, who had suddenly found themselves impoverished and unprotected, as the result of the arbitrary re-arrangements of national boundaries by well-meaning but uninformed officials of the League of Nations. With this force, France maintained order in her African, Syrian and Far Eastern possessions, while her own countrymen remained at home, built the Maginot Line and accepted its philosophy.

The German armies of 1940 owed much of their success to Falkenhayn.

When the Republican Congress voted America out of the League of Nations which Wilson had laboured so earnestly to create, they were giving effect to a national desire to isolate America, if possible from the rest of the world, but particularly from Europe. The vast majority of the inhabitants of the New World were Americans simply because they or their ancestors had found conditions in the Old World intolerable – and this latest display of bad temper and mismanagement among the European nations merely confirmed American opinion that the Atlantic could with advantage be made both wider and deeper.

Once the American Army returned home in 1923, the average American saw little need for its continued existence. Mr. Hoover himself had announced that 'This Country's business is business' – and what percentage of profit was to be yielded by the capital invested in armed forces, when it was the national intention that those forces should never be embroiled in other people's affairs again? The Army – and indeed the entire war effort – fell into some disrepute, and the young nation's natural desire to look to the future instead of the past, was so insistent that its treatment of ex-soldiers was ungrateful, and of those with shattered bodies or nerves, uncivilized.

With Pershing at the head of military affairs, the discipline in the American Army was tightened to a degree akin to that of the British Army in the days of Wellington – which was all very well when the Army was 'the scum of the earth, enlisted for drink', but was hardly likely to attract the country's better elements into the ranks, in days of a quickly expanding economy. This factor too, affected the men coming forward as potential officers, for a man possessing the imagination, initiative and administrative ability to make a good general, could also make a hundred times a general's pay in industry or commerce – and there were no family traditions which put service to the country higher than financial considerations, especially in a country which seemed vaguely ashamed of its latest military adventure, and even of the force which had carried it out.

The Army which had turned the balance in Europe dwindled in numbers, existed on ever-reduced financial votes, and was kept so much out of the public consciousness that it almost ceased to be an accepted part of the American life. In such circumstances, it was hardly likely to become a very potent factor in international affairs.

The Armies of the victorious powers therefore languished during the inter-war years, largely as a result of public apathy – an attitude considered excusable by many of those who adopted it, since under the terms of the Treaty of Versailles, Germany's armed forces had been drastically pruned. They would have been well advised to remember that the operation of pruning is usually employed to promote strong and healthy growth.

Among the advisers to the German delegation at the Peace Conference was a short, dapper man, always faultlessly dressed, of urbane manner and sophisticated wit, monocled in the tradition of the German military caste. His name was Hans von Seeckt, and during the war he had held a wider diversity of posts than any other German Staff officer. He had been Chief-of-Staff to one of the corps of the German First Army at the battle of the Marne in 1914, then Chief-of-Staff to Mackensen's Eleventh Army which in 1915 drove the Russian armies into the Pripet marshes, and later crushed both the Serbs and the Roumanians. In 1916 von Seeckt had been made Chief-of-Staff to the Austrian Archduke Karl in command of an Austro-German-Bulgar army group, and late in 1917 he went to the Middle East as Chief-of-Staff to the Turkish field armies.

The width of his experience was thus coupled with another great advantage – that his areas of influence had not been such as to earn him undue notoriety with the Western Powers who dominated the Conference. His nomination to head the extremely limited force of which the post-war Reichswehr was to consist, was therefore acceptable to the Allies and could hardly have been bettered from the point of view of Germany herself.

The military terms of the Peace Treaty were laid down with the express intention of preventing a regeneration of the German Army. It was to be limited to 100,000 officers and men, and in order to ensure that no vast reserve was quickly built up, officers were to serve for a minimum of twenty-five years and other ranks for a minimum of twelve. The formations of the Army were specified at seven infantry divisions, three cavalry divisions and the Staffs for two corps, and it was to have no tanks – which seems odd in view of the lack of importance apparently attached to these weapons by the commanders of the Allied Armies. Germany was to be allowed no air force, and a navy restricted to 15,000 officers and men.

Faced with the task of creating a potentially powerful army within these cramped limitations, von Seeckt was able immediately to turn those limitations to one immense advantage: if he could not have quantity, he could at least insist on quality – and from the wreck of Ludendorff's and Hoffmann's armies could easily be found far more than 100,000 of the toughest and most experienced soldiers Europe had ever produced. Even the domestic climate in Germany aided him, for the snarling political chaos which descended upon Germany in the immediate post-war years provided an admirable blanket under which he could work, and as always, the mass of German peoples looked to the Reichswehr for some degree of stability in national life. Immediately it showed some of the old, familiar and well-loved signs of authority, the Germans were as unable to avoid giving it their wholehearted support, as a normal mother is to avoid loving her children.

Perhaps the greatest aid that von Seeckt received in forming a highly efficient new army, was from the fact that Germany had lost the war. Although the immediate and subtle promulgation of the 'Stab-in-the-back' legend was a useful piece of expedient propaganda for public consumption, the military minds wanted to know exactly how the military defeat – which they were prepared to admit amongst themselves – had been brought about, and as von Seeckt possessed mental abilities of no mean order, he was able to pick others of keen and analytical intellect in order to probe the question. This they did with the painstaking thoroughness typical of the traditional

German Staff attitude to its problems, and from the conclusions drawn were learned many valuable lessons. These were immediately applied to the training of the new army.

As a result, while the British Army formed fours and polished its saddlery, and the French conscripts endured their year's service with boredom and complete disinterest, the Germans replaced much of their own close-order drill with competitive sports and training in special aptitudes, and encouraged each man in the army to consider himself a valuable part of it. Keenness and enthusiasm combined with national instinct to form superb soldiers, and as each man was trained for a year in infantry tactics, for a year in the use of machine-guns, for a year as an artilleryman, and for a year as part of a combat team which included specialists from each military arm, they all received a thorough grounding in the fundamentals of warfare.

Such was the training which was to produce the famous generals of the Second World War. Von Rundstedt was a divisional Chief-of-Staff in this Army, von Manstein a frontier guard, whilst Rommel and Guderian were both infantry officers avidly reading the works of Liddell Hart, who had been discharged from the British Army by the Chief of the Imperial General Staff succeeding Sir Henry Wilson. This Brigade of Guards Peer saw no reason why Liddell Hart's ability to think deeply and write lucidly should cancel out the fact that wounds received during the Battle of the Somme rendered him unfit to serve as an officer in any part of the British Empire.

Even the fact that von Seeckt's army was allowed no heavy artillery or any of the more modern military equipment, was turned to advantage, for technical details of every new development in weapons were quickly obtained during the inter-war years, their models used in training, and there was no political pressure to cling to out-dated weapons and out-dated ideas for the sake of financial economy. Even as late as 1939, the British still possessed large stocks of 1918 weapons and ammunition, and their soldiers were to a large extent still trained upon them: but as Germany had been forbidden possession of many types of weapons, once the German political leaders defied the terms of the Versailles Treaty, the Army could buy the latest models, without the embarrassment of having to jettison vast stocks of munitions rendered obsolete by mechanical and industrial development.

What was true of out-dated weapons was also true of out-dated ideas and the men who held them. None of the commanding generals of World War I was allowed to serve under von Seeckt – even had they wished to – so Ludendorff, for instance, was given no chance of influencing again the moulding of the German Army or the fate of his Fatherland. It would seem, moreover, that during his term of exile from Germany, Ludendorff's transition from competent soldier to inept politician – which began with his assumption of dictatorial powers to the Supreme Command – was completed, for his next appearance in German public life was in the front rank of the marchers upon Berlin on November 8th, 1923, who wished to overthrow the Government and set up an anti-communist dictatorship. This – and this alone – seems to have been the declared aim of the 'Munich Putsch', as the attempt was called. It had little or no political aim beyond the re-establishment of autocracy, although at the subsequent trial (at which Ludendorff, alone amongst all those arrested and to his intense disgust, was discharged without fine or imprisonment) it did seem that many of those in the dock were of the opinion that International Jewry was directly responsible for all of Germany's troubles. The mental atmosphere of von Seeckt's Army had no place for muddled thinking of this nature, whatever lip service it would pay to theories of Aryan Supremacy in the time to come.

As the years passed, the efficiency of the 100,000-man army reached its optimum, and the problems of increasing its size without too obvious and too violent an infraction of the Terms of the Versailles Treaty arose. The answer was found easily and simply in the natural existence throughout Germany of such social amenities as rifle clubs, hunting clubs, riding clubs and even rambling, mountaineering and sailing clubs. If a member of a British or American rifle team were told to stand to attention when addressing his team captain, he would probably react with violence and even some degree of profanity – and join another club. But the Germans loved it, and when experts were attached to each club from von Seeckt's army in order to encourage the respective sport and raise the club's standard of proficiency, their enthusiasm knew no bounds.

So by the middle 1920s, von Seeckt commanded the finest fighting unit in the world, and given the opportunity, could double its strength in a matter of days. All that was needed for a thorough

recrudescence of German military power, was a Government prepared to subsidize the social clubs to such an extent that every member could devote himself to each particular 'sport' all day and every day without the need otherwise to earn a living, or – preferably – a Government strong enough to repudiate openly and with powerfully backed defiance, all limitations imposed on Germany at the Peace Conference.

But where was such a Government to come from? Certainly not from any of the liberal or pseudo-liberal parties which floundered in the morass of German politics in the days of the Weimar Republic. Only the Communist Party seemed to possess the necessary ruthlessness both to need an army and to fly in the face of world opinion in order to possess one, and von Seeckt and his Army would have voluntarily disbanded rather than serve them or associate in any way with the Bolshevik rabble in Moscow.

Thus it was necessary to wait and hope, watching all the time for a system which could give again to Germany the control and discipline exercised in the past by the House of Hohenzollern. Many indeed, were the regretful dreams of what Germany's position in the world could have been, had the last Hohenzollern to occupy the Prussian throne possessed some of the qualities of the first – or better still, of his most illustrious ancestor, Frederick the Great.

In the early hours of November 10th, 1918, nine motor-cars had left the German GHQ at Spa and driven north for forty miles. The convoy reached the Dutch frontier not far from the village of Eysden just before seven o'clock, and as it was a Sunday morning, repeated hootings were necessary before a sleepy police sergeant made his appearance. At the sight of the bemedalled and braided German officers, the sergeant resolutely refused to remove the barrier and allow them entry into Holland, but in due course he was persuaded to telephone for an officer, who arrived shortly after eight o'clock.

Major van Dyl was possessed of a sense of responsibility and initiative, and he was sufficiently well aware of world personalities and events for him to recognize the Kaiser and the situation which had brought him to Holland so early on that particular morning. Drawing aside the chains which barred the road, the Dutch major invited the German officers to descend from their motor-cars and enter Holland, and he then accompanied them to the small railway station nearby. In due course, as a result of the last piece of administrative duty which the Staff of the Supreme Command was to perform for its War Lord, the royal train arrived from Spa and the Kaiser and his suite entered it to take up residence for what might have been an extended period.

However, once Major van Dyl had informed the Dutch Government of the arrival in their country of one of the most controversial figures of recent history, its officials set about endeavouring to arrange accommodation for him, earnestly hoping that his presence would not prove such an embarrassment as they feared. Upon inquiry, the Kaiser intimated that he would appeal first of all for hospitality to Count Godard Bentinck at his home in Amerongen, some fifteen miles south of Utrecht; and upon the Count's return in the early evening after a day's hunting, he was informed of the royal wish by his own Government.

Count Bentinck's first question was not unnaturally with the regard to the size of the suite for which he was asked to provide shelter, and being informed that in due course it would rise to as many as thirty persons, he tendered his regrets that his establishment was not large enough to provide adequate accommodation for so large a party. The following day, however, a letter arrived from the Kaiser, calling upon his fellow Knight of the Order of St. John to remember the vows of their order, and to provide him with sanctuary. Upon this, the Count acquiesced, and the royal train arrived at Maarn railway station nearby during the afternoon of November 11th, in damp foggy weather which added nothing to the pleasure of the occasion.

It was the first time that the Count and the Kaiser had met, and the preliminary exchanges between them included an inquiry from the Kaiser as to whether his host was a Freemason. Upon being assured that the Count was not, the Kaiser expressed his pleasure and then called, rather surprisingly, for a 'cup of tea, hot English tea!'

During the days which followed, the Kaiser settled in to the four rooms which Count Bentinck had set aside for him, while the rest of his Staff found themselves what accommodation they could. The Kaiserin arrived, some members of the Staff were compelled by financial considerations to beg leave to return to Germany, and as day followed day, a fixed routine was established which enabled the Kaiser to enjoy some feeling that his life was still running upon smooth and well-ordered lines.

At seven o'clock each morning, he rose and walked in the gardens – wearing, we are told, a plain blue suit such as he used to wear during the yachting seasons at Kiel or Cowes – and at a quarter to nine there would be a short religious service at which he would read the lesson. After breakfast he would open and read his mail, a considerable part of which during the first weeks consisted of insulting and threatening letters from all over the world. He would then occupy himself for the rest of the day learning Dutch or taking exercise by sawing or chopping wood in the grounds of Amerongen House, in silent contemplation, or in conversation with some chosen and appointed member of his retinue. Tea was at half-past four, dinner at eight.

This routine was disturbed on November 28th by the arrival of several men dressed in black, visiting him at the request of the German Council of the People's Delegates. The leader of the delegation was Count Ernst zu Rantzau, who produced from his brief-case a large white document headed with the Imperial Eagle. It read:

I herewith renounce for all time my right to the Crown of Prussia, and to the German Imperial Crown connected therewith. In doing so I release all officials of the German Reich and Prussia, all officers, non-commissioned officers and men of the Navy, the Prussian Army and the troops of Federal contingents from their oath of allegiance which they have sworn to me as their Emperor, King and Supreme Commander. Until the institution of a new order in the German Reich, I expect them to assist the holders of the actual power in Germany to protect the German people from the dangers threatening through anarchy, famine and foreign rule.

This was surprisingly short and concise for so momentous a document, but it had the advantage that there were few points over which doubt or argument could arise. After a few moments' deliberation, the Kaiser drew it towards him, wrote 'Signed and sealed by our hand and the affixed Imperial Seal. Given at Amerongen, the 28th November, 1918'.

He then signed it, largely and vigorously – Wilhelm; and became from that moment a private citizen, living in exile.

His quarters were comfortable at Amerongen, indeed splendid, for Count Bentinck was a wealthy man and properly conscious of the treatment the aristocratic world expected him to extend to one of their number in distress. The rooms were hung with Flanders tapestries and furnished superbly, and if they were alien in atmosphere, they were far better than the accommodation in which the Kaiser's cousins 'Nicky' and 'Alix' had spent their last days, in far-off Siberia.

Christmas came and went, the year drew to its close. It had been one of epochal events. The whole of the Kaiser's life had been a cavalcade of stirring enterprise and national – and indeed personal – triumphs: now, in twelve brief months, all its glories and achievements had been brought to nought. Defeat, exile, and then the abdication ending the long rule of his House; truly he had food for thought.

As the New Year began, the last Hohenzollern to occupy a throne pondered the past.

*   *   *

Just over four hundred miles south-east of Amerongen, between Munich and Salzburg and only fifteen miles from the Austrian border, lay the small town of Traunstein. Unlike the greater part of rural Germany, Traunstein did show some external sign that the country of which it was a tiny part had been engaged in war. Not, of course, that the sign was one of war's devastation, for no shattered roads or causeways, no burnt-out shells of barns or homesteads disfigured Traunstein's Christmas-card beauty. It was an addition to, not a subtraction from, Traunstein's accommodation facilities which signified Germany's prosecution of the war – for some two miles east of the town's outskirts sprawled the barrack-blocks and barbed-wire compounds of a large prison-camp, its harsh outlines blanketed during the closing hours of 1918 under two feet of snow.

Despite the ending of hostilities, German sentries still guarded the camp, and its administration by the German Kommandatur had not been relaxed one iota with the signing of any of the armistices – for the vast majority of the inhabitants of the camp were Russians, and none of the Fatherland's rolling stock had been spared as yet to transport them back to a homeland which was as uninterested in receiving them as most of the prisoners seemed to be in returning to. As the local authorities had no wish to add to their problems by releasing thirty thousand uncouth and possibly vengeful moujiks to terrorize the area, these therefore remained penned behind barbed wire, fed when food could be found for them, singing during the evenings vast rolling choruses of doleful incomprehensibility, trudging for exercise in swaying columns around the compounds, fighting amongst themselves for scraps of food; starving, and dying.

During the last hour of the year, silence lay upon the camp, for the prisoners had been shepherded into their blocks shortly after dusk and now lay on the thin, filthy straw which covered the floor, huddled together for warmth in dark, snoring, mephitic squalor.

Outside, the air was cold but clear, frost sparkling in the moonlight. At midnight, the guards changed. Files of men behind the guard NCOs trudged along the slushy paths between the high double fences which surrounded the whole camp area, and at each sentry box the last men in the files dropped off, perfunctorily performed the doll-like ceremony of relieving the previous sentries, after which each pair stood in muttering commiseration until the NCOs returned, trailing behind them other files, this time of the thankful, stumbling, bone-cold men going off duty.

By half-past twelve, all was silent and still again. The new guard sheltered inside their wooden boxes, cursed the cold, stamped their feet, bemoaned their lot in solitary communion, and wondered if the cold and the guard commander's sense of duty would be sufficient to keep them awake during their entire stag, or whether they would be able to snatch a doze and thus pass a few of the interminable minutes less conscious of their discomfort.

One of the sentries, however, had no intention of sleeping, for there was too much to think about, and too much dissatisfaction, corroding disappointment, thwarted longing and potential hatred seething in his soul to give him rest. He stood in his box, unaware of his present discomfort, his mind busy with a hundred half-formed, shadowy ambitions, his pallid, nervous face twitching with cold and concentration.

Obergefreiter Adolf Hitler was pondering the future.

BIBLIOGRAPHY

From some of the publications listed below I have quoted short extracts in my own text. I would like to thank the publishers and copyright owners for allowing me to do so. For those quotations where there is not in my text a direct reference to the author or the title of his particular book, I have provided after the Bibliography a list of sources.

ALBERT I: *The War Diaries of Albert I, King of the Belgians* (Kimber, 1954).
ALLEN, Arthur B.: *Twentieth Century Britain* (Barrie and Rockliff, 1958).
ASQUITH, Hon. Herbert: *Moments of Memory* (Hutchinson, 1937).
ASTON, Sir George: *Foch* (Hutchinson, 1929).
BEAVERBROOK, Lord: *Men and Power, 1917–18* (Hutchinson, 1956).
BINDING, Rudolf: *A Fatalist at War* (Allen and Unwin, 1929).
BIRNIE, Arthur: *The Art of War* (Nelson, 1942).
BLUMENTRITT, Gunther: *Von Rundstedt* (Odhams, 1952).
BLUNDEN, Edmund: *Undertones of War* (Cobden-Sanderson, 1928).
BULOW, Prince Von: *Memoirs* (Putnam, 1932).
BYRON, R. (Editor): *King's Royal Rifle Corps Chronicle, 1918* (Wykenham, 1919).
CHAPMAN, Guy (Editor): *Vain Glory* (Cassell, 1937).
CHURCHILL, Winston S.: *The World Crisis, 1916–18* (Thornton Butterworth, 1927).
   Great Contemporaries (Thornton Butterworth, 1937).
CLEMENCEAU, George: *Grandeur and Misery of Victory* (Harrap, 1930).
COOP, J. O.: *The Story of the 55th (West Lancashire Division)* (Liverpool Daily Post Printers, 1919).
COOPER, Duff: *Haig* (Faber, 1935).
CRUTTWELL, C. R. M. F.: *The War Service of the 1/4 Royal Berkshire Regiment* (Oxford, 1922).
CUTLACK, F. M.: *The Australians: Final Campaign, 1918* (Low, Marston, 1919).
EDMONDS, Sir J. E.: *A Short History of World War I* (O.U.P., 1951).
FALLS, Cyril: *The First World War* (Longmans, 1960).
FREDERICKS, Pierce G.: *The Great Adventure* (Dutton, 1958).
FRISCHAUER, Willi: *Goering* (Odhams, 1951).
GARDNER, R. B.: *The Big Push* (Cassell, 1961).
GAULLE, Charles de: *France and her Army* (Hutchinson, 1945).
GOUGH, Sir Hubert: *Fifth Army* (Hodder and Stoughton, 1931).
GRAVES, Robert: *Goodbye to All That* (Cassell, 1957).

GUEDELLA, Philip: *The Two Marshals* (Hodder and Stoughton, 1943).

HAIG, Sir Douglas: *Despatches, 1915–1919* (Dent, 1919).
   Private Papers, 1914–1919 (Editor: R. Blake) (Eyre and Spottiswoode, 1952).

HANKEY, Lord: *The Supreme Command, 1914–1918* (Allen and Unwin, 1961).

HARINGTON, Sir Charles: *Plumer of Messines* (Murray, 1935).

HITLER, Adolf: *Mein Kampf* (Hurst and Blackett, 1939).

HOFFMAN, Max: *The War of Lost Opportunities* (International, 1925).

ICKS and ANDREWS: *Tanks and Armoured Vehicles* (Duell, Sloane and Pearce, 1945).

INGLEFIELD, Captain V. E.: *The History of the Twentieth (Light) Division* (Niskett, 1921).

JERROLD, Douglas: *The Royal Naval Division* (Hutchinson, 1923).

JÜNGER, Ernst: *Storm of Steel* (Chatto and Windus, 1929).

KEYNES, J. M.: *The Economic Consequences of the Peace Treaty* (Macmillan, 1919: quotation made by permission of the Trustees of the Estate).

KURENBERG, Joachim von: *The Kaiser* (Cassell, 1954).

KUTZ, C. R.: *War on Wheels* (Lane, 1941).

LAWRENCE, T. E.: *Seven Pillars of Wisdom* (Cape, 1935).

LIDDELL HART, Captain B. H.: *Reputations* (Murray, 1928).
   Foch (Eyre and Spottiswoode, 1931).
   A History of the World War, 1914–1918 (Faber, 1934).
   Through the Fog of War (Faber, 1938).
   The Strategy of Indirect Approach (Faber, 1941).
   The Other Side of the Hill (Cassell, 1948).
   The Tanks (Cassell, 1959).

LLOYD GEORGE, David: *War Memoirs* (Nicholson and Watson, 1936: quotation made by permission of the Beaverbrook Foundations).

LUDENDORFF, Erich: *My War Memories* (Hutchinson, 1919).

LUNT, James: *Charge to Glory* (Heinemann, 1961).

LUTZ, R. H.: *The Causes of the German Collapse in 1918* (Stanford University Press, 1934).

MASON, F. van Wyck (Editor): *The Fighting American* (Jarrolds, 1945).

MAURICE, Sir Frederick (Editor): *The Life of General Lord Rawlinson* (Cassell, 1928).
   The Last Four Months (Cassell, 1919).

MILLIN, Sara G.: *General Smuts* (Faber, 1936).

MONTGOMERY, Sir Archibald: *The Story of the Fourth Army* (Hodder and Stoughton, 1926).

NEWMAN, Bernard: *Spy* (Gollancz, 1935).

BIBLIOGRAPHY

NEWMAN and EVANS (Editors): *Anthology of Amageddon* (Dennis Archer, 1935).

NICHOLLS, T. B.: *Army Medical Service at War* (Baillière, Tindall and Cox, 1940).

Official History of the War, Military Operations, France and Belgium, 1918 (Macmillan, 1935 et seq.).

PAGET, R. T.: *Manstein* (Collins, 1951).

PANKHURST, Sylvia: *The Home Front* (Hutchinson, 1932).

PEEL, Mrs. C. S.: *How We Lived Then* (The Bodley Head, 1929).

REYNOLDS, Quentin: *They Fought for the Sky* (Cassell, 1958).

RIDDELL, Lord: *War Diary, 1914–1918* (Nicholson and Watson, 1933).

ROSE, G. K.: *The Story of the 2/4 Oxfordshire and Buckinghamshire Light Infantry* (Blackwell, 1920).

SEYMOUR, Charles (Editor): *The Intimate Papers of Colonel House* (Benn, 1928).

SPEARS, Sir Edward: *Prelude to Victory* (Cape, 1939).

SUETER, Rear-Admiral Sir Murray: 'Evolution of the Tank', *Airmen or Noahs* (Hutchinson, 1928).

TSCHUPPIK, Karl: *Ludendorff, the Tragedy of a Specialist* (Allen and Unwin, 1932).

TUMULTY, J. P.: *Woodrow Wilson* (Heinemann, 1922).

WATSON, A. M. K.: *The Biography of President von Hindenburg* (Marriott, 1930).

WEERD DE, H. A.: *Great Soldiers of the Two World Wars* (Norton, 1941).

WILHELM, Crown Prince: *My War Memories* (Thornton Butterworth, 1922).

WOLFF, Leon: *In Flanders Fields* (Longmans, 1959).

WYRALL, Everard: *The History of the 62nd West Riding Division, 1914–1919* (The Bodley Head, 1924–5).

The East Yorkshire Regiment in the Great War (Harrison, 1928).

YOUNG, Desmond, *Rommel* (Collins, 1950).

Newspapers of the period and since.

SOURCES

(Full details of the publications noted here can be found in the Bibliography)

Chapter 1
Page

12. 'The Western Front was known': Robert Graves, article in *The Observer*, 'What Was the First War Like Sir?', November 9th, 1958. Quoted by permission of Roturman S.A.

20. ' "Jerry's got a gun" ': Robert Graves, *idem.*

Chapter 2

33. 'His mind opened': Churchill, *Great Contemporaries.*

Chapter 3

56. 'The P.M's house': Haig, *Private Papers.*

57. 'I think I can fairly claim': 'The usual statement': Haig, *idem.*

68. 'I was much struck': Haig, *idem.*

Chapter 4

84. 'I had given strict orders': Major R. Ogier Ward, article in the 'Journal of the Honourable Artillery Company', quoted in Chapman: *Vain Glory.*

89–90. 'Again that morning' *et seq.*: Herbert Read, *In Retreat*, quoted in Chapman, *Vain Glory.*

91. 'I must say': Lt.-Col. R. Feilding in 'War Letters to a Wife', quoted in Chapman, *Vain Glory.*

95. 'Pétain struck me': Haig, *idem.* ' "If you withdraw" ': quoted in Liddell Hart, *Foch.*

100. Conversation at Douellens Conference: quoted in Liddell Hart, *Foch.*

Chapter 5

111. 'The King said': Haig, *idem.*

112. 'Generals Bliss and Pershing': Haig, *idem.*

113. ' "I come to tell you" ': quoted in Liddell Hart, *Foch.*

124. 'I found Foch selfish': Haig, *idem.*

126. 'The operation would immobilize': quoted in Liddell Hart, *Foch.*

Chapter 6

145. 'In our opinion': quoted in Liddell Hart, *Fog of War*.
152. 'Suddenly the roads': Churchill, *World Crisis*.

Chapter 7

162. 'A strong picquet line': Churchill, *idem*.
166. 'Paris was calm': Churchill, *idem*.
168. ' "If we can hold" ': Quoted in Liddell Hart, *Fog of War*.

Chapter 8

185. 'If the dispositions': Haig, *idem*.

Chapter 9

205. 'No one who has been': Churchill, *idem*.
206. 'Cavalry cantered': Churchill, *idem*.
210. 'The attack on Mont St. Quentin': Sir A. Montgomery, *Story of Fourth Army*.

Chapter 10

222. 'Just a word of caution': quoted by Haig, *idem*.
223. 'What a wretched lot': Haig, *idem*.

Chapter 11

241. ' "I see that it is necessary" ': ' "We can no longer" ': quoted in Tschuppik, *Ludendorff*.
242. ' "Why bring up Belgium?" ': quoted in Tschuppik, *idem*.
244. 'One is able': Jünger, *Storm of Steel*.

Chapter 12

275. 'The mighty framework': Churchill, *idem*.

Index

INDEX